Shakespearean Genealogies of Power

Shakespearean Genealogies of Power proposes a new view on Shakespeare's involvement with the legal sphere: as a visible space between the spheres of politics and law and well able to negotiate legal and political, even constitutional concerns, Shakespeare's theater opened up a new perspective on normativity. His plays reflect, even create, "history" in a new sense on the premises of the older conceptions of historical and legal exemplarity: examples, cases, and instances are to be reflected rather than treated as straightforwardly didactic or salvific. Thus, what comes to be recognized, reflected and acknowledged has a disowning, alienating effect, whose enduring aftermath rather than its theatrical immediacy counts and remains effective. In Shakespeare, the law gets hold of its normativity as the problematic efficacy of unsolved – or rarely ever completely solved – problems: on the stage of the theater, the law has to cope with a mortgage of history rather than with its own success story. The exemplary interplay of critical, cultural and legal theory in the twentieth century – between Carl Schmitt and Hans Kelsen, Walter Benjamin and Ernst Kantorowicz, Hans Blumenberg and Giorgio Agamben, Robert Cover and Niklas Luhmann – found its speculative instruments in Shakespeare's plays.

Anselm Haverkamp is Professor of English at New York University. He is also a Professor of Literature and Philosophy in Berlin and Munich, and has held visiting appointments at Yale University, the EHESS in Paris, and the Cardozo Law School in New York.

Discourses of Law

Series editors: Peter Goodrich, Michel Rosenfeld and Arthur Jacobson
Benjamin N. Cardozo School of Law

This successful and exciting series seeks to publish the most innovative scholarship at the intersection of law, philosophy and social theory. The books published in the series are distinctive by virtue of exploring the boundaries of legal thought. The work that this series seeks to promote is marked most strongly by the drive to open up new perspectives on the relation between law and other disciplines. The series has also been unique in its commitment to international and comparative perspectives upon an increasingly global legal order. Of particular interest in a contemporary context, the series has concentrated upon the introduction and translation of continental traditions of theory and law.

The original impetus for the series came from the paradoxical merger and confrontation of East and West. Globalization and the internationalization of the rule of law have had many dramatic and often unforeseen and ironic consequences. An understanding of differing legal cultures, particularly different patterns of legal thought, can contribute, often strongly and starkly, to an appreciation if not always a resolution of international legal disputes. The rule of law is tied to social and philosophical underpinnings that the series has sought to excoriate and illuminate.

Titles in the series:

Nietzsche and Legal Theory: Half-Written Laws
Edited by Peter Goodrich and Mariana Valverde

Law, Orientalism, and Postcolonialism: The Jurisdiction of the Lotus Eaters
Piyel Haldar

Endowed: Regulating the Male Sexed Body
Michael Thomson

The Identity of the Constitutional Subject: Selfhood, Citizenship, Culture, and Community
Michel Rosenfeld

The Land is the Source of the Law: A Dialogic Encounter with Indigenous Jurisprudence
C.F. Black

Shakespearean Genealogies of Power: A Whispering of Nothing in Hamlet, Richard II, Julius Caesar, Macbeth, The Merchant of Venice, and The Winter's Tale
Anselm Haverkamp

Forthcoming:

Novel Judgments: Legal Theory as Fiction
William Macneil

Crime Scenes: Forensics and Aesthetics
Rebecca Scott Bray

Sex, Culpability and the Defence of Provocation
Danielle Tyson

The Rule of Reason in European Constitutionalism and Citizenship
Yuri Borgmann-Prebil

Visualizing Law in the Age of the Digital Baroque: Arabesques and Entanglements
Richard K. Sherwin

The publisher gratefully acknowledges the support of the Jacob Burns Institute for Advanced Legal Studies of the Benjamin N. Cardozo School of Law to the series *Discourses of Law*.

Anselm Haverkamp

Shakespearean Genealogies of Power
A Whispering of Nothing in Hamlet, Richard II, Julius Caesar, Macbeth, The Merchant of Venice, and The Winter's Tale

Brilliant, intense, and original. Like Benjamin, whose book on German baroque drama is comparably difficult, Haverkamp rewards every bit of concentration and labor. Just when it seemed impossible to write about Hamlet in a fresh and exciting way, Haverkamp comes along and shows how it can be done. His work will have a serious impact on anyone interested in the application of theory to Shakespeare.
Stephen Greenblatt, Harvard University

Anselm Haverkamp writes *in*, but also *to*, the European Shakespeare tradition, a stage shared by Hegel, Freud and Benjamin as well as Beckett, Brecht and Heiner Müller. His readings pursue the emergence and mutation of Shakespeare's futures in response to the refiguring pressures of theatrical performance, philosophical engagement, avant-garde adaptation, and epochal catastrophe. This study of Shakespeare's ongoing effects is the most stunning account to date of what it means for Shakespeare to be our contemporary – and why we should care.
Julia Reinhard Lupton, University of California, Irvine

Armed with the double-edged saber of historical erudition and textual acumen, Anselm Haverkamp storms the Fortresses Elsinore and Dunsany, but also most of the *idées reçues* of contemporary Shakespeare criticism, and in the process challenges readers to radically rethink and reread what they thought they knew – not just concerning *Hamlet*, *Macbeth* and *Richard II*, but about power, violence, theater and literature in the modern world.
Samuel Weber, Northwestern University

Shakespearean Genealogies of Power

A Whispering of Nothing in *Hamlet,
Richard II, Julius Caesar, Macbeth,
The Merchant of Venice,* and
The Winter's Tale

Anselm Haverkamp

Routledge
Taylor & Francis Group
LONDON AND NEW YORK

First published 2011
by Routledge
2 Park Square, Milton Park, Abingdon, Oxon OX14 4RN

Simultaneously published in the USA and Canada
by Routledge
270 Madison Avenue, New York, NY 10016

Routledge is an imprint of the Taylor & Francis Group, an informa business

© 2011 Anselm Haverkamp

The right of Anselm Haverkamp to be identified as author of this work has been asserted by him in accordance with sections 77 and 78 of the Copyright, Designs and Patents Act 1988.

Typeset in Minion by
RefineCatch Limited, Bungay, Suffolk
Printed and bound in Great Britain by
CIP Antony Rowe, Chippenham, Wiltshire

All rights reserved. No part of this book may be reprinted or reproduced or utilized in any form or by any electronic, mechanical, or other means, now known or hereafter invented, including photocopying and recording, or in any information storage or retrieval system, without permission in writing from the publishers.

British Library Cataloguing in Publication Data
A catalogue record for this book is available from the British Library

Library of Congress Cataloging in Publication Data
Haverkamp, Anselm.
 Shakespearean genealogies of power : a whispering of nothing in Hamlet, Richard II, Julius Caesar, Macbeth, The merchant of Venice, and The winter's tale / Anselm Haverkamp.
 p. cm.
 ISBN13: 978–0–415–59344–1 (hbk)—ISBN13: 978–0–415–59345–8 (pbk)—
ISBN13: 978–0–203–84028–3 (ebk) 1. Shakespeare, William, 1564–1616—Knowledge—Law. 2. Shakespeare, William, 1564–1616—Knowledge—History. 3. Shakespeare, William, 1564–1616—Poltical and social views. 4. Law in literature. 5. Politics in literature. 6. Law—Political aspects. 7. Power (Social sciences) in Literature. I. Title.
 PR3028.H38 2010
 822.3'3—dc22

2010032766

ISBN13: 978–0–415–59344–1 (hbk)
ISBN13: 978–0–415–59345–8 (pbk)
ISBN13: 978–0–203–84028–3 (ebk)

Contents

	Acknowledgements	viii
	The Argument	1
1	*Perpetuum Mobile:* Shakespeare's Perpetual Renaissance	7
2	The Ghost of History: Hamlet and the Politics of Paternity	17
3	Lethe's Wharf: Wild Justice, the Purgatorial Supplement	39
4	*Richard II*, Bracton, and the End of Political Theology	47
5	The Death of a Shifter: Jupiterian History in *Julius Caesar*	57
6	The Future of Violence: Machiavelli and Macbeth	73
7	A Whispering of Nothing: *The Winter's Tale*	87
	Tailpieces	107
8	But Mercy is Above: Shylock's Pun of a Pound	109
9	Habeas Corpus: The Law's Desire to Have the Body	117
	Notes	129
	Names, Words, and Things	169

Acknowledgements

The book was a long time in the making and has acquired a history of its own that is by far too long to be related in detail. Most parts were written and thought in English, revised and rethought in German, only in order to be reworked and translated back, in the accumulated bilinguistic reflection, into the English from which they came. Therefore, the help and influence of competent travelers between the languages were instrumental and deserve special gratitude, among them less obvious names like Jacques Derrida and Samuel Weber, superb readers between Nietzsche and the French connection of advanced American criticism, but also Peter Goodrich, intuitive genius without German but with a lot of French and, more important, the intimate feeling for centuries of Shakespearean British. Daniel Hoffman-Schwartz, Barbara Natalie Nagel, and Kirk Wetters have helped me greatly in detail; to them the actual shape of the text owes a lot. To Stanley Cavell and Stephen Greenblatt, I owe the courage to deal with Shakespeare, to Christoph Menke, the stamina to stay with Hegel. From Peter Goodrich and Cornelia Vismann I learned how to take the law. Rüdiger Campe, Cynthia Chase, Martin Harries, Jacques Lezra, Philip Lorenz, Michèle Lowrie, Julia Reinhard Lupton, Bettine Menke, Björn Quiring, Katrin Trüstedt and Juliane Rebentisch gave kind advice in matters theoretical, theatrical, and historical.

All previously published material has been thoroughly revised and reshaped for this book. All texts have been terminologically adapted to each other by the author with the help of Daniel Hoffman-Schwartz and Barbara Natalie Nagel.

"Perpetuum mobile" was published in *Theaterschrift* 11 (1997) on "The Return of the Classics." The original English version by Anthony Reynolds was reworked and adapted to the present volume by Daniel Hoffman-Schwartz and Barbara Natalie Nagel.

"The Ghost of History" developed from the Inaugural Lecture at the European University Viadrina in 1997; an earlier version, written in English, was given as a seminar under the title of "Twilight of the Literary" at New York University, 1994, SUNY Buffalo, 1995, and Harvard University, 1997. The German lecture was reprinted several times under the title "Hamlet, Hypothek der Macht," before it became part of *Hamlet, Hypothek der Macht* (Berlin: Kadmos 2001, 2nd edn. 2004); the American version, as re-translated by Kirk Wetters and published in *Law and Literature* 18 (2006), owes more than one point, including its most fitting subtitle "Hamlet and the Politics of Paternity," to Peter Goodrich.

"Lethe's Wharf," originally with the subtitle "The Tide of History," was written for a conference on "Cultural Memory," organized by Annette Schwartz and Cynthia Chase at Cornell University in 1999; it was repeated in versions in Amsterdam, Utrecht, and Hanover.

"Richard II, Bracton, and the End of Political Theology" was written for Hent de Vries' conference on "Political Theology" in Amsterdam in 2001, repeated at the British Shakespeare Association in Leicester in 2002, in SUNY Buffalo and the Johns Hopkins University in 2004; printed in *Law and Literature* 16 (2004).

"The Death of a Shifter" was written for a workshop on "Theo-Political Renaissance" organized by Philip Lorenz at Cornell University in 2008 and repeated for the Cardozo Law conference "Political Theology" in 2010.

"The Future of Violence" was written for the Bochum Institute of Genocide and Diaspora Research in 1999 and appeared in *Zeitschrift für Genozidforschung* 2 (2000). The English translation is Daniel Hoffman-Schwartz and Barbara Natalie Nagel's.

"A Whispering of Nothing" was written for the conference "Tragödie-Trauerspiel-Spektakel," organized by Bettine and Christoph Menke with Juliane Rebentisch in Berlin in 2006 and appeared in a first version in the volume of that title in the series *Theater der Zeit* (2007). It had been presented at LMU Munich in 2005, Yale and Johns Hopkins Universities in 2006. The English translation remains largely Kirk Wetter's.

"But Mercy Is Above" was only recently written for Hans Ulrich Gumbrecht's project on "Latency" and is meant to clarify my use of this term. The English version owes much to Daniel Hoffman-Schwartz and Barbara Natalie Nagel's translation and to Julia Lupton's first reading of it.

The "Habeas Corpus" piece is the oldest of the book and serves as a backdrop for the juridical genealogy of the project as developed with Giorgio Agamben. It was written in collaboration with Cornelia Vismann for the opening event of the Amsterdam School of Cultural Analysis in 1996 and published in the conference volume *Violence, Identity, and Self-Determination*, edited by Hent de Vries and Samuel Weber (Stanford University Press, 1997). I am deeply grateful to Cornelia Vismann for letting me repeat this text here again, if only for the sake of its unmanaged latencies, in its tentative, original form, occasionally supplemented and slightly touched up towards the end.

The predecessor volume *Hamlet, Hypothek der Macht* (Berlin: Kadmos, 2000, 2nd edn. 2004) includes related pieces and earlier versions of some chapters.

The Argument

This is not a Foucault book. Rather, the term genealogy, notorious as it may have become through the work of Foucault, refers back to a method implicit in Hegel's *Phenomenology of Spirit*, which also proceeds genealogically: as a history of the mind's and subject's legal, institutional, cultural embeddedness. Like Foucault, however, whose *Archaeology of Knowledge* – a title not without Hegelian resonances – refutes all attempts at a history of the mind's sole life in a post-Hegelian *Geistesgeschichte*, this book conceives of a different history: a history including the latent moments of its coming to pass instead of sublating the latent in the succession of a "subject" successfully aware of, and in full accord with, its own terms. For this kind of historical research, the venerable metaphor of archaeology, handed down from Rousseau and Freud to Collingwood and Foucault alike, seems too weak a reminder of what might be at stake. "Genealogy," on the other hand, if we take it as a metaphor subjected to the service of Hegel's phenomenology, points to a generic implication of method – its teleological aim beyond the culturally unconscious – which is closer to the literary sphere than the metaphorical fields of excavation will suggest. "Power," another key of Foucault's and subject of his archaeologies, is less susceptible to ideology, against whose functioning the method is to be safeguarded, than it is to legitimacy, whose logic of representation it addresses. Genealogy in this sense follows a logic of empowering, and it is one aim of the book to show the theater of Shakespeare as the place where this logic as a logic of positioning is discovered and exposed. But Power, after all, is only one term, the God term whose rule is presented and dismantled – deconstructed – on the stage after this same stage's predecessor, the universal representation of Christ's Incarnation on the altar of every church, had put on, from the beginning of its institution, the destruction of worldly power before this power's divine manifestation. The difficult ending of Walter Benjamin's *Critique of Violence* also marks the end of this trajectory.

"Political Theology," the jurist Ernst Kantorowicz's label for the medieval logic of political representation, took for a self-conscious, self-reflective, at moments self-deconstructive, analogue the emergence of what Stephen Greenblatt has most fittingly termed *Shakespearean Negotiations*. The things negotiated in this space allowed for a sense and concept of a "Political" beyond the rhetorical divide – in the aftermath, in fact – of Carl Schmitt's ominous conception of *Political Theology*. Here, Hans Blumenberg's critique of Schmitt proved devastating and final. As far as the negotiating part is concerned, however, there is any amount of historical amendments in place and a lot of theoretical supplements to be provided. Most decisively, the "eventuality" – not to call it the event-character – of Shakespeare reception asks for a deeper understanding of literary effect and transport. The term I have come more and more to favor is "latency" which, from the Latin "latere" in Ovid's "ars adeo latet arte sua" down to the "latent content" of Freud's *Interpretation of Dreams*, underwent a veritable "latency period" of its own, and the "Literary" – that much Ovid and Freud knew alike – seems its very phenomenology.* Thus, the genealogy of power in Shakespeare's trajectory, far from subscribing to that power, brings to the fore what his late Romantic admirer John Keats intuited with the loose but pregnant opposite formula of a "negative capability."

Adapted from the Late Shakespeare's *Winter's Tale*, "A Whispering of Nothing" refers to the seminal role of latency in Shakespeare's theater with respect, last but not least, to the law. As a visible space between the spheres of politics and law and well able to negotiate legal and political, even constitutional concerns, Shakespeare's theater opened up a new perspective on normativity. Specifically, Shakespeare offered a perspective that reflects, even creates, "history" in a new sense on the premises of the older conceptions of historical and legal exemplarity: examples, cases, and instances are to be reflected on rather than treated as straightforwardly

---

* See my books *Figura cryptica: Theorie der literarischen Latenz* (Frankfurt/M: Suhrkamp, 2002), and *Latenzzeit: Wissen im Nachkrieg* (Berlin: Kadmos, 2004), as well as *Metapher: Die Ästhetik in der Rhetorik* (Munich: Fink, 2007), for the rhetorical–technical background of the latency concept.

didactic or salvific. Thus, what comes to be recognized, reflected and acknowledged, has a disowning, alienating effect, whose aftermath rather than whose immediacy counts and remains effective. Hegel, who since his childhood remained a close reader of Shakespeare, found in Shakespeare's theater one of the sources of his philosophy of history and law, including the law's role in history. At the same time, the concept of latency – of invisible schemata governing visible forms – surfaced from Bacon's essays. It captures the far-reaching performative potential of Shakespeare's mise-en-scène, the inexhaustible quality of his designs, the *perpetuum mobile* as a mode of theatrical exposition that seems to run forever.

The first chapter "Perpetuum Mobile" introduces latency's formal, technical, rhetorical – in short, functional – implications for this extraordinary reception history of a canonical author and confronts it with the appropriate consequences of a historical redescription. Written in 1997, this piece remains marked by the theatrical momentum of the day, impressed by Artaud's *Theatre of Cruelty* and dominated by Peter Brook's diagnosis of Shakespeare's crucial role for the theater after Brecht. But there was more to say than met the eye at the time, much more than the tedious critical investigation of historical conditioning brings to light: a deep-seated latency of appeal that accounts for the enduring acuteness of a renewed rhetorical *actualitas*. The proto-political urgency that it promotes is indicative of an economy of latency, which informs Shakespeare's theater over the centuries, a latent thrust whose depth and reach can hardly be better measured than in reading his texts – in a reading that is no longer the poor supplement of actually watching its many ways of being performed.

Coming to terms with the "latent content" of Shakespeare's work leads to a rather laconic rephrasing of what has been most emphatically named the Renaissance. Already Hegel's philosophy of history implied in its many uses of Shakespeare a re-evaluation of the Renaissance as a re-description and re-inscription of the modern self-conception of law and history. Shakespeare's stage creates a type of history of its own, resetting legal and constitutional histories. Towards the end of the twentieth century, the machine is dismantled by Heiner Müller, taken apart and put together again. Against its own premise of an entirely "natural" working of violence, in the interest, rather, of its deep-seated, hidden juridical underpinnings, Müller's *Hamlet-Machine* is to be seen as the symptomatic result of a re-evaluation, which raises the historical threshold while deepening the underlying latencies.

The "Shakespearean Genealogies of Power" to be envisaged here trace this mode of the modern back to and beyond the notorious dead end of melancholia, as it had been recognized and fought over ever since Burton's

Anatomy of Melancholy and became the central trope for all criticism after Benjamin's *Trauerspiel*. The two tailpieces of this volume on the presentation of Shylock's case in *The Merchant of Venice* and on the writ and act of *Habeas corpus* indicate the larger theoretical frame, in which the main part elaborates, in seven exemplary readings, the interaction of law and latency in Shakespeare – from the meta-theater of *Hamlet* through the conflicts over the state and format of sovereignty in *Richard II*, *Julius Caesar* and *Macbeth* to the post-dramatic theater of Late Shakespeare's *Winter's Tale* and *Tempest*.

The second, central chapter focuses on "The Ghost of History" in "Hamlet and the Politics of Paternity" and excavates in the common ground of decades of *Hamlet* scholarship the legal and constitutional underground of what happens in *Hamlet*, and how what happens in *Hamlet* has been sensed all along in the uncommon reception history of the play from Nietzsche, Freud and Benjamin to Stanley Cavell, but also how and why this point was categorically missed by Carl Schmitt and political activists of all quarters. Writing and staging what is latent in history is what happens and makes things happen in *Hamlet*.

In addition, the third chapter considers "Lethe's Wharf" as the latent spot in the text, where "Wild Justice and the Purgatorial Supplement" supplement the *Hamlet* syndrome with its crucial point in legal philosophy, according to Hegel's refined though also utterly cryptic reading. The difference of revenge as "wild justice" and law corresponds to the difference of memory and history. The recent "turn" to memory and religion is thus exposed as – indeed, turns out to be – a turn against history and the historical achievement of the law.

The fourth chapter on "*Richard II*, Bracton, and the End of Political Theology" takes a step back in the canon of Shakespeare plays to the striking move against the politico-theological ideology and mystical foundation of the earlier British monarchy around 1300. Here, the Carl Schmitt debate is reset through the fundamental critiques of Hans Blumenberg and Giorgio Agamben, supplemented by the older state of the debate in Erik Peterson's and Ernst Kantorowicz's work. At the same time, and against the grain of the constitutional agenda, the specific poetological irony of the play becomes visible: in deposing himself, the king is, and remains, above the law.

The fifth chapter "The Death of a Shifter" comes to a crucial moment of this trajectory with Foucault's intuition, taken from Georges Dumézil, of a "Jupiterian History" in Julius Caesar's mortgage: the question of what comes after the dismantled political theology of the later Middle Ages is left behind, possibly in the interest of the British Empire's administrative power elite and newly established nobility. Thus, Shakespeare's *Julius Caesar* offers the flip side of the *Hamlet* impasse, a constitutional problem that remains up to now embarrassed by a historically unsettled question. Shakespeare takes his own evaluation in the spirit of Tacitus vs. the modernist versions of Livy after Machiavelli, and this Tacitean turn will inform his further dramatic career and development from *Hamlet* to *Macbeth* on the one side, and to *The Winter's Tale* and *The Tempest* – so-called Late Shakespeare as a genre – on the other.

The sixth chapter "The Future of Violence" shows *Macbeth* as the grim caricature of a Maclavellus answering to Machiavelli's Borgia and his exemplary use of violence. The exemplarity question, with which the Tacitean turn in *Julius Caesar* concluded, finds a new model in Machiavelli's influence on *Macbeth*, historically the mythic law maker, who is overwhelmed by the violence unleashed, but also, and more importantly, by the merciless futurity emerging from it and foreshadowing a problematic governmentality to come.

In the seventh chapter, finally, "A Whispering of Nothing" is found in *The Winter's Tale*, which begins with the Romantic aftermath of the Machiavellian scene and is put into perspective by a new sense of the Political in Heine's, Marx's and Benjamin's, rather than in Carl Schmitt's sense of an ending: as "tragic humor," rather than "political Romanticism." Late Shakespeare, far from withdrawing into Romance, rewrites the older historical designs into intricate examples of a latent Latinity, which in dramatic variations of Montaigne's essayistic mode of presentation produces deep historical insights, in this case a reconceiving of *Hamlet* in a *Winter's Tale* without Hamlet, but with a lost son nevertheless. The art that had failed in vengeance need not refuse itself reconciliation.

Both tailpieces, "But Mercy is Above: Shylock's Pun of a Pound" and "Habeas Corpus: The Law's Desire to Have the Body," the most recent and the oldest piece of the book, respectively, indicate aspects and consequences for the debate on structural violence from Benjamin and Agamben to Robert Cover and Niklas Luhmann. History and pre-history of *Habeas Corpus* coincide with the Shakespearean genealogies of power, violence, and mercy.

CHAPTER 1

Perpetuum Mobile: Shakespeare's Perpetual Renaissance

Like the Hamlet-machine, the whole of Shakespeare is a *perpetuum mobile*; it runs as if from itself and produces ever anew the matter that it needs: History, the ever-same old story. What makes the idea of the machine so appealing is the assumption that it would run on endlessly, although this is the last thing a machine would do – they do just stop from time to time. History is that which keeps on going: "History in its natural state," which is to say: History as "Nature."[1] When we think of the fatal mechanical course of history and compare Shakespeare to a *perpetuum mobile*, what we actually mean is the spirit, rather, that breezes through it: a Spirit which drives the machine where it would never go on its own, nor even tend to go from its own power. The Hamlet-machine, and with it all of Shakespeare, hides a philosophy of history with a built-in spirit induced from Shakespeare's theater. It speaks from the beyond and drifts into the beyond, out of which it – from beyond the stage – speaks: a ghost of the theater.

The theater that summoned this spirit cannot get rid of it. Shakespeare invented it, here Heiner Müller is right, and in *Hamlet* it literally entered the stage; as a ghost it haunts the theater and shows itself, dead father and king, as the ruling principle from the beginning: it embodies – or rather, bodilessly appears as – the spirit that drives history. When this, history, at the play's end goes on with the armed force of a Fortinbras, we catch a glimpse of the machinery. Since instead of simply producing theater, Shakespeare's theater showed the theater-machine at work in the production of history. This means that it did not merely show the functioning of history on stage but rather the functioning of the theater in the production of history: the origin of history from the spirit of theater; history as we know it and as we believe ourselves to be in it; of the concept we have of it as something that goes on around us.

We have grown accustomed to this conception of history; we think we have a grasp on it. We call it historical just as one called the course of nature historical before modern science withdrew this understanding of nature from history.[2] The new concept of history is a self-evident second nature in which we self-evidently know our way around. We have taken it to be so evident that it is difficult to make comprehensible how – or even that – it once *emerged*. This conception is so deeply embedded in the givenness of our life-world that it has become impossible to imagine any course and occurrence of events without it. That it was brought to a concept by Shakespeare and Elizabethan theater – that it was made comprehensible *as* a mode of theatrical representation – has been lost in the self-evidence of the quasi-natural grasp on things passing or coming to pass. Nietzsche for one had an idea of the revolution that dwelled within this new concept when he referred to Shakespeare again and again in his *Birth of Tragedy*. Benjamin deepened this intuition when he recognized the baroque stage as the site where history as we know it – against the concept of the old, classic tragedy, which we no longer know – is brought to a definition.

The confusion of theater and history, like that of literature and life, goes deep; it is part of the theater-effect, and Shakespeare's stage not only factored in its emergence but also deepened its effect in unforeseeable ways. What Shakespeare is said to have indeed invented, however, according to Shakespeare-adepts and admirers since the eighteenth century, would not be history – for this had already become patently clear – but character: the *individuum ineffabile* with its inimitable nature and abyssal particularity, a singularity, which allows it to surpass the role it has to play on the stage of this world. Yet what in fact surpasses the limits of the stage and bestows this format upon its protagonists is, precisely, the history they leave behind. For by now it is certain that history could not appear simply as itself or have effects as that which is remembered in annals and chronicles as stories and legends. While History itself – this makes the ghost of Hamlet, the witches of Macbeth, or the dreams of Richard III so extreme – neither speaks nor speaks for itself from out of the stage-machine, it crystallizes, nevertheless, in the characters of the protagonists. Resounding from within the machine, detached from it under the groans of those who bear its voice, history emerges as History. What the actors leave behind and beneath them is the stage on which they act – *as* history. Their characters make History readable as a script, as hieroglyphics in a human form. And as we read history in these characters, it disappears in the figures in which it enters the stage: of these figures of history, thus, we perceive nothing but their character as the trace of the readability of History. The history of which they are a part is drained away from them; while the characters, who are not real but only fictively brought into a human form, remain with us. In taking these figures literally, we have come to grasp History as theater.

The modern success of Shakespeare, starting from the Romantics, is the success of these characters. What they represent in the place of history, as its residue, is the modern *individuum* as ineffable: as the elusive subject of histories, which makes exemplary in a wondrous way what, as an *ineffabile*, cannot very well be exemplary; singularly, as it presents itself and stages itself, it is unpicturable: "Hamlet is the difference Shakespeare made."[3] Psychoanalysis puts this paradoxical *exemplum* to the test: no real human beings could be more productive for psychoanalysis than Shakespeare's characters. Hamlet's Oedipus-complex, which Oedipus himself could not very well have had yet, brings before the eyes of the modern individual what all repression must, wide-eyed, mistake. What the public does not notice about Hamlet's melancholia, but it itself actually helps to bring about, is nothing but its own condition and entanglement. Since then, there has been no double-binding force, no entanglement that Shakespeare's theater could not represent and call forth, could not produce and provoke. "Shakespeare and – once again – no end." Goethe's notorious title was more than a timely *bon mot*; just short of a prophecy, it betrays a deep insight into the historical efficiency of Shakespeare's theater.

If embodied history is always the same – say, bloodthirsty – then too the heroes in it are always the same – like, unfathomable. This is a concept that is clear to schoolmasters and dramaturges alike. One never ceases to be amazed – Jan Kott's slogan "Shakespeare Our Contemporary" attests to it – how his genius intuited a human nature that seems marked as if unalterable in the course of things, and, more astonishingly, how he was able to foresee time and again the full amount of anthropological knowledge that has been gained since. There is no insight or perversion that Shakespeare would not have already predicted *avant la lettre* – just as one would say of Nature herself, except that there one would not find it. Thus, a new historicism, which aims for this kind of a readability of human nature within history, found it immediately in Shakespeare.

The value of Shakespeare as a historical source elucidates the success of his plays in impressive ways: the two run parallel to one another, from the Romantics via Psychoanalysis to the New Historicism, which makes the implicit historical thrust of the former fully explicit. It is this parallelism which in turn is highly revealing: the parallel of a continual and by now almost patented success on the fields of anthropology, psychoanalysis and other cultural sciences, whose validity is measured against and confirmed by the evidence established on Shakespeare's stage. For Stephen Greenblatt, the actuality of the Hamlet-machine as well as the actuality of the Oedipus complex, the brutalities of natural history as well as the latencies of cultural history, are effects of "social energy."[4] The energy in question is the Latin *actualitas*, and Shakespeare produces this actuality to the extent that it transforms the Greek *energeia* into a principle of dramatic presencing – a "bringing before one's eyes" in Aristotle's *Poetics*, where it was called *enargeia* (both terms were conflated at the time, and as one sees, with a reason).

The question then is: what in the *enargeia* of theatrical presentation could secure the perpetual actuality of Shakespeare's stage? Is it really nothing but the exposed brutality of history, as in the version of Heiner Müller, which is meant to extend Marx's continuation – or, rather, his correction – of Hegel's understanding of Shakespeare? Or is it, more to the point, the persistent blindness of the actors of this history, as in the psychoanalytic tendency of Freud's version? How do we arrive at this stunning transparency of history, given the opacity of the characters ensnared within it? Following Greenblatt's conclusion, it is the strikingly effective force of "cultural transactions" that in Shakespeare becomes aesthetically presentable: aesthetically in the sense that these transactions are brought from their more or less concealed cultural functioning into the full light right before the eyes and draw from there the force of negotiation on and beyond the stage. This hypothesis provides not only a most plausible genealogy of the modern "public sphere."[5] It attempts and manages to found the very plausibility that it produces on the basis of its own self-evidence. In the manner of a self-foundation, which promises to ground no less than a "cultural poetics," the enterprise of Greenblatt's new historicism resembles, and brings into the open, the implicit historicism of psychoanalysis. The new historicist explanation delivers nothing less than a full transposition of the method, practice, and cure of psychoanalysis. That this transposition actually works is due to the concealment of its origin, which appears on stage as the visible violence of history. In the characters of the protagonists, it appears as repressed desire, as a form of an at best half-conscious involvedness: in short, as the pressure of the very history that has disappeared in them and returns, dramatically incorporated, in the form of the individuated stories that, according to their scripts, the characters are brought to act out.

Freud and Jones have shown, and Lacan, Green, Abraham, Girard following them, how the concealment of the potential effectivity of Shakespeare's stage keeps on functioning the better in and through the state of latency, under the continued cover of repression. Greenblatt, Fineman, and Shell each show how the self-thematization of the stage in the disclosure of social energy reproduces itself aesthetically, as revelation, and it is the continuation rather than the original, historically-bound disclosure, which succeeds and proliferates in the circulation of social energy and self-representation. In this doubled explanation – of the persistence of repression and of the proliferation of self-representation – the theater has become a double-theater: a stage with a double floor. In the long run, what would secure the interest of the audience would be the second floor on which the first – which in itself has turned into an entirely opaque and historically contingent ground – would have become universal, and thereby serviceable for either self-reflection proper or the focusing of collective energy.

The stage, which since then has come to signify the world, carries the latter out of itself. It is no wonder that it was the Romantics who enriched Shakespeare's stage with the addition of the second floor of "reflection" and established theatricality as a "mediality of reflection" in the early Benjamin's sense [*Reflexionsmedium*]. But whatever one's relation to the inbuilt Romanticism of the new historical challenge may be, it does not serve to explain Shakespeare's undiminished actuality, the *actualitas* of his *enargeia*, the effects of "presencing" on his stage. It demonstrates rather than explains this actuality. Like all machines, the *perpetuum mobile* called Shakespeare runs by itself only inasmuch as it continually affirms itself. As a consequence, post-Romantic Shakespeare interpretation is imprinted with a sort of self-fulfilling prophecy. The programmed mis-interpretation or foreshortening of interpretation becomes effective as some other, milder type of repression: it resembles – at best – the self-misunderstanding of the histories represented. They come to appear as the merest arbitrary stuff, depotentiated to the dramatic fuel of the machine. And history comes into appearance as a ghost haunting the machine, inscrutably shadowing over the stage.

In this respect, Shakespeare's effect conforms not to that of Freud but to that of Marx, after all, and *Hamlet* is the first and oldest of Derrida's *Specters of Marx*, the proto-ghost of a history, which never comes to itself, a spirit, which does not occur as revolution, but stagnates. Shakespeare's stage is the place of this not-taking-place of history; it is, one might say, the place of the discovery of a movable, labile stage in lieu of a place: a nonplace, where a caesura in history is announced, which would – perhaps, at best – in the meanwhile remain nothing but a proleptic presentation of the stage. That the ghost of Hamlet allows Time to slip "out of joint" and lays claim thereby to a model of history as upheaval (be it as renaissance or revolution), betrays the energy within the *enargeia* that was to be accounted for. Thus, what does not allow the performance to come to a rest, but allows the ghost on the contrary to achieve great form is the collected social energy of history, which the ghost of Shakespeare's theater lets enter the stage as a ghost of pre-history: the ghost of an old, unfinished story. In the ghost of old Hamlet the specter of history plays itself; the specter of this history is, as I read William Empson's intuition, the emergence of the theater itself. A theater, which in *Richard II* only and simply *is* – is powerlessly there, bare theater. But which in *Richard III* is no longer content merely to *be* there – instead, history as catastrophe enters, re-volution in the literal sense [*Umwälzung*]. Ernst Kantorowicz's indecision as to whether *Richard II* merely ended the Middle Ages or was already preparing for the revolution of the modern was a scandal and concern already for the contemporaries including their queen, the great Elizabeth. *Richard II* reveals the flipside of the Romantic genius in whose guise *Richard III*, a Hamlet's walk on the wild side, sets history in motion and causes it to lose its common composure.

That History in this manner simply keeps going *is* the catastrophe, wrote Benjamin in the *Central Park* fragments, meaning the catastrophe of Hegel's "ethical order," from whose permanence Hegel wanted the phenomenology of his Spirit to escape (illustrating his claims through Shakespeare characters). However one would like to describe the career of this spirit, it remains a ghost of the stage, haunting the double floor of the theater in order to speak from there without interruption. That this ghost of Hamlet gives acting lessons to Brecht's Arturo Ui in Heiner Müller's last Berlin production and, more tellingly, from the mouth of Marianne Hoppe, reveals how plausibly history keeps going – provided it does so – in stage productions from Brecht to Müller and beyond.[6] Matthias Langhoff's Paris production of *Richard III*, good for every graphic consequence, displays the boundaries, and beyond these, the fading out, of the old world with its drama of the ethical. In Langhoff's *Gloucester Time*, Richard III undergoes an elaborate series of transformations, joint by joint, from act to act: he turns from the Elizabethan villain into the Robespierre of the *terreurs* and inevitably into Hitler, ending up in recording the latest warfare from desert storm and drowning out old Hamlet's ghost voice in the acoustic coolness of a certain General Schwarzkopf (already forgotten), before which Shakespeare's good old bad times crumble away as almost again worthy of good old melancholia.[7]

Thus, Joan of Arc serves as a remedy in the metamorphosis of brutal Tudor history, in a pointed pre-revolutionary irony that works as a prelude to desert storm. "Supporting our tropes" (as Avital Ronell proclaimed at the time), Saint Joan leaves us with the whole ethical world caught between pre-history and the post-histoire. No longer "our contemporary," Shakespeare has turned into the ghost of ancestors from a pre-history, which the myth of the modern has kept in store for us. This pre-history, which modernity wards off with the ghost of Shakespeare's stage, continues with undiminished violence. It endures in the mediating form of a modernity which, even in Shakespeare, was never, at any time, the master of its pre-history. This makes Shakespeare the precursor of Freud and the epitome of the Western canon. Such continuation is that of a certain knowing: a knowing how to defend oneself: a defense in the *tristes tropiques* of the theater as well as a defense mechanism in the more or less gay skepticism of theory. In the spirit of Nietzsche and following Freud, Stanley Cavell has summed up the skepticism that is acted out in Shakespeare as a cheerful science rather than a form of tragic non-knowledge: his dramas – "like those of Freud," Cavell assures us – "propose our coming to know what we cannot just not know; like philosophy."[8]

What one in such a defense does not know, and yet cannot just not know, the full range of repressed traumas, of bygone wars, has turned into a foreknowing that leads the Shakespearean stage beyond the morality of an ethical order. As an antidote to philosophical skepticism, this type of non-knowledge, or negative knowledge, is a reaction to the epistemological formation of the modern, which goes all the way to the end with modernity – although it does not come to an end there; Cavell refers to such a moral of immanence as "the acceptance of days." The "subjectivity effect" of modern consciousness, whose emergence Joel Fineman found in Shakespeare, is that of a self-skeptical and never more than half-conscious knowledge, completed in a "self-fashioning" by way of the theatricality of history. As a curious appetite for knowledge, this consciousness knows what, as a subject, it precisely does not and cannot very well know; it *is* the not-knowing of this subject: an itself-not-completely-knowing and an itself-also-not-completely-being (I underline the "also-not" of this theatrical mode of "being"), whose theatrical existence, as it enters the stage by the spirit of History, is moved and animated by a theater-ghost.

Shakespeare's continued Renaissance thrives upon a "strategic opacity," superbly thematized in *Hamlet* but implicitly at work all along.[9] Its metahistorical character is reflected ever after, particularly in the reflective genre of Late Shakespeare. Opacity is a good name for the appearance of energy and force on Shakespeare's stage in general, but there is more to its efficacy than meets – or, rather, in all its opaqueness escapes – the eye of the beholder. The law of Shakespeare's stage is counter-determined by, and thus prevails on, the unexplained premises of a latency far before the law, whose threat the law is barely able to keep at bay, and whose transgressive nature has been only precariously mastered in classical myth. In this respect, Ovid was crucial; he is the historical threshold from which Shakespeare operates. The double-bind that forces law and myth of old is "something rotten," cites Benjamin Hamlet; its rottenness is the latent ground on which Shakespeare's theater takes its uncertain place. The history of its effects – call it reception – is not one of the changing opinions on an ongoing same substance – call it the Human – but asks for an elucidation of the rotten ground taken in each case. To arrange the cases – plays – in chronological order, historical, biographical or generic, will not do. Latent traits and their ways of theatrical manifestation are of no systematic order. History is to be grasped in the events of their singular latency's manifestations – in the text, in short – rather than in the bare facticity, that these occasions are to be localized, as it were, in the broken chain of occurrences.

200 Years of Shakespeare Reception, Mostly *Hamlet*

Georg Wilhelm Friedrich Hegel, *Phänomenologie des Geistes* (1807)
August Wilhelm Schlegel, *Vorlesungen über dramatische Kunst und Literatur* (1809)
Friedrich Nietzsche, *Die Geburt der Tragödie* (1872)
Sigmund Freud, *Die Traumdeutung* (1900)
T.S. Eliot, "Hamlet and his Problems" (1919)
Walter Benjamin, *Ursprung des deutschen Trauerspiels* (1928)
G. Wilson Knight, *The Wheel of Fire* (1930)
William Empson, *Some Versions of Pastoral* (1935)
C.S. Lewis, "Hamlet: The Prince or the Poem" (1942)
E.M.W. Tillyard, *Shakespeare's History Plays* (1944)
Ernest Jones, *Hamlet and Oedipus* (1949)
Harold C. Goddard, *The Meaning of Shakespeare* (1951)
William Empson, *Essays on Shakespeare* (1953–1968)
Carl Schmitt, *Hamlet oder Hekuba* (1956)
Ernst Kantorowicz, *The King's Two Bodies* (1958)
Jan Kott, *Shakespeare our Contemporary* (1962)
Frances A. Yates, *The Art of Memory* (1966)
Tom Stoppard, *Rosencrantz and Guildenstern Are Dead* (1967)
Peter Brook, *The Empty Space* (1968)
Emrys Jones, *Scenic Form in Shakespeare* (1971)

Nicolas Abraham, "Le fantôme d'Hamlet ou le VIe act" (1975)
Jacques Lacan, "Desire and the Interpretation of Desire in Hamlet" (1977)
Heiner Müller, *Hamletmaschine* (1977)
André Green, *Hamlet et Hamlet* (1982)
Malcolm Evans, *Signifying Nothing* (1986)
Jonathan Bate, *Shakespeare and the English Romantic Imagination* (1986)
Joel Fineman, *Shakespeare's Perjured Eye* (1986)
Stanley Cavell, *Disowning Knowledge* (1987)
Stephen Greenblatt, *Shakespearean Negotiations* (1987)
Joel Fineman, *The Subjectivity Effect in Western Tradition* (1991)
René Girard, *A Theater of Envy* (1991)
Marc Shell, *Children of the Earth* (1993)
Julia Lupton and Kenneth Reinhard, *After Oedipus* (1993)
Jacques Derrida, *Spectres of Marx* (1993)
Jonathan Bate, *The Genius of Shakespeare* (1997)
Richard Halpern, *Shakespeare Among the Moderns* (1997)
Harold Bloom, *Shakespeare: The Invention of the Human* (1998)
Stephen Greenblatt, *Hamlet in Purgatory* (2001)
Margreta de Grazia, *Hamlet Without Hamlet* (2007)

CHAPTER 2

The Ghost of History: Hamlet and the Politics of Paternity

Wildharrend/ in der furchtbaren Rüstung Jahrtausende.
— Hölderlin[1]

Adieu, fantômes! Le monde n'a plus besoin de vous.
— Valéry[2]

Shakespeare's *Hamlet*, following the Bible and possibly the Koran, has been subject of the most and best commentary of any text in the world. This situation, documented in huge bibliographies, is so overwhelming that it can no longer in itself be commented on. This does not mean, however, that there is nothing new to be said about *Hamlet*. Whatever might be new would never be so entirely new that it would have remained completely untouched in the endless network of the accumulated literature, but the impression of an infinite commentability of literary works that is often taken as historical proof of literary quality through reception is nevertheless a deceptive effect. It only proves, assuming it proves anything at all, the persistence of desires that are deceptively rewarded in literary works. This is not only true of *Hamlet*, but of all great works. They give rise to the idea that they achieve their greatness through progressive development as types of fascination — an endless spiritual preoccupation through which culture is cultivated and renews itself. This self-delusion does not reside in the fascination that keeps the reader imprisoned, but rather in a deceptively deepened perception of the works' identity.

Centuries of commentary have inevitably touched upon what they could neither conceive of nor over time not conceive of, but were all too willing to leave alone, ungrasped. In the case of *Hamlet* there are mountains of literature on such forms of defense or denial, and every attempt at a new interpretation must inevitably run the risk of its own belatedness, which consequently confronts it with the obvious question: why didn't someone come up with it before? Even in the densest of receptions like *Hamlet*'s, the latency of that which has not been discovered lies relatively motionless beneath the surface of thousands of known details of a story that has been retold and replayed thousands of times. It was the success and the achievement of a new historicism that it was able, schooled in the reading of Shakespeare, to bring such latencies into motion. But it remains a widespread error to assume that this motion was affected by an ever broader historical contextualization and by an ever greater precision in connecting the texts back to the historical referents they contain. It is indeed rather the reverse: Every new observation in a text, brought from its latency into a manifest state, does so thanks to a radical de-contextualization, which must occur before interpretation can become fertile again in the light of historical details and produce a new historical context. Every new reading of literature allows history to be rewritten, and this is in fact its point. This is what makes it literary: that it allows the old stories of history to be reconceived and rewritten.

Shakespeare's theater revolutionized this rewriting of history, and re-conceptualized the function of literature – its ability to reconceive of history – in the epochal sense of a transformative "Copernican Revolution" in the Kantian and also in the Freudian sense.[3] It was Walter Benjamin who recognized the overturning of the concept of classical tragedy in Shakespeare's *tragical histories,* and has understood *Hamlet* as the quintessence or meta-drama of a modern, historical concept of the tragic, in which history emerges in the place of older mythical constructions.[4] In *Hamlet,* the transition produced by this reinvestment takes its effect, indeed, in a kind of Copernican reversal. Unlike the tragedies of antiquity – say, *Medea* – *Hamlet* cannot presuppose, memorialize and represent myth as the constitutive moment of its production. Instead *Hamlet* must establish the priority of the mythic event as a quasi-mythic analog within its own reception. In *Hamlet* this necessity seems so perfectly accomplished that the modern history of its reception has promptly re-mythified it, and in retrospect has celebrated it as the perfect return of classical tragedy within modernity.

Nietzsche's *Birth of Tragedy* had re-inscribed this effect, *Hamlet*'s modern intensification of the tragic, into the form of the Dionysian origin of ancient tragedy. It was from this that Freud's *Interpretation of Dreams* drew its negative account, recognizing in Dionysian Hamlet the return of "Dionysian man" *par excellence*: the increase of a cultural repression that had caused Hamlet to fall victim to the same Oedipus complex that held his audience under its sway.[5] *Hamlet* was bound to present the syndrome produced by its own influence as a pre-existing parameter of old narratives (like Oedipus for Freud) and could not but confirm it in its historical, mythical function. Thus, even today, we tend to take the ghost of *Hamlet* at face value, as an objective ghost through which justice and order impose themselves during a time that has gotten "out of joint" (as Hamlet comments on the appearance of the ghost) and the great mass of post-Romantic interpretations, finally those following Nietzsche, take this as an enigmatic but universal, transhistorical matter of fact. They interpret Hamlet's task as the mission of the modern subject itself, who must stand up against incomprehensible forces of murderously violent power-relations and must rid states like Denmark of whatever may be "rotten" in them.[6]

> *The time is out of joint. O cursed spite,*
> *That ever I was born to set it right.*
> (1.5.196–197)

A word of great pathos whose irony, like all pathos in this play, is first illuminated from its ending. The grandiosity of a great birth is, as will come out in the course of the acts to follow, a curse – "O cursed spite" – that includes the righteous act he is called upon to perform, the act by which right relations are to be re-established not only in the state, but the state itself is to be restored. As a curse rather than a blessing, Hamlet parodies the happy annunciation of the Christian epochal transformation and discovers in the rebirth that is supposed to be a renaissance nothing but the return of a repressed. And, as the ghost unmistakably makes known, this repression is Christian: The name of the bedeviled Claudius seems to locate *Hamlet* as an ultra early Christian mise-en-scène from the time of a Seneca or, more precisely, of Tacitus' history of the Claudian royal house under Nero.

To start with, I will address the "curse," the term by which Hamlet comprehends the time that has gotten "out of joint," and thematize it in three theses, which strike me as more or less overdue given the current state of scholarship. These propositions have, over the last hundred years, come into view and have more recently had a number of occasions to manifest themselves. They have emerged, however, without ultimately making it beyond the threshold of the commonplaces that they are indeed about to turn upside down.

My first thesis has to do with the ghost whose witching hour represents for Hamlet the occasion for the announcement that the "time is out of joint." This spirit – my first thesis, according to an old suspicion – *is a liar:* He is a phantom who is not the ghost that he claims to be; it is the ghost in which History takes the stage and presents itself as a phantom full of lies.

The second thesis concerns the historical relation of Hamlet to Fortinbras and the state of exception that threatens from the margins of the drama, threats that characterize the present disjointedness of the state of Denmark at the time of the play's action. *Hamlet* – my second thesis – is not, as it appears, only the story of Hamlet, but is – last but not least on account of the ghost – the *anamorphosis* of a different story and history: there is always another history buried in History.

My third thesis pertains to Hamlet's relation to Claudius and Gertrude, which, in the course of the drama, uncovers a third kind of disjointedness pertaining to Hamlet himself. It is entirely possible and conceivable – this is the third thesis – that he is not even the son of the dead King, but of his murderer, Claudius. It is this specific uncertainty that makes him ask – last but not least – the question whether "to be or not to be." The uncertainty of conception – one's being as being of uncertain origin – is a mortgage that fuels history.

A possible fourth thesis, which is already implicit in the third, but is not easily included without further supplementation, belongs to the "joint-ress," Hamlet's mother Gertrude, with regard to whom he refers to the time as "out of joint." It is the power of the mother, and the role of Queen that goes along with it, in which the hidden historico-political point of the play is invested. Gertrude makes *Hamlet* into Shakespeare's Elizabethan drama *par excellence,* and maybe his farewell to Elizabeth.

Unfortunately a sketch cannot include everything on which it depends. For this reason I will concentrate on Hamlet's ghost and the role of Fortinbras, but I will have not enough time for this drama's other drama, the story of Polonius, Laertes and Ophelia. I will treat the story of Claudius and Gertrude, but largely neglect the background of Nero. Unfortunately I will also largely neglect the closer analysis of Shakespeare's language, even though I owe my findings, where I deviate from the commonplaces on *Hamlet,* to a closer analytic reading, and that which I argue for, based on aspects of constitutional and criminal law, is the result of a rhetorical analysis. Since the theses are too interconnected to allow them to be treated completely separately, I have subdivided the material into two parts according to the conventional concerns of *Hamlet* scholarship, to which I also specifically hope to respond. The first deals with the appearance of the ghost and the political situation of revenge thereby defined. This aspect is conventionally understood as a historical problem. The second develops the psychological problem through the analysis of Hamlet's character and the delay of vengeance. The psychological dimension of the mortgaging power redefines both the theatrical impact and the historical profile of the play.

The Historical Enigma

Recall first the story, as we know it: The ghost of the father at the beginning of the play is the occasion for a great number of subsequent uncertainties. Without ourselves believing in ghosts, we have thought it necessary, ever since Romanticism, to take this spirit as a given of a superstitious era. A preliminary decision is thereby made, but it is one with which the hero of the play has significant difficulties. It is, after all, by no means true that either he or his contemporaries unquestioningly believed in ghosts, and this is certainly not inconsequential for the course of the play's events. If one takes the ghost of the father and his call for vengeance as the voice of justice (which in all seriousness it cannot be), then the remainder of the play heads inexorably in the direction of the plodding completion of a task whose detours can only lie in the weak character of the protagonist. Freud's formulation still hits on this point: "The play is built upon Hamlet's hesitating to fulfill the task of revenge that is laid upon him. Whatever the reasons or motives for this delay may be, they are not admitted in the text; even the most elaborate interpretive attempts have been unable to say what they actually are."[7] *Wilhelm Meister*, Freud's primary point of reference and implicitly that of the entire interpretive tradition, was the source that provided the most auspicious reading by its empathy with Hamlet's situation: "a great deed placed upon his soul that was not adequate to the deed." This is the key to a play in which, for Wilhelm, "the hero has no plan, whereas the work itself reflects design."[8]

Taking to the stage in the character of melancholy man, Hamlet's responsibility for his own actions is limited, and this seems to be his tragedy, because rather than resolving to avenge the murder of his father, doing away with the murderer and taking over the power due to him by inheritance, he begins by killing the father of his beloved, the secretary of state Polonius, thereby driving the beloved Ophelia herself to suicide. He then sends two friends of his youth, Rosencrantz and Guildenstern, to their horrible deaths, in order to finally bring the whole thing to a devastatingly good close by killing his unfaithful mother Gertrude – and all of this ultimately only to accomplish a by now somewhat costly vengeance against the brother and murderer of the old King, his father. In the process Laertes, brother of Ophelia and son of Polonius, who meanwhile has more than a little occasion to want revenge against Hamlet, also loses his life, as does, for good measure, Hamlet himself. Only two survive: Horatio, friend and witness, and Fortinbras, secret competitor and eventual successor.

There are three questions that take shape in this coarse overview of the plot: questions concerning the beginning, the middle and the end – one after the other. What does the specter have to do with the dramatic events that it sets in motion? Why is it unable to carry out the deed in question in the way it is pronounced? What is the logic of these events if they are not determined by a deed to be committed but only by their own enigmatic deferral? What is the significance of an ending that is only an end at all insofar as the actors are suddenly dead and the stage accordingly empty? The play begins wildly and violently with the supernatural apparition of a ghost, and it ends, as if coincidentally, with a series of lethal cases of mistaken identity, which bring the whole thing to a close after it can no longer be brought to an end with any proper sense of its own. Unable to get an overview of events, neither at the beginning nor of the close, the machinery redoubles itself in the middle of the play as doubly doubled theater of a theater within the theater. If one reads the duplication in reverse, then the piece becomes as opaque as the pantomime that is performed as the prelude of the play within the play, the dumb show, in which the ghost's story of murder is mutely exposed.[9] Nothing, in other words, appears more unambiguous than the pre-history, the veracity of which is attested, for us as for Hamlet himself, only by the ghost. And thus nothing appears less clear than the resulting story, which passes over us in confusing detail.

As far as the ghost is concerned, it has been attempted, with great effort, to keep the Catholic aspects separate from the pagan ones, so as plausibly to turn the ghost into a compromise-formation from older, feudal days. This hopeless endeavor creates great difficulties, however, for the figures of Hamlet and Horatio, reformed students from Luther's Wittenberg, and Shakespeare's own public would undoubtedly have had an equally hard time with it. This ghost is not believable and the task incredible. It is true though that revenge, after Shakespeare and through his theater, changed its character and became an essential element in the course and motivation of courtly intrigue. But these find their momentum in themselves and could just as well do without antiquated commissions of the older, feudal kind.[10] Bacon's definition of revenge as "Wild justice," which applies to the prehistory of *Hamlet*, from Kyd's *Spanish Tragedy* to the supposed *Urhamlet*, turns overnight into a social play of intriguers, and the ghost who requires the revenge is transformed into, or becomes equivalent to, the rumors produced by the many courtly Iagos, to whom Shakespeare would deliver their timely diagnosis in *Othello*, directly following *Hamlet*. Spying and secrecy do not only characterize an over-complicated realm within the represented action, in which revenge becomes the maxim and essence of political action, but they moreover reflect a radically new presupposition for theatricality itself.[11] As a ghost of the older kind, the spirit of old Hamlet is an untimely fellow whose business is just as passé as his task is ignoble – and equally ignoble from all perspectives, theological, ecclesiastical, or juridical. In contemporary terms it is an evil spirit and his apparition therefore not the simple plot-device that later eras have taken it for, while seeking to raise it to the level of great auspiciousness in the formation of the modern individual. As out of date and even as ridiculous as it must have appeared in the new era of the intriguer, this ghost must have served as an even better, though at first sight puzzling, mirror of the new relations of revenge and intrigue.

As Hamlet and his audience knew, and Horatio puts it in the most precise formula, the ghost can only be false, a deceiving phantom.[12] It takes the stage in the armor of the old King, which he had worn for a very particular occasion, but it otherwise bears no individual features that the son could recognize. Its speech emerges from nothing but this mask, as an "it," but never as a "he" that could be the father it appears as. In the eyes of a Christian *communis opinio*, beyond all differences in types of confession, it can be nothing other than a devilish phantom. It is therefore not at all easier to deal with him than, for instance, with a *visitatio* of the dead in the Middle Ages, when it was still possible, or advisable, to trust a ghost. To the contrary, as a false and devilish apparition, this ghost moves according to a different trajectory than that of a revelation from the beyond. He may for his own part even be presenting a truth, but it is a distorted truth like that spoken by the damned in Dante's *Inferno*.[13] His desire for revenge proves how far he is from making atonement for his earthly crimes, "the foul crimes done in my days of nature" (1.5.12). Incorrigibly entangled in his vengeance, this ghost takes the stage in the shape of one who comes from purgatory, but the way he speaks gives away that he must come from hell. He comes from the inferno, while at the same time pretending with the greatest cunning that he comes from purgatory and is deserving of pity – a pity that Shakespeare does not even deny him completely: Mixing the infernal thrust of his rhetoric with the symptoms of an unspeakable suffering, this rhetoric appears to be tragically overwhelmed by its own falseness.[14] It is a spirit, in other words, who uses the pretext of the fires of atonement – and cannot but use it in the infernal repetition compulsion, that defines the condition of being in hell – in order to accomplish a hellish intention that is the mark of the devil and the theater alike: to draw what comes after into the same deceitful orbit of compassion.

The demand of revenge thus both marks and masks a mystery that is anything but resolved or clarified – as the call for vengeance would have done in earlier ages – by the deceitful shape behind which it hides. "It" takes the stage and is assessed by Horatio according to the rules of art ("crossed" is the specialized expression), but Hamlet himself is not in the position to bring it under control. "It" unleashes something in him that lies hidden in the revenge demand. Insofar as "it" in no way causes its desired revenge to appear in the form of the pointless delay that it will eventually become, the ghost is able to construct a highly sophisticated double-bind: It proves revenge *as* a double-bind by doubling the amount of the losses, whereas the loss that was supposed to be avenged is merely sealed off in the vengeance. Not only can no revenge make up for the loss, revenge provides the retroactive justification for that against which it reacts. It "avenges itself" in a double sense in that it hurts itself in deepening the trauma, and this likewise conforms to the structure of Dante's *Inferno*, which Machiavelli took as the general state of human blindness, not just in hell but always already in this world.[15]

This is an interesting double-bind for an audience, and defines a new type of theatricality, that a ghost in which the public does not believe – a belief, which is in fact doubly forbidden, both religiously and morally – achieves its effect by way of the audience's retrospective comprehension. The ghost, in other words, in its particular effectiveness, in the truth of its untruth, cannot actually be doubted in the slightest. Freud, who discovers the Oedipal situation in *Hamlet*, at the same time also found the reason for a similarly necessary self-misrecognition of the modern audience. Whatever the case may be with Oedipus, Freud was able to clearly see that – and how – the phantom's spectral influence on Hamlet extends itself to the audience. As little as the ghost is real, it is the stage itself, and as undeniable as the phantom is, it is the theater itself. The enigmatic nature of the ghost is indeed a self-thematization of the stage (and the equal of Nietzsche's later speculations) as an apparatus of historically immemorial insinuations.[16] Revenge is the haunting of History ever after the murder of Cain at the dawn of time. With advancing modernity and finally, since

Romanticism (though they had put it behind them), Hamlet nails the audience fast in ghostly entanglements that it had tried to avoid from the beginning and which, in the end, it appears to have successfully escaped: The ghost does not appear on stage again at the end, as the convention would have demanded, offering instead indirect confirmation that it is not this ghost's revenge that has found its fulfillment in the ending of the play, its running out of time.

In the end not only the fratricidal usurper Claudius meets with death, but all of the *dramatis personae*, with the exceptions of the witness Horatio and the winner Fortinbras, are dead. The former, Horatio, has been seen at Hamlet's side during the entire length of the play, while the other, Fortinbras, has been a topic of discussion from the beginning and is seen, however fleetingly, crossing the stage with his army in the middle of the play. Both of his appearances are just long enough to allow the audience to recognize him when he comes back to play his role at the play's closing and takes over political power. Horatio, on the other hand, is bid by the dying Hamlet to bear witness to the very events the audience has just witnessed on its own: With his back to the audience and as its double, he appears, despite all sympathy we may have with him, not really up to the task. Fortinbras receives in the "dying voice" of Hamlet the *votum* that secures him the princely succession and thus also his inheritance. He, Fortinbras, is the *alter ego* of one who was not born to play the hero, Hamlet, but who became one *malgré lui*, and who is only instated into his rights after the fact by the one whose succession he admits with his dying word – thus in death reacquiring the princely inheritance of which he was robbed during his life. The play ends with the corpse that Fortinbras, in the most emblematic fashion, lays out – the corpse of a King who Hamlet had never been in this play.

But Fortinbras is more than a *rex ex machina* in the place of the *deus ex machina*, who brings order at the end to the proverbially "rotten state" of Denmark. He is not just the reversal of whatever was "rotten in the state of Denmark," the rottenness responsible for conjuring up the *diabolus ex machina* in the first place, in the shape of the specter of old King Hamlet. The appearance of Fortinbras' army in the middle of the play (unexpected, poorly motivated, often cut) permits an external political threat to come suddenly into view: a threat from beyond the stage, from an elusive off-stage, whose dislocation into the beyond makes it comparable to the threatening spirit at the beginning. If all of these indications at the margins of the drama are taken and added together – something which, as mentioned, rarely happens – the story of Hamlet appears all of a sudden transformed and displaced into an episode on the edge of a quite different story: that of the Norwegian conquest of Denmark made possible under the pretext of an invasion of Poland. It is in this capacity Fortinbras comes up at the beginning and is seen crossing through Denmark on his Polish expedition – just in time to put himself in place and assume power in Denmark.[17]

In this barely perceptible framing of the vengeance plot, which the ghost sets in motion, a backstory is concealed that need have nothing to do with Hamlet himself, if he would only follow the words of the ghost, but which in the end does pertain to him, and indeed in such a way that, in the advent of the ending – if it ends up having to do with revenge at all – the revenge cannot be that *of* old Hamlet but, rather, of Fortinbras *on* old Hamlet. Because did not the latter, old Hamlet, in the pre-history of the play, have the treacherous murder of Fortinbras' father on his conscience and the usurpation of the Norwegian throne? This was of course not the Danish version of the story, as Horatio makes clear in his assessment of the initial situation, in which he refers entirely to rumor and hearsay, and quite explicitly says so: "At least the whisper goes so" (1.1.84). And did old Hamlet – "our valiant Hamlet (For so this side of our known world esteem'd him)" (1.1.87–88) – not wear on the occasion of his conquest the same armor by which Horatio – not Hamlet – is able to recognize him? It is Horatio who recognizes him and not Hamlet, while the latter is of the same age as Fortinbras, even born on the day in question. Directly following this report, still in the same first act, when Hamlet meets with the new King to speak about current official business, we hear more about Fortinbras in Claudius' grand welcoming monolog, in which he presents his politics – on how he plans to use the turnover of power to his advantage in Denmark. "Now follows," Claudius concludes the declaration of his takeover that he delivers to Hamlet, who has only just arrived, "that you know young Fortinbras . . ."

> *Now follows that you know young Fortinbras,*
> *Holding a weak supposal of our worth,*
> *Or thinking by our late dear brother's death*
> *Our state be disjoint and out of frame.*
> (1.2.17–20)

Not only do we learn about Fortinbras' threat and about the Norwegian estimation of the Danish situation as "disjoint" (which will, only a little later, following the entrance of the ghost, be echoed in Hamlet's sentence "The time is out of joint"), but only slightly earlier we heard the legal definition whose terms tie Claudius' succession to the marriage of the Queen:

Therefore our sometime sister, now our queen,
Th'imperial jointress to this warlike state,
Have we . . .
[interrupted by four lines on a laughing and a crying eye]
Taken to wife. . . .

(1.2.8–14)

Both Hamlet and Fortinbras doubt this joint, irrespective of the "jointress." The latter, Fortinbras, does so in his unmistakable affirmation of the state of exception, the "warlike state" – which is in turn the reason for Claudius' haste. The ghost of old Hamlet, who makes his entrance at exactly the same time as Fortinbras, and who thereby accompanies the danger embodied by him, could just as well be the ghost of old Fortinbras, who like Claudius passed on his inheritance to his brother and not his son. The conclusion of *Hamlet* does even allow the revenge of the one son to be distinguished from the revenge of the other. *Hamlet*, rather than the drama of Hamlet's revenge, might as well be taken as a shrewd anamorphosis of the revenge of the other prince, Fortinbras. Already in *Richard II*, in many respects a dramatic predecessor of *Hamlet*, Shakespeare had used the sophisticated technique of *anamorphosis*, the representational device of a cylinder showing an indecipherably distorted image that is to be decrypted through the reflection of a surrounding mirror.[18] Likewise Hamlet's story, in the hidden mirror of a princely code, reveals the story of Fortinbras, while remaining, viewed in and of itself, strictly unrecognizable: mired in melancholia. The loss of Hamlet's story to Fortinbras corresponds to, and even serves as the basis for, the loss of the father that Hamlet must mourn, and the loss would be decidedly not the one that the ghost called upon him to avenge; on the contrary, it would be its mirror image only – revenge exposed as a sham of justice.

However one wishes to comprehend the doubled revenge-plot in its framing function, the legal position of new King Claudius is left untouched by it. Claudius, like his counterpart in Norway, apparently understood how to avoid the right of the firstborn or to defer it and even, with the Queen as jointress, to acquire the cabinet and the acclamation of the people without taking recourse to the dying voice of his predecessor.[19] The legal transition signifies the legitimacy of Claudius and displaces Hamlet (like Fortinbras in Norway) to the next place in the line of succession, a place which Claudius ostentatiously confers to Hamlet upon his homecoming: First, in calling him "my cousin Hamlet, and my son" (parallel to "our sometime sister, now our queen"), and then when Hamlet will not let pass the thoughts of his father, in the official proclamation

> ... for let the world take note,
> You are the most immediate to our throne,
> And with no less nobility of love
> Than that which dearest father bears his son
> Do I impart toward you. ...
>   (1.2.108–112)

Claudius' irreproachable and statesmanly attitude has been constantly noted as a reaction to Hamlet's excessive grieving, but also as an attempt by Claudius to console his nephew over the loss of the immediate succession, thereby simultaneously recognizing his grief and attempting to allay his concrete political loss.[20] More difficult to get a hold of is the possibility that Claudius may at the same time be engaging in some deception regarding his brother's murder. His effort to keep the duped heir to the throne at home instead of giving him leave to his distant life as a scholar in Wittenberg does not suggest it. Rather, he seems to believe Hamlet capable of the same thing he has just diagnosed in Fortinbras: mustering troops against him. Hamlet, who does not allow himself to be contented, wears the mask of madness instead and, with entirely apparent intentions, stabs the secretary of state Polonius, who was certainly not uninvolved in the uncle's coup, and only at this point does Claudius attempt to get his nephew out of the way by sending him on a diplomatic mission to England. Hamlet shows how little he actually is the crazy melancholy figure incapable of action – the characterization through which Polonius wants to sideline him – in the display of the brutal bravura by which he withdraws himself from the affair at the expense of Rosencrantz and Guildenstern.[21]

Claudius protrudes out of the Danish–Norwegian double-mystery that serves as the frame for Hamlet's story and into the Oedipal saga, but the psychological intricacies of the latter have caused many to forget the politically conditioned framework that literally appears at the outer edge of the family romance. The framework itself might be quite simple and easy to forget if it did not so strikingly accentuate the fact that beyond this frame – except for the triumph of Fortinbras – nothing remains. "The rest is silence" are Hamlet's last words (5.2.363), before Fortinbras' troops take the stage and Horatio's touching "sweet prince" eulogy echoes "And flights of angels sing thee to thy rest" (364–365). At the funeral of Diana, Princess of Wales, this song was to be heard in its most recent actuality; it is an angel's song that can hardly penetrate the silence of the "rest" upon which *Hamlet* ends. As always in Shakespeare, the pun is intentional: Hamlet's final rest is a silence, in which the angelic procession brings him to rest. So confirms the accredited witness who is supposed to protect the rest from sinking into silence.

The Psychological Enigma

What attracted the attention from the beginning, and finally that of the modern audience, was the psychological effect of the ghost upon the son, which in the course of the plot becomes so fixated upon Hamlet that the whole outer history begins to vanish before his inner story.[22] The psychoanalyst Nicolas Abraham spoke of a "bait" through which the phantom (as the spirit of the father) is able to make its demands so irresistible. The secret of this bait, according to Abraham, "masks another secret, a real and authentic one, with which the father has burdened his own conscience without the knowledge of the son."[23] What is the nature of this open secret that has eluded the son and with him the audience, which identifies with the task imposed by the father in the mask of the phantom? The structure of the secret is laid bare in the story of the Prince's alter ego Fortinbras and is comprehensible when viewed from the margins of the story. Fortinbras and Hamlet, in strict parallel, are both born upon the same day, both lost their father to murder, and both lose the succession to their father's brother. Both stories are furthermore complementary (though no longer parallel) in that the father of the one (old Hamlet) overcomes the father of the other (old Fortinbras) through treachery, and both display inverse complementarity in that the ghost appears at the same time as Fortinbras, and the murder of old Fortinbras is committed by the same means of a poisoned blade in a duel. It is the same means used in the third revenge-story of the play, Laertes' revenge against Hamlet for the murder of his father Polonius and the death of his sister. Laertes executes the revenge on Claudius with the same blade, and Hamlet realizes its poisonousness in the same instant, thereby famously making Fortinbras the heir of the one who killed his father and robbed him of his own inheritance. The anamorphotic reversal is inscribed, as Hegel possibly saw, in the *punto riverso*, the exchange of weapons that shifts the poisoned rapier from Laertes' hand to Hamlet's – a highly refined detail of fencing technique, which corresponds to the *anamorphosis* of the tragical outcome – tragic, precisely, in the "external" role of chance.[24] In the execution of this revenge, the vengeance of another is inscribed and avenges itself upon Hamlet. Thus he pays, through the justice that he allows to be passed upon his father, for the injustice of the same father. But this is not the whole story.

Only in death, when he experiences the poisonous treachery upon his own body, does Hamlet come around to the realization of that which had begun to reveal itself as the secret of the ghost. In the belatedness of the enigma's solution Stanley Cavell discovered Shakespeare's crucial Freudian accomplishment. That which had been withdrawn as the secret of representation and could only take its effect *in* its withdrawal achieves a remarkable, retrospectively "deferred representation."[25] In the equivalency of the two stories, which takes root in the co-originarity of their claims, Shakespeare is able to allow both strands to run their course until they abruptly reach their end and dissolve in a nothing. The mock moral of the story is a moral that the older revenge-tragedies before Shakespeare did not possess and could not have contained, because this non-moral would have made them impossible by revealing a basic a-morality in uncovering that which is lacking in their (as well as their hypocrite audiences') ethical order. *Hamlet* leads the revenge tragedy (which could have been the content of the hypothesized *Urhamlet*) into the absurd by showing how deceptively, behind the backs of the sons, the mortgaged power of dead fathers extends itself and is executed. Mortgage, a concept borrowed from the French during Shakespeare's time, originally referred to the money that we owe to the dead – the dead to whom we remain permanently indebted without need of repayment: a mortgage due to the dead whose spectral intercession can only further entangle in always greater debts of even more and deeper unknown proportions.[26] In the best-case scenario of theatrical retrospection, as Freud, no coincidence, found confirmed in *Hamlet*, it may become "negotiable" (in Greenblatt's use of the word) *following* the performance on stage. *In reading* the latent within the performative, it may become possible to achieve a kind of "enlightenment" whose trace Hamlet follows and which he may even in the end have achieved for himself.

This is not, however, to say that Shakespeare used such a generalized historical moral as the material point that would update his *Urhamlet* and bring it into line with some more contemporary, enlightened understanding. The background standard of political morality, if not political correctness, that we must grant to Shakespeare and his time, is only what first places him in the position to make his dramatic point and to elaborate what hides as the "unspeakable ignominy" postulated by Abraham, and to highlight it as an unparalleled scandal of, as it turns out, transhistorical proportions. In this articulation of standards, *Hamlet, Prince of Denmark* acquires the traits of an abyssal Mirror of Princes, concerning the tragic story of Kings on the verge of enlightenment. Shakespeare inscribes the drama of the auto-enlightenment, which Hamlet allows himself to undergo within the course of an apparent deferral – the deferral of a revenge to which Hamlet is summoned by the feudal *raison d'être* of the spirit of History that is precariously present in the ghost of fathers. What summons him to this calling is a morality prior to all reason, and a reason prior to every moral. Thus the question gains momentum: What is it that may be called the "unspeakable ignominy" of a King, who can leave nothing to his son but the ruinous form of a revenge in which the bankruptcy of the very foundations of his rule is revealed and the realm lost? When the ghost calls to the son and whispers to him "remember me," it is not the memory of a beloved father Hamlet is reminded of, but a restitution of members, the re-membering of a King who has been robbed of his power to beget offspring – robbed of the member by which the son was begotten and fit for success according to the primogeniture of the succession.

The murder of the King alone and by itself, even the murder by his own brother, one might imagine, might or might not have been defensibly avenged according to the ancient code of honor. The ghost represents its applicability in the way he represents the possibility of his own redemption as redemption out of purgatory. Except that in his case an additional circumstance arises which endangers this logic of the succession and makes the possibility of restitution undecidable: the same circumstance that makes up the silenced ignominy makes it as irreparable as it is unspeakable.[27] It is the same reason why the ghost sues for a revenge that has no chance, thereby turning his revenge against the circumstance itself. In this shame his kingdom is extinguished as if he had produced no offspring at all: Along with his life, his brother not only robbed him of his Queen but also of his son. The risk of the *pater semper incertus* has always presented a classical form of destabilization, which could, however, be resolved by well-defined codifications, and which was in fact legally resolved long before through the declared implication that all children born within a marriage were begotten by the father and to be legitimized through him. The great Elizabeth herself, throughout the entire period of her reign, was never completely secure in her legitimacy and was only able to be seriously threatened by Maria Stuart for the same reason, because Elizabeth's mother Anne Boleyn was successfully accused of high treason by Henry VIII: High treason meant endangerment of the succession through matrimonial infidelity, for which she was in fact put to death. Elizabeth had been declared legitimate by her father and admitted into the succession, but this condition remained easily to be contested in the light of her mother's subsequent fate.[28]

In the ghost of the murdered King Hamlet's accusation, ignominy insinuates itself into the image of vengeance and outweighs the mere murder, in the telling of which the repressed truth presses hopelessly for expression. One should not misunderstand or falsely psychologize this scenario, nor Hamlet's obvious entanglement in it. Freud's ingenious intuition, and Goethe's perspicuity before him, was to see the genesis of the modern subject as a mortgage, taken out on an older, feudal constellation, according to which the trauma of princes became the model of narcissistic injury and castration anxiety, and the dissolution of the feudal *familia* with its principle of delegation – including the commissions and curses put into effect by family ghosts – turned into the repertoire of the dynamics of the Oedipal relation.[29] Goethe and Freud read this filiation of the modern subject into *Hamlet* – but this reading is already Hamlet's historical consequence and not inherent to him. The shameful aspect, according to the ghost's tirades, is not unspeakable in those parts that the spirit utters nor in those that Hamlet theatrically amplifies behind the melancholy mask of madness.

Nietzsche brought this to bear, in the implicit reading of *Hamlet* offered in *The Birth of Tragedy*, with the "terrible wisdom of the forest god Silen," according to whom the "very best" thing would have been "not *to be* born" at all, which means, as Nietzsche emphasizes, in a remarkable inversion of the meaning of *being*, "to be *nothing*."[30] Nietzsche is right, and much more literally than he was aware, when he read Hamlet's "to be or not to be" as "to be born or not to be born." In fact, "That it were better my mother had not borne me" says Hamlet himself (3.1.123), and that may have inspired Nietzsche.[31] What bothers Hamlet is the question of birth and the unspoken but virulent question of the act of conception. What the ghost does not say and still does not completely conceal (but to the contrary makes apparent in his instruction that the mother is by all means to be spared from the revenge) is the full measure of his wife's complicity: Her complicity, not so much in the murder of her husband as for her doubling of the regicide through the annihilation of the succession.

> *A second time I kill my husband dead,*
> *When second husband kisses me in bed.*
> (3.2.179–180)

The confession of the Player-Queen, which Hamlet presents in the play within the play performed before the royal couple, is scandalous not only in its parodistically inverted Petrarchism, according to which the "little death" of orgasm, *picol' morte*, deepens the "big death" in that the latter antecedes the former in this case instead of preceding and foreshadowing it: This second death seals and consummates the first one, to which it could otherwise only metaphorically have alluded. The thematized theatricality of the meta-play of the mousetrap reveals the logic of "thrift," turning perlocutionary force into a performative trap – a trap in which "the object

Ophelia," as Jacques Lacan has named it, figures as "piece of bait."[32] In exposing the latent within the performative, I have said, Hamlet forces locution into perlocution. In the mouth of the Player-Queen second death affirms the flat and literal way of all flesh in "base respects of thrift, but none of love" (3.2.178). Hamlet, who laments the proverbial weakness of woman from the start – "Frailty thy name is woman" – even before he hears any accusations from the ghost (1.2.146), does so not out of repugnance at that "incestuous, that adulterate beast" (1.5.42), which his father's spirit proclaims the fratricide to be who has drawn the mother into the adulterous bed. The implication which the ghost cannot admit, and which it can only partially cover up with its railing against incest, is the existence of the infidelity already when he was still alive. That much was already present in the source Belleforest and has been emphasized since Bradley's *Shakespearean Tragedy*, without necessarily being completely sure of what to make of it: "she was false to her husband while he lived."[33] The consequence, which everyone keeps avoiding to this day, is the possibility that Claudius might be Hamlet's father. The ghost, who post-mortally assigns the mission of his re-membering as father and King, cannot very well admit it, neither as a possibility nor as a reality, but he can count to a certain extent on the son's cooperation in this point.

The sheer possibility is sufficient – the mere suspicion makes all proof superfluous – to make the story's irony palpable: a completely literal irony in which all metaphors become true in an instant, at the same time as all revealed truth becomes metaphorical. Thus, for instance, in the apparent metaphor by which Claudius makes Hamlet into his "son" and thereby declares him as "his" heir, Hamlet finds himself declared as a son that he would have never wished to be, but as whom he now learns to be fearful of his new status. His mother says that much directly to his face, when she instructs him:

> *Do not for ever with thy vailed lids*
> *Seek for thy noble father in the dust.*
> (1.2.70–71)

Where, if not in dust and ashes, would the real father be sought? Not as a specter to be sure: Gertrude completely overlooks this shape, which appears to her son in her bedroom to urge him to more promptly fulfill his revenge. "Do you see nothing there?" the son asks in a panic; "Nothing at all," she says, cool, "yet all that is I see" (3.4.122/123). The apparition of the father fades before the reality of the mother; the ghost can never have been more than the phantom of the father's ideality. The irony is completed by the fact that the succession comes out the same either way for Hamlet, regardless of whose son he is. Hamlet is the heir to the throne, even if he were not the old King's heir, and even if he is not the son of the father whose son he is supposed to be. Instead he would be the son of a murderer, through the murder, though, of his biological father, and through his mother, who is incestuously implicated in this murder. It would thus remain impossible for him to separate himself from cause and occasion of the murder.[34] And so, at the end of the play, an ending, which for this reason can no longer reach its anticipated end, Claudius is dealt a vengeance at Hamlet's hand that could just as well be a vengeful patricide. In the name of the father (in short: of old Hamlet) "young Hamlet" kills a biological father (Claudius), whose name he does not carry, but in whose name he is equally implicated as the usurper of that which had belonged to him under the rule of the old legitimacy.

A "common theme/Is death of fathers," Claudius mocks (1.2.103–104) and points up the style of Machiavellian Princes, to whose number Hamlet does not wish to be counted. "Sovereign is he who determines the state of exception," we may have perhaps too quickly assimilated: in his application of this rule of thumb, Claudius tries to close the check without ever asking for the bill.[35] The sovereign in the state of exception is the one who controls the principle of thrift that Hamlet's Player-Queen calls by its name. In a time that has gotten out of joint, the only one up to date is the one who makes transitions "fitting" – in other words: a "joiner" like Gertrude the jointress. What remains in the state of exception, that "warlike state" proclaimed by Claudius, is the jointress Gertrude, whose weakness is her absolute strength. She loved her son, one way or the other, but was unable to secure the succession for him as soon as he wanted to know too much. She is not the Virgin Queen Elizabeth, in whose final days *Hamlet* first took the stage, but she illuminates the underpinnings upon which Elizabeth's decision – hardly understood to this day – brilliantly emerges, the decision not to allow her reign to be corrupted by "incestuous sheets" (according to a semantics that we would no longer use). As the Fairy Queen unreachable by sexual politics, she unhinged the politics of the Princes.

The incest that is spoken of so incessantly in *Hamlet* is of a symptomatic significance. In the supplementary role of a family politics for the supposed body politic, Marie Axton has perceived the Elizabethan crux of the metaphor of the Two Bodies of the Queen instead of a King. She invokes within Elizabeth's thought – unfortunately without consideration of *Hamlet* – an idea to which Shakespeare may have even alluded in Claudius' offer to Hamlet: "that if Mary [Stuart] would accept a husband chosen by the Queen of England, Elizabeth would [thus literally cited from Camden's *Annals*] 'declare her, Her Sister, or Daughter, and England's Heretrix, by Act of Parliament.' "[36] As Queen, Elizabeth had quickly rejected the various alternatives posed by a politics of succession. Raising the image of the Virgin Queen and the claim of a monarch above the problematic sexual–political pressures, she had felt the pressures on her own body nevertheless before she came to stand above them. In *Hamlet*, it seems, Shakespeare shares Elizabeth's momentary utopia. He represents Elizabethan tragedy at the moment when the fabulous apotheosis of the Fairy Queen was coming to an end and the heir was at the door.[37]

Postlude in the Theater

Elizabeth dies in March of 1603 and resolves the question of her succession only in the last minute. James, as the son of the executed Mary Stuart and the favorite of Elizabeth's cabinet, finally receives her dying voice and arrives in London from Scotland at the end of 1603. Prior to his arrival, he holds court for the first time at Christmas at Hampton Court. Everyone with hopes of accomplishing anything under his reign did everything possible to be in attendance. One of the first official acts of the King and his Danish Queen (a tireless lover of the theater who knew all of the plays of the period) was the elevation of Shakespeare's troupe to *The King's Men*. They turned the royal estate at Hampton Court into a theatrical happening of the first order, which dominated the court's social proceedings between Christmas and *Twelfth Night*.

Hamlet, one speculates, may have been on the program of Christmas 1603 at Hampton Court, where it must have represented an excessively bold idea for the celebration of these days. The piece was certainly not written for this diplomatic context, which only coincidentally may have come about, but many extremely fitting and unfitting aspects would be brought to light by this staging (and it may perhaps offer some explanation of the deviations undertaken in the first quarto-edition of 1603).[38] In the royal box the Queen from Denmark follows the show with her Royal Lord, both of them surrounded by a state that is on high alert in the excitement of governmental changeover. And indeed, for the first time after fifty years of the Fairy Queen, there was a King and a Queen, who would have found themselves confronted with the Player-Queen and Player-King, in a mirror inversion putting King James across from Queen Gertrude and her theatrical double of the Player-Queen – a staging that in its allegorical features was approaching the most fashionable theatrical genre of the future, the court masque. A certain toning down is imaginable this way, yet it remains necessary to explain the tolerance needed in facing the provocation that this particular play in the celebration of this particular day – the Birth of Christ and the new state of a Christian Majesty in elaborate conjunction. In short, this performance is only acceptable as a contra-factual speculation and it may be as such not completely useless, since it simultaneously illustrates and refutes the chances of relating *Hamlet* (or *Macbeth,* or *Lear,* at that) to James' politics and interests, and thus to define, as unequivocally as the name of "The King's Men" suggests, Shakespeare in the new sovereign's service.[39]

On the threshold between Elizabeth and James, *Hamlet* displays a political alternative with excessive sharpness, in which the restored ideology of Divine Right seeks (as we know, without much success) to reestablish the pertinence it had lost, precisely, under Elizabeth. *Hamlet* had not only implicitly stated the ultimate loss of the Divine Right of Kings, but had exposed its vain nullity. The solution presented in Elizabeth was thanks to the luck of the draw, but this chance was not only over in 1603, it could hardly even be perceived anymore by the majority of a public, which would continue to drift apart towards an incorrigible *ancien régime* on the one side and Protestant anti-theatricality on the other. In 1603, *Hamlet* had already been historically surpassed; in Hampton Court its acid irony would have caused the occasion of the festivities to fade away in the after-pains of the Elizabethan epoch. *Hamlet* (as the *Hamlet*-reader *Werther*) is secretly dated at Christmas, indeed; this much is certainly correct, but Hamlet's epochal turning-point occurs in the negation of precisely this Son, and the father who reclaims him for himself is nothing but a ghost, the spirit of a deceitful, theatrically overblown era, of History (with capital H), and thus there is nothing heartening in this for a holder of Divine Right with a royal spouse, who is a Princess of Denmark.

The nothing of the thrift contained in the jointress Gertrude (pronounced by her son's Player-Queen as the principle of nothingness) could have been for James at best some historical humbug. The fact that it lasted for as long as it did is almost unbelievable, an irony of history that historians still have no great idea what to do with. Let us simply say: She, Elizabeth, was ahead of her time, just as Shakespeare was ahead of his – thus ahead and, like all literature, always already long past. "The King," complains Hamlet to Rosencrantz and Guildenstern, after he has stabbed the secretary of state Polonius, "is a thing," and he adds – following their horrified response, "A thing?" – "Of nothing" (4.2.27–29).[40] He, the King, is the accidental product of a thrift, which Elizabeth was nonetheless able to suspend for the duration of half a century. The Queen – Gertrude, like Elizabeth – establishes "the thing that's the king;" after her – Gertrude, like the Fairy Queen – the future of Princes remained broken to the present day. Even the son of the second Elizabeth and his Diana, furnished with the mythical name of a Virgin Queen, in whose requiem Hamlet's consolation was sung, cannot but attest to it in a distant echo of the theatrical thunder of 1603.

CHAPTER 3

Lethe's Wharf: Wild Justice, the Purgatorial Supplement

Ghost. I find thee apt.
    (1.5.31)

Nothing satisfies like a pun, as in this case the anagram of Lethe in the name of Hamlet, especially in its original Nordic spelling Am-lethe: a weird coincidence that equals the strange invocation of the same Greek name by old Hamlet's ghost when "it" comes to deal with his learned son. It does not equal, but still resembles, the fundamental inscription of Lesmosyne, forgetting, in her sister Mnemosyne's name: the lessening of evil in the name of memory, the mother of the Muses.[1] But while the hidden presence of Lethe in Hamlet seems to have her come out, against the grain of the father ghost's defense, in the son's notorious melancholy conduct, lesmosyne remains a rarely thematized implication of the Muses's manifold work, a well-established work of mourning on whose premises rhetorical memoria unfolds her mnemo-technique. Against the mythic trajectory of this commonplace, Shakespeare's theater invokes and registers the intrusion of what a modern episteme calls History, a master trope beyond memory's rhetoric whose apparition resides in the machinery of the stage itself. Hamlet's ghost announces the advent of history and its dubious relationship with a memory that is no longer her muse and mother. The invention of history rather than the "Invention of the Human" advertised by Harold Bloom is the achievement of Shakespeare's stage, an achievement that seems to reveal its full force only after it has outrun its course and memory's comeback is about to reset the stage.

One of the many mysteries that remain in Shakespeare's text is how Hamlet's, of all ghosts, comes to cite the Greek Lethe and, more precisely, "the fat weed/ That roots itself in ease on Lethe's wharf" (1.5.32–33). Sitting on the wharf of the Hades river – Lethe's wharf – while waiting for Charon's boat, the dead who are to cross the river are bound to meditate with horror the dull fat weed announcing oblivion's work, a last reminder and remainder of the worldly flora of rhetoric perverted by oblivion and in the service of nothing but oblivion's memory, whose domain they are about to leave. All of that makes sense for a humanist compiler, but does it for a Christian ghost, however tainted by ancient Senecan associations? A ghost from hell rather than purgatory, pretending to come from purgatory, but with a devilish rhetoric and a perverted pagan imagery that must be Greek to him. Surprising as it is that Lethe may come from the mouth of someone who claims to be on leave from "sulphurous and tormenting flames" (1.5.3), it corresponds to Hamlet's classical use of language and feeds into his final reaction to the ghost's tale, the "table" speech on memory which takes on in appropriate classical terms the ghost's last word, "Remember me" (1.5.91).

There is more than one thing to be put together here, to be re-membered, various kinds of mnemonical places and techniques to begin with: two thresholds are to be crossed with yet one other threshold of a different order implied that qualifies the difference of the two others, ancient and modern, as a historically decisive divide. It is this second order, or historical difference, which separates Hamlet from current "analogies between Renaissance and postmodern melancholies."[2] Like the ghost, who poses as a "purgatorial agent" (I borrow this phrase from Beckett's reading of Joyce's "work in progress" where it is used with respect to Dante, whose conception of *Purgatory* and *Inferno* – of both in relation to each other – is to be recovered from the background), Hamlet poses as a melancholy agent of show.[3] Insisting on "that within which passes show," Hamlet insists, ultimately, on history – history as surpassing show. We have to twist his words here only slightly to include his insistence on history in the immediate context of the Queen's speech delivered before (1.2.85).

The table speech following the ghost's revelation puts on an appearance of the memory disorder of melancholia, in order to counter the history disorder encountered as the ghost. "The time is out of joint" is Hamlet's apt remark at the end of the ghost's show (1.5.189), and "revolution" the name of the notorious specter haunting Europe not much later.[4] How come, History comes about and imposes itself, in the poses of a show, as *coming about*? As we learn in *Hamlet* (if ever we learn a thing), it does not just happen (if ever it happens).[5] If ever, it happens against "Lethe's warf," and "what happens in Hamlet" (the question famously investigated by Dover Wilson) is just this: how it comes about. It comes with the ghost of fathers, and it comes with a vengeance, a call for "wild justice," as Bacon has aptly named it.[6] It comes with a vengeance masquerading as remembrance, the banks of Lethe its only wharf.

Before *Hamlet*, and possibly connected with a supposed first version of it (the *Urhamlet*), the "biggest theatrical hit of the early 1590s," Thomas Kyd's *Spanish Tragedy* had begun with the entrance of a "stage-manager" called Revenge, "a figure from ancient Roman tragedy" in secularized, "classicized version of the medieval image of God looking down on the theatre of the world." Jonathan Bate, editor of the last Arden edition of *Titus Andronicus* (Shakespeare's roughest and presumably earliest play, which was beside *Hamlet* of exemplary interest for Heiner Müller), has put this attempt at secularization, which puts revenge in the vacant god-position, into a juridical perspective: "where Christian iconography had God and Kyd had Revenge, Shakespeare [in *Titus Andronicus*] begins with human, secular authorities in the commanding position aloft," that is, literally above, in the upper stage of the Globe theatre.[7] In Kyd, the theatricality of history is the pay-off of revenge masquerading as God. Whereas in *Hamlet*, to begin with, justice as the dire necessity and urgency of secular law is mocked by the ghost of history calling for remembrance.

Let me recapitulate. *Hamlet* 1.5: "Enter the Ghost and Hamlet." The Ghost speaks at last: "Mark me" (1.5.2) and Hamlet gives it the "serious hearing" asked for: "I am bound to hear" (1.5.6). The binding force of "hearing" is crucial in what comes, after all, as a visual apparition, because hearing transcends vision and induces knowledge; and with this, "with wings as swift as meditation or the thoughts of love," Hamlet finds himself "sweep" to his revenge (1.5.29–31). Whereupon the ghost promptly acknowledges "I find thee apt" (1.5.31). The *aptum* that seems to govern the scene as a whole is wholly rhetorical and presents us with rhetoric's greatest trick, its art of self-affirmation. Hamlet's apt invocation of swift aptness, as in the juridical qualifications of premeditation and affect (he may have been to Law School in Wittenberg, after all), meets the demand of the ghost's rhetoric, and what it overcomes, reminded of by the ghost, is "Lethe's wharf," the dullness of the way of all things, fate in classical tragedy. That paves the way, in the ghost's show, for the ghost's tale of the father's murder through the ear: the self-stabilizing representation through the ear of what happened through the ear. The ghost's self-presentation three times "horrible, most horrible" remains uninterrupted;

but it culminates in a threefold "Adieu," which puts the matter – blasphemously – to God (à dieu), in order to leave it, as a matter of fact, with Hamlet. The "Remember me" (1.5.91), with which the apparition vanishes, is not without the pointed threat of a return. Hamlet faces it with no chance of an intervention, all alone in front of the audience – which is not the least point to be reckoned.

With memory and revenge in his ears, Hamlet faces the necessity of proof in the legal and historical sense of evidence. The opening of *Hamlet*, recalling the classical setting of Agamemnon, asks for more than hearsay. There is more of Aristotelian tragedy in *Hamlet*, claims Kathy Eden, than meets the eye at first glance: "The Ghost marks with the fullest dramatic ambiguity the point of intersection between the psychological image and legal evidence."[8] But, as much as I agree with her claim that Hamlet is "a literary theorist of some sophistication" (180), so little do I find Hamlet "act completely in character" (181). On the contrary, in a remarkable *parekbasis* that is sheltered in melancholia, Hamlet sophistically withdraws from what he enacts. His fully conscientious resistance to the character he is in theory does not contradict the Aristotelian terms, but constitutes the dramatic ambiguity that *is* tragedy – in order to leave it behind. The *Trauerspiel* of History shall catch up with him, and this is the one and only point left to him. He decides to take the ghost literally, it seems – "I know not seems" will be his maxim but all along (1.2.76) – *as if* no threat was involved. But if the "commandment" to remember is in fact nothing but the reinforcement by threat of the command to revenge, one might surmise that he hides the threat in what he is to develop in his further moves as the guise of the melancholy man's memory disorder.

To cut a longer analysis short and bring it to the relevant point, Hamlet's table speech contains, hides and reveals at the same time, the open disconnection of memory and history, revenge and judgment. The melancholy show put on as a guise suggests, even points out, what is misleading in the ghost's ill-designed commandment and makes melancholy's inability to come to terms with what happened its pretext of action. Hamlet does *not fall* for the ghost's command to remember through revenge. He, Hamlet the son, keeps up appearances with the appearance of the father, but as his rhetorical swiftness shows and extracts from the visitor's anxiety, the tide of history flooding Lethe's wharf is not consistent with the story and command of revenge; it appears and imposes itself, presses and is repressed. Hamlet refuses to act it out but brings it to act out itself: to happen against the grain of its first appearance, as irony of history instead of memory's allegorical superstition.[9] The irony inscribed into the allegory or, rather, in the mime of an allegory comes with the ghost's tell-tale of the murder through the ear: the representation through the ear of what happened through the ear, binding through the ear what is said to have happened through the ear – that is, the question of faith searching for insight, *fides quaerens intellectum* in Canterbury's scholastic formula. Evidently, the ghost's evidence is an evidence barred from the eye that would constitute evidence in tragic as well as legal terms.

Answering the ghost in its absence, after it has vanished, Hamlet's table speech performs the pantomime of an answer while the show goes on. Twice, the rhetorical mime of a gesture: "Remember thee?" echoes the vehicle instead of the tenor of the message, revenge. It pays back the devilish rhetoric of the ghost, the confounding of memory and revenge, in the same currency and does not fail to mention the currency's currency: "Ay, thou poor ghost [an 'Ay' consonant with the I of the speaking subject, as well as with the eye on watch], whiles memory holds a seat/ In this distracted globe" (1.5.96/97). Frances Yates was helpful to mark in this speech, delivered in the Globe theatre, the mnemotechnical implications of the theater of memory for *Hamlet*.[10] Here is important to add that Hamlet does not only uses this commonplace, but that he does so with respect to "Lethe's wharf." The audience of the Globe cannot but be distracted, distracted as all audiences until today, by the ghost's infernal rhetoric of revenge. Sheltered by "Lethe's wharf," the audience is to the same extent deceived by, as it is afraid of, the ghost's rhetoric of history, history's false claim of action on the grounds of remembrance. If only at second sight (if you come to think of it), Hamlet makes fun of the ghost in the table scene. To the uneasy surprise of the audience that is barely aware of it, he makes fun of the ghost all the time, most ostensibly when he has "it" cry, blind "old mole," under the stage at the end of the scene (1.5162).[11] The "cellerage," from where the ghost calls upon them, betrays the irony of allegory (and it may be "a stage-metaphor about the 'platform' of Elsinore" for the stage of the Globe on top of it).[12]

"Indeed," Cavell has pointed out, "Hamlet's table speech seems to go out of its way to show that the line (Hamlet calls it his 'word') containing the words 'remember me' is *not* what he sets down in his tables."[13] The moment of writing – in the stage direction prescribed as "Writes" – is to be performed in the air, rather than into some notebook that would literalize the mnemotechnical metaphor and prove Hamlet as mad enough, at this point, to perform his writing as a genuine way of obedience to the ghost; this would show Hamlet as always already so mad as to offer in a genuine display of irony the literal transcription of the ghost's "word" into his poor notebook, as if that was the action asked for, and reinforced by the ghost's words "remember" and "me." "Poor ghost," indeed, since that is what

Hamlet has in memory's tropological store for him. Hamlet's decision is to give up not the burden of the past, but the assignment from the past's innumerable ghosts and to instead take up the burden of "giving in" to the responsibility left as the mortgage of history.[14]

Towards the end of his *Phenomenology of the Mind*, which is also a phenomenology of the Spirits put to rest in this book, Hegel comes to reckon in *Hamlet* how tragedy comes to an end: "History comprehended" is Hegel's last word.[15] "History comprehended" means "at once the recollection *and* the Golgotha of the Absolute Spirit," recollecting and containing in its conception Hamlet with the skull of Yorick in his hands, that most famous of theatrical scenes in Hegel's time, but moreover, beyond that most famous mime of a baroque *meditatio mortis*, a sense of Hamlet's near escape from tragedy's fatal, classical limitation emerges in Hegel's reading. In Hamlet's dispute with the "father ghost" Hegel recognizes a "purer consciousness," ready for dialectical reconciliation: "Versöhnung des Gegensatzes mit sich," whereby the popular etymology of *Versöhnung* echoes the fate of "sons" as the Christian Christ Son's prime matter of all reconciliation. Of this "purer consciousness" Hegel observes that it transcends the classical "Lethe der Unterwelt im Tode." In his much later lectures on aesthetics, anticipating Nietzsche's account in the *Birth of Tragedy* (which may actually have been influenced by this passage), Hegel rewrites, which is to say translates and sublates, "Lethe's wharf" into the "strand of finitude" [*Sandbank der Endlichkeit*] where, as it would seem, Hamlet tried hard not to get beached. "Sandbank der Endlichkeit" describes a finitude of which, it seems clear to Hegel, cannot satisfy Hamlet – "sie genügt ihm nicht" – and what follows for Hegel in the *Lectures on Aesthetics* is a deeper understanding of Goethe's *Meister*'s notorious analysis, an analysis unquestioned until Freud.[16]

The text of Hegel's *Phenomenology* is cryptic and hard to read, it is (as I said) a crypt of his times's philosophical ambitions.[17] Shakespeare's *dramatis personae* loom large in this cryptic account. They are rarely ever explicitly named in the text, but remain implied and come close to philosophical allegories. Classical and modern *personae* are telescopically juxtaposed and appear to be mutually implied: Oedipus and Orestes turn into Hamlet and Macbeth (Freud made famous use of the Oedipus–Hamlet transposition). What counts in Hegel's recognition of "Lethe's wharf" is the doubling of the two Lethes in the transcendence from the classical pagan strand of forgetting to a modern Lethe bordering relief: "Absolution, not from guilt (for consciousness cannot deny its guilt, because it acted), but from the crime; and also its expiatory pacification [which is the *Sühne* of *Versöhnung*]" (448). In the case of Macbeth, the relapse into classical Lethe is graspable as the instance of an unsurpassable, mythically blind latency of "the power that conceals itself and lies in ambush" (446), says Hegel – whereas in the case of Hamlet the "expiatory pacification" (448) that for Hegel looms "already in tragedy in general" (449) is in force. The "purer consciousness" that Hamlet embodies has outgrown the old tragedy – even though Hamlet in his "childlike trusting" threatens to fall for the "Ghost of the father," just as Macbeth fell for the "ambiguous sisters of fate" (446).[18] But although even Hamlet's "purer" consciousness remains "estranged," it masters in this estrangement nevertheless its "negativity" (321–323): this consciousness is radically superior to the "hypocrisy" of tragic "compassion," about which Hegel does not deceive himself. Even though Hamlet could not shed the mask under which "art does not contain the true authentic self" (444) in the end, he would undoubtedly – "I have that within which passes show" – have figured it out: "I know not seems" is precondition and proof.

The recent preference for memory, cultural memory in particular, which has turned an antiquarian item from Aby Warburg's and Frances Yates's treasure house of *Mnemosyne* into a catchword for the Humanities at large, marks and seals the end of history in its humanist understanding. As a latency in the Freudian sense, the latest turns to memory and religion bridge the generational gap of post-war times. They give up on history in the very manner that created the historicist delusion in the first place, in favor of a memory masquerading as history, with revenge on its lips. As a re-creation of that delusion, it presents us with a return of no repressed, but of its cause, repression. History is to flood the dull banks of Lethe, its weeds instead of flowers; the cries of revenge as of justice, memory's unfailable other, foreshadow the necessity of history to be rewritten endlessly. History as the mnemo-trope to be settled once and for all, the mnemo-fetish of the modern, has outrun its rhetorical course. At the end of *Finnegans Wake*, in the return of a "commodius vicus of recirculation" – in both, the infernal irony of Beckett's "purgatorial agent" and Nietzsche's all too human but also all too Greek "eternal return of the same" – we hear the anamorphotically me-distorted echo of Hamlet's ghost cry for "a lone a last" time, "mememormee!" (me, me, more me!)

CHAPTER 4

Richard II, Bracton, and the End of Political Theology

Not unlike ideology, political theology exists in two versions, a weaker and a stronger use of the term.¹ In the weaker variety, political theology seems merely ideological. In this ideological sense of the word, political theology is of a descriptive value for the sociology of religion, while sociology itself is the secularized replacement or political successor of a theologically grounded politics of religion. Thus Deborah Kuller Shuger's recent *Political Theologies in Shakespeare's England* deals with an ideological functioning of theological politics.² In the stronger sense of the word, however, this socio-ideological surface is the historical function of a translation or commerce between theology and politics whose notorious definition is Carl Schmitt's thesis that "significant concepts of the modern doctrine of the state are secularized theological concepts."³ Here, as Schmitt continues, it is not so much the transfer "from theology to the theory of the state, whereby, for example, the omnipotent God became the omnipotent lawgiver" that is decisive, but the transfer's "systematic structure, the recognition of which is decisive for a sociological consideration of these concepts." Unlike Shuger who, happily and most fortuitously, elaborates "the massive transfer of sacrality from church to crown" and thereby recognizes in *Measure for Measure* a reflection "on the post-Reformation crossover of the sacred from ecclesial to temporal polity," this chapter puts the second, more fundamental, constitutional thesis to the test, a test whose witness for Ernst Kantorowicz is Shakespeare's theater in general and *Richard II* in particular.⁴

In *The King's Two Bodies* of 1957, Kantorowicz does not (want to) mention Schmitt.[5] Nor does Hans Blumenberg seem to have read Kantorowicz, when he declared in 1966 that Schmitt's *Political Theology* was a "metaphorical theology," in order to accuse him, more precisely, of a "theology as politics," in which the "cynicism" of "theological politics" is barely hidden.[6] Nor seems Schmitt – when he finally, in 1970, tried to assemble everything available to refute Blumenberg's assessment and to escape the consequences of his attack – to have known Kantorowicz, whose subtitle, *A Study in Medieval Political Theology*, seems to cite his own title. Only occasionally, in the notes to a smaller study of the early fifties, Kantorowicz had put a date to his own use of the term: "the early thirties."[7] He refers, presumably, to Erik Peterson's essay *Der Monotheismus als politisches Problem* of 1935, whose subtitle, *Ein Beitrag zur Geschichte der politischen Theologie im Imperium Romanum*, parallels Kantorowicz's.[8] Kantorowicz does not touch Peterson either, although he does make the "exchange" of imperial and sacerdotal semiotics, the mutual mimicry of Roman emperors and popes in the representation of their divine rights, the point of departure of that study, but without particular interest in the theological dimension. Instead of Peterson, he quotes Percy Ernst Schramm, who speaks of an "exchange of privileges" between *sacerdotium* and *regnum* but limits his approach to the history of ideas.[9]

Carl Schmitt, on the other hand, takes Peterson as pretext and hostage, in order to counter what must have come to him as a shock with Blumenberg's attack: *Political Theology II* of 1970 shifts attention to the older, outdated Peterson layer of the debate only to displace Blumenberg's argument to the point where the metaphorical transfer from theology to politics is said to have originated in the Christian takeover of the Roman empire. The subtitle of *Political Theology II* is *The Legend of the Final Refutation of Any Political Theology*, and its target is no longer Peterson alone, whom Jacob Taubes, Blumenberg's colleague from the research group *Poetik und Hermeneutik*, in a letter to Schmitt, calls Schmitt's "best friend."[10] What is uppermost on Schmitt's mind is "the contemporary problem situation," and that is, as his afterword makes explicit, *The Legitimacy of the Modern Age*.[11] All of a sudden, Blumenberg's title appears to be nothing less than the decisive threat of a "final refutation." In seeking out and positioning Blumenberg, under the cover of Peterson, as the exemplary enemy of his work, Schmitt manages to restate his argument on a new plane and to replay the battle whose mythical, Manichean dimension he finds dismantled in Blumenberg's late Augustinian metaphorology.[12] Now the question – by far more than a mere methodological question – remains as to how Kantorowicz's metaphorological topic, the juridical allegory of the king's two bodies, relates to Blumenberg's truly "final refutation" of *Political Theology II* in the rewriting of the *Legitimacy* book in 1974.

" 'Political theology' is itself the very idea [*Inbegriff*] of the results of secularization," Blumenberg writes, "which veils that what is meant is 'theology as politics.' It is almost *a priori* conclusive that a juristic positivism must ally itself with history as a given [*dem Geschichtsfaktor*], which withdraws from perception the contingency of institutional positings [*der positiven Setzungen*]."[13] The decisive point of Blumenberg's final critique is not solely (as it had been before) the literalized metaphor of the sovereign's *Divine Right*, whose juridical figure had been reconstructed by Kantorowicz; nor is it the missing of legitimacy that had been covered up and compensated for, by Schmitt, through secularization. Rather, for Blumenberg as well as Kantorowicz, the demand for a political theology behind the divine right of kings seems to be created, necessitated rather than reinforced, by the dead metaphor, or catachresis, of a theology in continuation of politics.[14] The juridical allegory, or *metaphora continua*, of the king's two bodies is the topos on whose grounds modern politics was negotiated as a result of secularization.

Nowhere else is secularization more obviously "a category of historical injustice," as Blumenberg had put it from the start in the title of Part I, than in Schmitt's "metaphorical theology," because it transforms the illegitimate into the potential of legitimacy [*Potentiale der Legitimität*]; theology is the name of that potentiality for Schmitt. In short, Blumenberg reads Schmitt as a Machiavellian rather than a Hobbesian, and he is right, if we take Shakespeare's word for it and interpret it in the light of Kantorowicz's reading of *Richard II*. In this reading, Kantorowicz makes the juridical topos of the king's two bodies a Shakespearean negotiation of the first order: "It is he [Shakespeare] who has eternalized that metaphor" (26). "Eternalized" is to be taken in more than the usual epideictic sense; it is to be taken in the stricter technical sense of a finalized metaphor, that is, catachresis. The former disciple of Stefan George may have thought of Hölderlin's "steadfast letter" [*der veste Buchstab*] or the famous maxim recently used by Giorgio Agamben: "What remains, the poets establish," since they establish, as Hölderlin had put it, through a "stiffening" [etymologically operative in *stiften*], the stiffening of metaphor within the state of a catachresis that eternalizes in the sense of its "remaining" [*quel che resta – was bleibet aber, stiften die Dichter*, in the late poem *Andenken*].[15] What Shakespeare has exposed, according to Kantorowicz, is the catachrestic positing and reiteration of the theological metaphor at that point in history (Shakespeare's and Kantorowicz's history of Richard II), when its potential for legitimacy was re-created and, at the same time, the representational logic of theology, its necessity as well as its mythic functioning, was about to change. With this change, the stage is revealed, among whose more recent theoretical effects the *deus ex machina* comes to the fore, which has been evoked by Schmitt under the apt name – the metaphor, in fact – of theology.[16]

Agamben, who knows all of this, I am sure, begins his first chapter on "The Logic of Sovereignty" in *Homo Sacer* with "The Paradox of Sovereignty" according to Carl Schmitt – namely, "the sovereign is, at the same time, outside and inside the juridical order."[17] It is both interesting and immediately understandable that Kantorowicz did not want to refer to Schmitt, and to make a fool of himself by doing so, if we learn that this formula is, indeed, medieval: *rex infra et supra legem* is the central crux of what Kantorowicz calls "medieval political theology" and discusses with the help of the thirteenth-century jurist Henry Bracton (143). Kantorowicz's use of Bracton has been severely criticized to the effect that in Bracton no such thing as a "King above the law" exists: no "features of a supralegal status" that would imply or necessitate theological considerations.[18] Indeed, it seems that Bracton is interesting for almost the opposite reason: he is exemplary in his approach to reducing theological motives that may have entered into the legal definition of Royal power, to workable legal procedures and regulations. This sobering effect of Bracton's work, the *De Legibus et Consuetudinibus Angliae*, put together toward the end of the thirteenth century when Richard's II reign came to its unhappy ending, is important, and Kantorowicz is therefore wise to have taken him on, because Bracton elaborates with admirable logical acuity how the law was to work with the underlying paradox identified by Kantorowicz and Agamben.

According to Bracton, there was no legal problem; Bolingbroke had "no legal claim."[19] As far as Richard's fate is concerned, there was a *political* problem. According to Kantorowicz's use of Shakespeare, Richard failed because he did not manage the king's two bodies – Bracton, it seems, notwithstanding. Curiously enough, Kantorowicz does not include Bracton in his reading of *Richard II*. In eternalizing the metaphor, as it were, Shakespeare would have obliterated the traces of what Bracton was working on. For whatever reason, Kantorowicz, of all people, missed the opportunity to point out the Bracton in Shakespeare; indeed, nobody has until now, although Kantorowicz came closest in juxtaposing Bracton and Shakespeare. Read in the light of Bracton's achievement – an achievement paramount both in Shakespeare's time and in Kantorowicz's book – *Richard II* discovers rather than merely manifests, illuminates rather than illustrates, the doctrine of the king's two bodies at the very moment its alleged religious force is transformed into the force of Bracton's law.[20] Or is it, more precisely, the other way round, and Shakespeare's point is that Bracton's juridical pragmatism, in order to reinforce the secular enactment of the law, provoked with the deposition of Richard an afterimage of what this king could not *be*, but, as king, could very well elucidate and expose through his deposition, the law's supra-legal foundation? In short, on stage, and only on the stage, the king is "above the law," and this shows, exactly in the sense in which Hamlet shall call himself an agent "of show," in the paradoxical performance of self-deposition.

Bracton's commentary, whichever way we read it (it need not be Kantorowicz's way), is striking. In order to focus his point as we find it inscribed in Shakespeare's play, some new historicist scenario would need to be in place, a historical background not unfamiliar to Elizabethans and available, most readily, in Holinshed's chronicle – although one has to read him with more than an interest in what Shakespeare took from him as a sourcebook. I cannot do this here, but can only point to one striking detail in *Richard II* with respect to the king's position above the law. Of the king's so-called "favorites," Bushy and Greene, who are executed in act III, Bushy was, in fact, speaker of the House of Commons, and their speedy execution through Bolingbroke, consequently, was no inner affair of the rival noble houses. Even though the very same Bushy had, in an earlier scene, consoled the Queen's sorrows (2.2.1–27), and this scene came to prefigure the tear work of the final deposition scene, the subterranean political focus is the Common's loyalty that will be torn apart by conflicting feudal interests.[21] Thus, John Hayward's scandalous account – and we do not know how much he owed to Shakespeare's *Richard* – quite frankly reports "how instead of the noble princes of his bloud, and peeres of the realme' hee [Richard] was wholy governed by certaine new-found and new-fangled favorites, vulgare in birth, corrupt in qualities, having no sufficiencie ether of councell for peace, or of courrage for warre."[22] In other words, it seems that Richard tried hard to build up a force of his own against the feudal politics that had come to an impasse and that would be manifestly at an end in Shakespeare's and Hayward's days. Above all, Bolingbroke's execution of the favorites, just and apt as it aims to appear in Hayward's presentation, betrays already at that early point the later revolutionary rhetoric of discrediting the king through his sexual aberration with the Commons, a political Layer in this play whose setting needs to be elucidated against the grain of the prominent power struggle between the houses of York and Lancaster. Not the least, although the least recognized, feature of *Richard II* is the legal subplot, which is by no means uninteresting for the Elizabethan contemporaries of Shakespeare. Incidentally, it is a plot precisely not, as has been surmised again and again – Kantorowicz and Carl Schmitt took it for granted – in favor of some noble competitor for Elizabeth's throne like Essex.[23]

Kantorowicz investigates the legal concept of the king's two bodies on another level, on the theatrical or liturgical plane in Shakespeare's play. While it seems, "that the speech of the Elizabethan lawyers derived its tenor in the last analysis from theological diction and that their speech itself, to say the least, was crypto-theological" (18), the scenic implication of that theological subtext is liturgical and Shakespeare's representation of it, while using the vehicle, cannot but highlight the tenor.[24] Many critics, therefore, have qualified Richard's speeches in the deposition and mirror scenes as sheer poetry. Walter Pater, in particular, whom Stefan George's pupil Kantorowicz does not fail to quote, has put special emphasis on the aesthetic quality of what Pater calls "so emphatic a reiteration [...] of the sentiment which those singular rites were calculated to produce."[25] Thus, Harold Bloom's notorious insistence that "Religion is bad poetry" is turned upside down in *Richard II*, where religion's empty rhetorical shell, stripped of its theological content, becomes the vehicle of poetry, and the poetry's truth is not the religion contained in it but the religion of which it disposes. This is not to say that King Richard in his deposition turns into a poet, but that, bereft of his kingcraft, he is the one and only king to expose this craft authentically in its paradoxical *exclusion within* the law: under the law above the law.

Kantorowicz, who trusts Shakespeare a great deal, does not follow him that far. He is content with the king's body eternalized; he is ready to sacrifice the body vehicle for the afterlife of the tenor of the idea eternalized, although he knows of, and keeps mentioning, its spectral return with the revolution accomplished. He keeps Bracton separate from Shakespeare in spite of his otherwise keen awareness (in the case of Dante) of the common rhetorical ground shared by law and poetry, a structural ground and shared economy in which the realm of the poetic thematizes the law's working. Shakespeare redramatizes, that is, re-enacts, what is supposed to work in Bracton: the force in England's laws. According to him, there is no outside of the law except inside, where the king resides more resolutely than any other, in the *plenitudo potestatis* transferred from the papal model to "the full sovereignty of a ruler in his realm."[26] It seems that Kantorowicz misses this point, but paradoxically so, because he puts the paradox in too orthodox a fashion, *infra et supra* (both, *et-et*): "a legislator above the Law and according to the Law," is his translation (Lewis' resumé, 149).[27] Bracton himself had more shrewdly put it "*non sub homine, sed sub deo et sub lege*," which means simply: "no writ runs against him," because he is not "sub homine"; on the other hand "God will punish his abuse of power," because he remains "sub deo et sub lege" (263). While Kantorowicz keeps to the rhetoric of the implied *et-et – et infra et supra* – Lewis highlights Bracton's pragmatic turn. There is, however, a remarkable refinement in Bracton's formula that escapes modern pragmatism. He destructs the syntagma *et-et*, laying bare its rhetorical bias, by confronting the sovereign balance with its theological foundation. The second doubling (again, *et-et*) is the implication folded into his being above, and it grounds the being *above* in God's Law. This is how Richard can, in reverse, "undo his kingship" in Shakespeare. It is not until now that we come to the core of *Political Theology II* and, retroactively, also to the agenda of Walter Benjamin's *Trauerspiel*, which Schmitt was eager to include and whose pertinence is revived in the Benjaminian Agamben's work.[28]

Bracton's actual formula, *non sub homine, sed sub deo et sub lege*, renders the Kantorowicz paradox, *rex infra et supra legem*, in its legally relevant form and thereby approaches the schematic representation elaborated by Agamben in *Homo Sacer*: what seems to state a paradoxical juxtaposition of *infra et supra* turns, by means of the implicit *et-et – et infra et supra*, into an included exclusion of the *supra* within the *infra*. In the state of exception they "show themselves to be inside each other," with the growing tendency, observed by Benjamin and advocated by Schmitt, to "coincide in absolute indistinction" (38). *Richard II* gives a first hunch of that tendency, albeit in the form Schmitt claims to avoid with the wisdom of Hobbes: civil war. Richard himself and the Bishop of Carlisle in his defense, for which he is duly incarcerated, foresee "the purple testament of bleeding war" (3.3.94), which is to arrive in the course of dramatic events right after the burlesque scene in which, at the beginning of Richard's monologue, Bolingbroke's right hand and emissary Northumberland is mockingly, in fact, self-mockingly asked, "how dare thy joints forget/ To pay their awful duty to our presence" (3.3.75–76). One of the charges brought against Richard, also to become stock repertory of revolutionary rhetoric, was his strange delight in the ceremonial exhibition of his presence, to which "to watch the fearful bending of thy knee," as he himself puts it (73), is the required response.[29] What Richard is able to perform in view of the third, "purple testament" of blood is a parodic review of the past second testament, which saw him as vicar of Christ requiring such "aw and fear."

It is the third, the "purple testament of bleeding war," that threatens and that is to be avoided at all cost by what Carl Schmitt calls (referring to Paul) the "katechon" [*den großen Aufhalter*].[30] *Political Theology II* is to deliver the Christological crux of *Political Theology I* and to explain, against Peterson's version of it, what the all-too-loose "metaphorical" use of the religious lexicon (Blumenberg's first complaint) gave away. Kantorowicz's explanation of the "crypto-theological" idiom of the Elizabethan lawyers in the more specific "terms of christological definition" (as quoted above) had paid particular attention to the twin nature, that is, the *persona geminata* of the *Rex imago Christi* ("rather than *Dei*"), which could not very well serve as a metaphorical model for the king's two bodies "since the divine nature [of Christ] is his Being" and, that is, no "office" at all: "the King as *persona geminata* is ontological and, as an effluence of a sacramental and liturgical action performed at the altar, it is liturgical as well" (59). Kantorowicz's complaint that this [the Norman Anonymous's] "dialectic threatens to break up the ontological oneness by playing off the two natures against each other," is only too relevant here. The same "dangerous facility" recognized by Kantorowicz in theory is what he overlooks in practice in his reading of *Richard II*. Shakespeare presents the problem dramatically as Bracton, in the historical Richard's time, had dealt with it constitutionally. Schmitt's reckoning with Peterson in *Political Theology II* recognizes with Peterson, though against the grain of his dogmatic defense, the onto-theological source of that "dialectic" within the trinitarian construction of God's Being Three and, more precisely, the resolution of the Father and Son of the Law conflict resolved within the triangle of the trinity, to the effect of a sublation of the first within the second, New Testament.

Blumenberg's final assessment in *Work on Myth* from 1979 is the most pertinent here. In overcoming myth, the trinity reveals myth's hidden work: the covenant, first and second testament, presupposes another, quasi-covenant within the trinity concerning the Son's mission and office, a mission whose own mythic character is hard to conceal.[31] It keeps Schmitt going like all gnostics before him. Here the "friend–enemy" relation resides; from here it contaminates the covenants to come. Blumenberg's final critique of Schmitt's metaphorological thesis must therefore be the de-construction of Schmitt's stasiological construct of theology, of the Manichean fight of a God against whom nobody but a God can stand up, the pagan *deus contra deum*, invoked in Shakespeare's great precursor – he was most certainly aware of it – Aeschylus. The *stasis* or revolt of Prometheus divides the monotheist model of politics endlessly into friend and enemy, Epimetheus and Prometheus, pagan figures of Christ, with Leviathan and Christ as their post-figural others.[32] The sober jurist Bracton's demystification of the mega-mythical latencies preserved in the crypto-theological idiom of his age enables Shakespeare to reveal the theatrical role of King made flesh in the king's body.

Agamben's *Homo Sacer* confronts and refutes Schmitt's mythic superstructure of the exception with its proto-typical application in Roman law. As *homo sacer*, and only in becoming a *homo sacer*, which is at the same time his revelation as *sacer*, King Richard fulfills the ontological qualification of his *being* a king. In his Christ-like passion he is to prove what his reign cannot prove, neither factually nor legally. Bolingbroke (later Henry IV) knows that much when he finds himself at the end of the play unable to wash his hands in innocence. He bans the "murtherer" of his "fear," turns him, a "Judas" in Richard's words, into an *homo sacer*, and promises to "wash [Richard's] blood off from [his] guilty hands" in a pilgrimage to the Holy Land (5.6.30–40). "In weeping after [the murdered King's] untimely bier" (last line of the entire play), the new king makes and declares the dead king's imitation of Christ a theatrical *arcanum*: a state secret to be exposed as such, comparable *cum grano salis* to the semiotic paradox of the Eucharist in France, not in reformed England, in the public realm of princely representations.[33] Such is the function of Shakespeare's theater, in the London of Elizabeth. The theatrical instrument of "mirroring the magistrates" takes its sharpness from the arcane dialectic, in which the Son's Law remains submitted to the Father's Law on the cost of the Son's sacrificial performance for a new covenant, *semper reformandum*. Schmitt takes to the father because he is paranoid about the son – contrary to Saint Paul.[34] In presenting "the Political" as an Arcanum, *Richard II* may be the first piece of theater to address, after a *lacuna* of 2000 years, as Ivan Nagel has observed, "the political itself," that is, to localize and approach the emergence of a political principle of structure beyond the contingency of dynasties.[35]

As far as Elizabeth was concerned, she "was" Richard – as she famously once put it: "I am Richard II know ye not that?"[36] – but in a sense almost opposite to what has been made of this statement by all those who wanted to read *Richard II* as a political allegory of sorts (Schmitt and Kantorowicz among them). Elizabeth was unafraid of being deposed like Richard even in the face of Essex, whatever her own administration may have feared. Shakespeare's play was never in danger even though, as a friend of Southampton, he may have been too close to the Essex circle for the taste of her secret service. In fact and practice – *Richard II* is the proof – Shakespeare understood her well enough. She was Richard not in his fall as a prince but in the epiphany of princes that came from this fall, after the "purple testament" had been brought to a halt, indeed, by the Tudor dynasty. More radically, as the Virgin Queen she decided to be the *katechon* of foul princely succession, denounced in *Hamlet*, at the end of her reign. The successor nominated by her council with her "dying voice," James I, was a belated, ardent advocate of the *Divine Right*, incorporated by his Virgin predecessor, but lost on his son the Martyr King Charles I, executed in 1649. The great Milton, no lesser man, accused him, on top of everything else, of reading too much and making too much – the wrong thing – of Shakespeare.[37] No wonder that Kantorowicz was impressed with the uncanny historical irony of Shakespeare's unintended prophecy that seemed to come true in the "Christ-like martyr king" and "that most unpleasant idea of a violent separation of the King's Two Bodies" (41).

A last word on the *arcanum* that motivates all *arcana imperii* after Tacitus came to name them, in the wake of Tiberius's reign.[38] Schmitt's as well as Kantorowicz's use of the term goes back to Lipsius and, more importantly here, James I's "Mysteries of the State."[39] *Richard II* is a most Tacitean *mise-en-scène* of this *arcanum*. The onto-theological God-structure usurped by Schmitt and denounced by Blumenberg and Agamben works on the hidden grounds of a substitutional logic that necessitates ontological claims for the role of kings but that, more importantly, allows for a visible distinction that the law itself (Bracton's law) is unable to make: the king under the law above. Mercy is his most justified prerogative, acknowledged most cogently by Hegel's *Philosophy of Right*. The difficulty is that this most rational but (for that very reason) most hated prerogative of kings, mercy, is to be only individually addressed and cannot, for that reason, entirely be reconciled with, and applied according to, rules. Structurally, the act of mercy seems the flipside of Schmitt's sovereignty, the better side of what Schmitt himself preferred, and acknowledged, according to his gnostic taste, as his fate as jurist. The performative of mercy thus is a meta-performative like the one practiced by the sovereign in the "state of exception."[40] Consequently, mercy was no longer the virtue of the Machiavellian princes (*Macbeth* is the mirror offered to James I). Bracton's and Shakespeare's Richard confirm Agamben's and Blumenberg's refutation of Schmitt, as they also confirm the vanishing of sovereign mercy. But they do not support the revolutionary perspective connected with their – that is, our – post-revolutionary point of view. The king's price was the king's Christ-like passion and the contingency – itself the last of *theologoumena* – of an abrupt ending.

In a way, this is the fate of every star above the condition of everyday life. The problem that may be more urgent than the successful performatives of the presencing industry, however, is the substitutional pattern of God's necessary exception from the everyday expectation of Law and Justice. There is no better or deeper example of linguistic latency than the God name's primal and fatal attraction. "In God's name," Bolingbroke declares with the disillusioned cleverness required from the new Machiavellian princes, "I'll ascend the regal throne" (4.1.113). And, "Marry, God forbid!" Carlisle intervenes (114) since there is, indeed, no legal claim that comes with God's name but a vacant place, indeed, the vacancy of decision.

CHAPTER 5

The Death of a Shifter: Jupiterian History in *Julius Caesar*

> Had Pyrrhus not fallen by a beldam's hand in Argos or
> Julius Caesar not been knifed to death? They are not
> to be thought away. Time has branded them and fettered
> they are lodged in the room of infinite possibilities they
> have ousted. But can those have been possible seeing
> that they never were? Or was that only possible which
> came to pass? Weave, weaver of the wind.
> – James Joyce, *Ulysses*, 2.48

After Political Theology

As far as Shakespeare is concerned, the question "What comes after political theology" seems simple enough.[1] After *Richard II* comes *Julius Caesar* as the first of what should amount to a "Roman Trilogy" including *Coriolanus* and *Antony and Cleopatra*. Within the Shakespeare canon, this constellation raises some follow-up questions, notably with regard to *Hamlet* where a certain Claudius looms large, and there are also *Titus Andronicus* and *Cymbeline* at the beginning and the end of Shakespeare's career to be taken into account, but all of this should fall nicely into place, as soon as we have a fixed point of interest to distinguish the tragical English histories up to *Richard II* from the Roman tragedies that followed with *Julius Caesar*, immediately after the cycles of the English histories of civil war and succession had been brought to an end. The sudden transition from the English Middle Ages back to ancient Rome is striking, but except for the scattered, unsystematic recognition of the fact, not much has been made of it so far. It may be necessary to admit from the start the unsatisfactory state of the art in this respect, a complete embarrassment in the face of the continued efforts of ever newer historicisms, a predicament that suggests some more than accidental, deeper disturbances beneath the mere lack of historical understanding.

Instead of exemplifying the sad state of affairs down to the more funny details of recent research, I propose a new beginning with the ostensible "end of political theology" in *Richard II*. Taken seriously as political diagnosis of Shakespeare's tragical histories of England, it is important to note that these events go back 300 years and have caused 300 years of enduring trouble (1300 to 1600, roughly); they beg the question of a rising actuality of Roman affairs after the end of political theology and, more precisely, of interest in the crisis of the Roman Republic that led to the highly auspicious form of the Empire. What was Shakespeare's interest in the end of the Roman Republic? What did he know that made the topic interesting beyond the archaic setting of *Titus* and *Lucrece*? Never was the question of influence so silly as when it came to the Roman plays and the varieties of Elizabethans in Roman garb. There is something to be found in the horizon of expectations shared by Shakespeare and his time, and there are interesting symptoms like, in the wake of political theology, the amusing translation of Caesar becoming *pontifex maximus* in North's Plutarch as "bishop of Rome" (not present in Shakespeare's play).[2] Before we come to recognize and evaluate the unexpected range and intuition of historical knowledge in Shakespeare's Roman plays, we need to put this knowledge into an adequate perspective, matching the advanced level of reflection to be found in his take on political theology.

Only very recently, the historical formation to which political theology belongs and from which it draws its undiminished actuality has been subjected to a historicization of its conditioning.[3] Still, from Carl Schmitt to Habermas and Agamben there seems little chance to escape the all-demanding challenge of legitimacy, to which political theology offers a feeble solution. In a late lecture series with the citational title "Society must be defended" – a text that remained, unfortunately, in a rather unfinished state – Michel Foucault has sketched out an alternative "economy of power," in comparison with which he calls the juridico-political theory of sovereignty, "the theory we have to get away from if we want to analyze power," even a "great trap."[4] Ultimately, Foucault's objective in these lectures is a "counter-history" which surfaces after Shakespeare and leads to the rise of modern bio-politics. In the perspective of such a counter-history an important continuity comes to the fore in the history of sovereignty after Rome: "It is 'Jupiterian' history," Foucault insists (68). But although it is of the greatest importance that "there was still a direct continuity between the historical practice of the Middle Ages and the history of the Romans," this does not mean, as Foucault has it very much against the grain of his own initiative, that the later ideological function is an early implication of that story. It is by no means evident that there was no different sense of the political operative in the *translatio imperii* that had North translate *pontifex maximus* with "bishop of Rome" (and, that means by implication, Caesar as a proto-pope). With the reference to Jupiter, Foucault implicitly quotes Georges Dumézil's tripartite functional order of *Jupiter, Mars, Quirinus*, which does, precisely, not include, even almost precludes, any theory of sovereignty in the politico-theological sense, not to speak of its legitimizing function in the *Divine Right of Kings* through the Middle Ages and its radicalization to full-blown ideology in modern times.

Dumézil, one of the important influences upon Foucault (but largely unknown in this respect), enables a more refined reading of Foucault's alternative theory of power, including his archeological suggestion of a "counter-history."[5] This seems to me of special interest, since Shakespeare's theatre in general and his Roman plays in particular do negotiate functional aspects rather than represent historical knowledge and ideological transport. Plutarch's role, for that matter alone, is a very limited one. Dumézil's triad of Roman gods, the Capitolinian triad of *Jupiter, Mars, Quirinus*, represents the double-binding force of a *re-ligio* that regulates, quite in Foucault's archeological sense, the deep structure of the political sphere as a system of conflicting forces and functions.[6] Thus, Jupiter in Shakespeare's *Julius Caesar*, Mars in *Coriolanus*, Quirinus in *Antony and Cleopatra* are models to be investigated in their economy of discourse. I restrict myself here to the isolated Jupiter-function, which must be of special interest for the genesis of the politico-theological paradigm. The mono-functional isolation of political theology is bound to turn into a trap and initiate a counter-history of war (Mars) and domestic affairs (Quirinus), which runs counter, in fact, only to place itself into the Jupiter-position.[7] As we shall see, *Julius Caesar* does not deal with a proto-politico-theological setting, nor does he allude much to contemporary similarities of political legitimization or (*cum grano salis*) "democratic" tendencies of parliamentary representation.[8]

An Embarrassment of Method

Before I come to this at greater length, a second point is to be clarified, which I'm afraid is mostly to blame for the political disaster of interpreting Shakespeare's Roman plays. Here, the prevailing tendency is still to conceive of these plays as more or less faithful presentations of a more or less dubious historical material, mostly Plutarch, in order to illustrate some humanistic plot of more or less, again, psychological, or maybe psychohistorical, human interest – with the growing awareness, however, that there must be more to it than just Roman disguise. The crux is not only one of reading Shakespeare. A most characteristic version of the problem is the mode of interpretation proposed by Lisa Jardine and Anthony Grafton for a "new" reading of the Roman historians in Shakespeare's period, a reading, namely, for action: "Studied for Action" is the keyword.[9] But what it amounts to in the fascinating material collected – mostly Gabriel Harvey's annotation of Livy for the purposes of political counseling – is a far cry from the sad story related in Jardine and Grafton's emblematic reading at the beginning: the execution of one Essex advisor after being implicated by his master – an action that turns out as no case in point, since in no case, as the jurists handling the case clearly saw, can the reading of a classical text serve as an excuse for any action whatsoever. What Harvey, however, illustrates against the grain of Jardine and Grafton's mindful narrative is the growing awareness of political principles of structure in the reading of Roman history, an awareness that shifts from the politico-theological sphere to a Machiavellian reinterpretation of that sphere, most tellingly in Harvey's fabulous reinterpretation of Augustine's evaluation of Livy in most astonishing Machiavellian terms. As far as Julius Caesar is concerned, Augustine ends up highest in Harvey's new sense of the political; a sense, however, that does not at all, in all its newly gained and deepened Roman exemplarity, "lead to action," as Jardine and Grafton jump to conclusions, but to a newly emerging discourse of political "negotiation" among those in power. Stephen Greenblatt's preference for this term proves valid here in a more precisely political respect than the most general sense of "collective negotiation and exchange" and "circulation."[10]

In order to get a better idea of what this new discourse of the political, as well as the new state of classical scholarship in its service, entails, some methodological considerations seem in place. Stanley Cavell's extremely careful essay on *Coriolanus* has stated the aporia best: in the sharp divide of "the political and the psychological" that has brought the philosopher to read between the lines of the psychological symptoms of this play – "the childishness of its hero," in short – the proto-politics of an advanced skepticism.[11] Cavell gives utmost credit to the psychoanalytically refined pathology of history that has been most cunningly drawn from Shakespeare's presentation of Roman life – character and gender – in the work of Janet Adelman and Coppelia Kahn.[12] They raise the stakes enormously with respect to the missing political link. I propose to take the well-contested psychoanalytical readability of the Roman plays, which seems to preclude any sense of the political except for the proto-politics of skepticism, as the pretext for an experiment in the opposite direction. The strength as well as the problematic of psychoanalytic criticism resides in its power to bracket intention and influence – the two factors unavailable in Shakespeare's case, particularly with respect to the state of Roman history in his time. A lot of scholarship will be necessary – Jardine and Grafton are a rather biased first step in this direction – and this will be, no doubt, successful if done.

Instead, I propose an analytical attitude comparable to the psychoanalytical standard of reading, that is, an investigation of the historical readability of Shakespeare's texts in the strictest sense of the most advanced reading possible of Roman historians, developed and shared by 15th- to 20th- (by now 21st-) century scholarship. A proposal like this would be vain, if it were not for the extraordinary examples, beside Georges Dumézil, of Ronald Syme or, more recently, John Henderson. Superb readers of sources, they are unmatched in their refinement, equaled only by Freud and Lacan who both were also learned in the field of classical scholarship. Syme and Henderson are obvious examples, because they have reconstructed the histories normally read as Shakespeare's sources in their interaction of views rather than in order to establish an objective, causal chain of occurrences. The result is not the Machiavellian scope that replaces in Harvey's reading the salvation-historical scope of history and confirms Augustine's world-historical diagnosis in the first place – Foucault's misunderstanding of a counter-history – but a skeptical account of political negotiation and function in scope and telos.[13] It is not possible to include in this first attempt how much Syme or Henderson's view of the sources owes to the historical work of Tacitus, whose influence on Shakespeare is particularly manifest in *Hamlet*. Thus a first, preliminary, and most superficial rendering of my answer to the question "What comes after political theology" in Shakespeare would simply be: Tacitus (along with, to a certain degree, Sallust, Seneca, and Augustine's reference Lucan).

Tacitus, however, has nothing, except in passing, on the subject matter of Shakespeare's Roman plays. Instead, his *Annals* and *Histories* offer a counter-statement to Livy before him and, by implication, Plutarch after him. Whereas Livy in hindsight of Harvey and his time conveys the exemplary political wisdom of Rome, a wisdom morally broadened by Plutarch and perfectly in tune with the imperial project of Augustus's continuation of the Republic, Tacitus's later review of this project's fate (preceded already by the horror of the by no means unknown Lucan) brought out and made readable what was at stake before, and was prepared in Sallust's work on Catiline in particular. Sallust's account of Julius Caesar, at a time his sponsor, has left traces in Shakespeare's play (as it had, by the way, in Augustine's *Civitas Dei*). It was Ben Jonson, not Shakespeare, who put Tacitus on the stage with the tragedy of *Sejanus*, which may be read as an almost direct answer to *Julius Caesar*, with the telling subtitle – *Sejanus: His Fall* – that indicates a difference to which I come in a moment. Jonson is at the bottom of Shakespeare's bad name whenever it comes to classicist matters; unfortunately, we have not yet come to a revision of this embarrassing commonplace, which pits the learned Jonson and his peers against a naively popular Shakespeare with nothing but the coffee table Plutarch in hand.[14] As a matter of late irony I might add that no lesser man than the greatest authority on Tacitus, Sir Ronald Syme, came at the end of his career to the suggestion that Tacitus himself had realized too late that his work *Ab excessu Divi Augusti* (the *Annals*) would better have begun with what it was to imply and work through in the most complicated manner of a depressing aftermath, the death of Julius Caesar.[15]

The Lesson of Contingency

"The tyrant in view is not hard to find," we find ourselves ensured by the last Arden editor's introduction to *Julius Caesar:* "Even elementary knowledge of Queen Elizabeth's policies in the years up to her death allows parallels between herself and a tyrannical Caesar."[16] Only very recently, Oliver Arnold was about the first to present the case in a different light. As his title indicates, we cannot reasonably assume that tyrannicide was on the agenda of the newly opened Globe in 1599, but the debates around the "Early Modern House of Commons" might form an interesting backdrop – although that need not entail, I would want to caution the next demand for action, any apt or timely suggestion of "democratic" change. On the contrary, the Tacitean tendency of Shakespeare (for the sake of brevity), which will take an even more stoic turn in Late Shakespeare, asks for a different theatrical conception, after political theology is gone (the Virgin Queen will have been gone), and the Machiavellian princes are on the threshold. Still, Arnold is right and explains in admirable detail what might be at stake in the Roman plays at the time:

> In *Julius Caesar* and *Coriolanus*, the tribunes are plebeian by birth, but their status as representatives has made them part of Rome's governing class, and they devote themselves to managing, controlling, bamboozling, and pacifying the plebeians. They are, in fact, as zealous as the patricians in limiting the people's power. In the first scene of Caesar, the tribunes suppress the people's celebration of Caesar's triumph over Pompey. In Plutarch, the people hate Caesar [...] Shakespeare makes Caesar the people's darling and the tribunes their scourge.[17]

The point is striking and the argument well put, but needs historical clarification. If we read Syme on the side, it becomes shockingly clear how much good intuition and well-informed knowledge Shakespeare is operating with. Whoever his "facilitators" may have been (Jardine and Grafton's term), Shakespeare's presentation needs no contemporary coloring in the prospective terms of class conflict. A perceptive reading of Livy will do for the start, although it takes Sallustus and Tacitus to identify Julius Caesar's problem, the advanced constitutional crux of dictatorship. As little as the Roman Republic has to do with democracy, as little has the institution of dictatorship to do with tyrants (both Greek to Rome).[18] Thus there is an up to now highly controversial, but well-defined and documented, over the centuries into every terminological crux debated, political scene presented by Shakespeare, whose very Roman exemplarity (Roman in the very sense that kept and keeps it exemplary) lies in its lasting importance for what we might be tempted to call the Roman concept of the political. For Shakespeare's Caesar, it is not Carl Schmitt's or Leo Strauss's (nor Alan Bloom's or Paul Cantor's)[19] concept of the political that would necessitate and initiate the political theologies, but the deep structure that surfaces after these formations have outrun their course; Machiavelli is a most ambivalent witness of this process.[20]

Dumézil's construction is helpful here, if only to underline the enduring split between the patrician families and the plebeian part of the population; a split, which, in Livy, turns up and becomes vital only after the end of the Etruscan kings. Livy takes pains at the beginning of Book II (Book I ends with Lucretia, the first Brutus's revolution and the fall of Tarquinius) to explain that the royal function remains fully in place, but is limited in time and divided in power. Namely, it is given to the administration of a group of father families, while what is excluded is the older royal Etruscan part of the city which, in the by now famously "inclusive exclusion" of a people's party, shall ask for enduring trouble.[21] Livy himself seems to have been highly ambivalent about the exemplary value of the regal period.[22] As

Dumézil has shown in many intricate details, the Jupiter-function remains intact, but retains the title of king in this withdrawal from the political sphere to a higher level, to which the theo-political role of the *flamen dialis*, but also the *pontifex maximus* belong (in short, Julius Caesar's alternative way to power). What from that time onwards seems to be defining in the smooth presentation of Livy's Augustan mind, is the self-control of the aristocratic families, their limited share in power, on the one hand, and the not to be pacified rest of the older part of the city, as well as later also that of the drastic expansion of the population. Among the ritualized means of conflict management, the feast of the *October equus* stands out, to which Dumézil has dedicated some of his most fascinating pieces.[23] It takes place at the Ides of October, and under the auspices of the Jupiter's day it stages for the troops, who traditionally return on that day for the winter until the Ides of March, a competition ritual between the two irreconcilable parties of the city. (It may not be entirely accidental that Mamillius, the king's son of *The Winter's Tale*, shall carry most casually the name of the Mamilii, the plebeian party in this winter's rite.)

An interesting point in *Julius Caesar* is the correspondence of the feast of the October horse with the *Lupercalia* at the end of the winter period, on the Ides of February, but most sensibly telescoped by Shakespeare onto the Ides of March, to which it does, in fact, lead up. In the ritual run of the consul Marc Antony, in which the need to secure the succession is implicitly thematized (as the *Winter's Tale*'s Mamillius is the spoiled success to an unlucky king), the regal crown is offered to Caesar in a most overdetermined and hard-to-read gesture. Within the context of the *Lupercalia* the reference is historically conventional; it is meant to keep up the royal past within the city, but it does so on these Ides of 44 in a particular manner: the dictator for life does not need it, because it is hardly to be distinguished from what its distant memory is to keep at bay. Instead it brings out – and it is Shakespeare who brings this out, as clearly as any historian of his time, including his rival in these matters, Jonson, could have wished for – what the agenda was at this point: dictatorship had changed sides.

Not only was Caesar one of the popular party of Marius through his first wife; not only were "many Marians in him," as Sulla had famously observed (echoed in most telling fashion in Augustine's *Civitas Dei* 5.11). Sulla was the last one who had exercised the office of *dictator*, and with a success both exemplary and devastating. After Sulla, the might of Pompey the Great had been great, indeed, but still it had amounted to nothing less than the unconstitutional exploitation of the provinces and brought about, if only indirectly, the threat of Catiline and his gang of friends from within the ruling aristocracy, which neither Cicero nor Cato were able to bring back to their old ways of sharing the power. Sulla had been exemplary in stepping back from the dictatorship after the work was done; but the work had been devastating, because it had ruined the substructure. The age-old instrument of limited power within the consular families had brought about – and could not have avoided – the supplement of the tribunician power of appeal (the starting point of Machiavelli's *Discourses on Livy* 1.3). The institution of dictator had been introduced in order to suspend this complicated space of negotiation via the tribunes for a limited time of urgency. After Catiline's warlike state of exception at the latest (Cicero was overly aware of this), what used to be expected as a limited state of exception had grown into a constitutive threat: "the Roman aristocracy was not to be permitted to govern and exploit the Empire in its own fashion" – thus Sir Ronald Syme describes Caesar's agenda (on the eve of the imminent end of the British Empire): "Being forced into an autocratic position," Caesar had to face a mixed opposition and to work with a very mixed party: "personal feuds and personal interest masked by the profession of high principle, family tradition and the primacy of civic over private virtue."[24] The resonances for Shakespeare's England are very clear, and a literary exemplum was available in Caesar's own writing, in his *Bellum civile* to begin with, whose well-calculated exemplarity features Caesar's antidote: a new politics of friendship, of *fides* and *clementia*, as means of political reformation through *amicitia*, the risk of violent "ingratitude" included.[25] Patronage – *amicitia* – is the dubious institution that needed revision.

The king-like position, into which Caesar was brought with a dictatorship that served both the plebeian side and the new needs was an anachronistic reminder of the failed integration and the lack of integrative power of the old order, while the rule of the old *nobiles* itself had become an anachronism in a world empire in which a different oligarchy of government emerged. Shakespeare portrays the "liberators" Brutus and his consorts' character masks with the greatest possible perceptiveness. No Queen was needed as tyrant from whom to be liberated. Shakespeare's historical interest went deeper; he was never a mere critic of the day. As an object, he has the evolutionary thrust of the early British Empire before his eyes that had outgrown the dimensions of late-mediaeval nobility and was in the process to regenerate itself into a new, upward-moving class of Machiavellian entrepreneurs. The *arcanum* of political change, as a Tacitus would name and describe it (*Annales* 2.36.1), was not to be found and pictured in the hypocrisy of these liberators.[26] As the term *arcana imperii* indicates (and King James's I own translation "Mysteries of the state" underlines),[27] there was a strong religious implication (in the Roman sense of *religio*); the *Julii* were a sacerdotal family and Caesar became a reformer of rites, the rationality of which is still to be admired in his calendar reform. Shakespeare does not fail to include the double-binding religious force of the older republican order, still functioning along Dumézil's lines. Jupiter needs the unpredictable Mars desperately (as the notorious nuisance *Coriolanus* proves in Livy as well as in Shakespeare), but both hinged on the domestic force of negotiation that came under the name of Quirinus. (So too, by the way, *Othello*, the next project in the Shakespeare canon, appears in a new light.)

Back to the crucial role of the *tribunitia potestas*, whose suspense first, and whose apotheosis later, was facilitated by Caesar's dictatorship. A risky office which, since the tribunes' power was easily corrupted, almost lends itself to corruption by the senatorial forces, and was therefore to be safeguarded by the sacrosanct status of the tribunes in this office; Caesar himself had claimed it for himself for life in 44, and so would Caesar Augustus when he handed over the *imperium* in 27. Whoever would touch him would be *like* (I underline: like) a *homo sacer* – to be killed without due process on the spot. The killing of Julius Caesar the dictator had turned sacrosanctness upside down in a thorough perversion of the established Lupercalian rites. The bloody side of this travesty has been well analyzed, as it had been analyzed already within the play itself and played out in Marc Antony's rhetoric. In spite of the pointedness of the allusions, the details in Shakespeare's application seem "more evidence of the perversion of traditional rites" than their correct description, one has complained.[28] Indeed, and with a reason. The murder of Caesar, besides being a politically senseless deed, stems from the perversion of what it claims, unwittingly, to save. That "virtually all of this is Shakespeare's invention," therefore, is a rather strange complaint: compared to Plutarch's scandalous entertainment version for the later born, Shakespeare's perversion has the sharpness of the Tacitean diagnosis of a perverted politics. Plutarch, in comparison, excelled with details like Brutus aiming at his possible father's "privities" in revenge for Caesar's lifelong relationship with his, Brutus's mother Servilia (possibly Caesar's closest ally over the years). Obviously, the congeniality of Plutarch to the ruling bad taste of Elizabethan audiences does not define Shakespeare's intention.

There remains, however, some Elizabethan "study for action" to be discussed, although contrary to the ambitions of the Harveys of the time. When it comes, in Act 3.1, to the situational pretext for the assassination, it is Caesar's innovation of the prerogative of *clementia* that is being questioned and turned into a duplicitous trap: a bind that perverts, before it shows the opposite of what it proves, the merciless pursuit of masked interests in the self-proclaimed liberators. Casca is put into the position to strike first and from behind (3.1.30), while a certain Metellus Cimber – former supporters of Pompey, the *Metelli* had supplemented Caesar's faction, precisely, through his clemency – asks for the pardon of his brother and is seconded by Brutus, but in a bad moment and obvious pretense: If Caesar falls for the flattery, he proves the partisan misuse of his power; if he does not, he proves the suspected partisan suppression of his aristocratic enemies. In any way, he becomes the target of revenge. In this emblematic predicament of position, he will be killed anyhow. But Caesar stands beyond the fights of factions and he says so: "constant as the northern star," he calls up one of the leitmotifs of the preceding deliberations, *constantia* (3.1.60). In Lipsius's treatise *De Constantia* of 1584 (a cult-book of the European intelligentsia of the time, published ten years after Lipsius's edition of Tacitus's *Annals* and fifteen years before *Julius Caesar*), constancy is treated as the one and only true fundament of liberty.

In independence and constancy of judgment Caesar literally falls – in a blatant irony, that is, of the constancy of his stance, in a self-performative pun of the Shakespearean kind. While the proverbial *clementia Caesaris* shall survive as the last and decisive prerogative of Kings until Hegel's *Philosophy of Right*.[29] In the act of his actual fall, manifested in the sheer Latin "Et tu Brute," Caesar appears monumentalized to the extreme: language could not be pronounced in a more distancing manner than in these last words. Now, History speaks, and the rest is silence before the return of civil war (the *Hamlet* motif to come). What we are left with is the vacant Jupiter-position, which had become unmanageable by the old aristocratic set of noble families, threatened of old by a Janus-faced Mars running wild – *Coriolanus* is the Republican screen memory for this threat to which Shakespeare shall soon return. Caesar had shifted the Jupiter-position from senatorial dictatorship to the plebeian side, with the effect of bringing the very same Mars back into the city, over whom the *Quirites* had lost control since Sulla the latest.

The critical plot thickens to the extent to which we do rival, up to now, with Shakespeare's evaluation of the story to be told: Caesar's tragical history in the face of Brutus's self-declared demand for higher tragedy. Let me, for the sake of brevity in the vast field of undecided historical questions, cite from a recent account that seems apt enough to settle the Brutus question for the moment:

> What, then [that is still the question], were the aims of the conspirators against Caesar? [. . .] despite the allegations, there is no

serious evidence that Caesar wished to elevate himself to the level of divinity. [...] Nor is there evidence to suggest that Caesar wished to be king in Rome; indeed, it is clear that he was aware of and sensitive to this charge, and wished to counter it. The stage-managed occasion when Caesar refused Antonius' offer of a golden crown was such an attempt. The campaign of disinformation was intended by Caesar's enemies to isolate the dictator and to justify what they were conspiring to do.[30]

As Shakespeare shows, this double-edged rhetorical strategy ended differently. In his will the dead Caesar continues to do something for the plebeian side, while Brutus in his address is unable to point to tyrannical acts of the dead but only to his ambition and the threat of a future tyranny according to the old model – a *futurum exactum* of dictatorship. In an unintended, as it seems, moment of irony, which, it turns out, is the dramatic irony of History, the monetary gift to the people reduces the critique of royal prerogatives from the politics of sovereignty to the sphere of business negotiations.[31] Or, to put it in Dumézil's terms: the gift of Caesar's legacy moves it, *corpus delicti*, under the threat of Mars, and in the name of Jupiter, to the negotiating power of Quirinus – a "giving in to the name" of Jupiter, mistaken by Brutus and Cassius (or Cicero, at that) in their stoic or epicurean outlooks, but less likely to be misunderstood by the rest of the everything but disinterested faction of senators.[32]

The hope of the self-proclaimed "liberators" was ill-advised and wide-eyed, a masquerade of lost values. The irony of Caesar's death – a constant star that was to fall – is countered by the irony of the liberators' only remaining liberty, namely, to die freely – as the "honorable men" ridiculed by Marc Antony, the proverbial runner, and ironized, in the icy manner of the winner, new Caesar Augustus. The bygone era expires in a show of freedom, in which the "history of liberty turns out to be" a "history of dramatic performance" – or so it appeared to an audience, which had gotten used to the modes of theatricalization of power in sovereign representation.[33] Thus, what comes after political theology for Shakespeare? The profane illumination that was, for one historical moment, the *clementia Caesaris* and that is, for the present moment, the stage. Constancy of mind, not Machiavellian activism is the message, if there is any. What used to be *catharsis* (Shakespeare did not care for the Greek) could not purge any longer: the many wounds of Caesar flowering in Marc Antony's speech, as well as the one wound of Brutus's Portia at home, had turned into the mouths and flowers of a rhetoric that could but state an example, though one useless for immediate action. This paradoxical uselessness, *nota bene*, had been also the paradoxical function of the examples employed by Machiavelli himself, which leads me to a tailpiece of exemplarity.

The Exemplary Turn

In this case, the paradox derived from no lesser man's hand than that of Caesar himself. John Henderson, who has excavated and reconstructed the exemplary coincidence of "writing for and fighting for Rome" in Caesar's self-commentaries, sensed the implied temporality, which is politically instrumental and produces also, in its theatrical efficiency, a Roman prototype of Shakespeare's dramatic technique.[34] Citing Freud's "deferred action," Cavell had described this technique as "deferred representation," a terminological preference which Michel Serres, in congenial anticipation of Agamben, brought back to its primal scene and screen memory in Rome: to its Roman and, that is (important to note), pre-Christian exemplarity: "When Rome, to end royalty, chases the kings out, it is not expelling royalty but defining it."[35] Shakespeare had demonstrated this specific belatedness for the end of political theology in Richard's II deposition. Serres recapitulates Livy, "Manlius was lynched in the senate, and this is what made him king." And "Likewise," Serres continues, mindful of Livy's Augustan confession, "Caesar was lynched in the senate, and this is what made him king."

A logic of deferred representation, then, seems to govern the end of the Roman Republic. "Brutus," invoked in Caesar's Latin by Shakespeare's Caesar in all his brutality – "Et tu Brute" – is the mask into which the proclaimed liberator has turned, leaving behind his name as the mortgage of a liberty going down the drain, drowned in blood. In the closest possible reading of political motivation and deep memory of the civil war to be found in the satirical idiom of Horace, Henderson has marked the lasting effect of Cinna's (the Younger) notorious, remarkable "echolalia" of "Liberty! Freedom! Tyranny is dead!" [3.1.78] – a stutter of brutal mnemonic force: "the raw figure 'Brutus' holds us, still."[36] Shakespeare gets hold of that figure in its far-reaching, lasting effectivity. Hamlet cites this hold of the brutal – "It was a brute part of him" (3.2.104) – in making fun of Polonius who claims to remember playing (Shakespeare's) *Julius Caesar* right before he gets stabbed. Hamlet's mock-question in this moment, "Is it the king?" (3.4.26), is the irony of Brutus's deed in retrospect and an even more ironic self-commentary of having him return in *Hamlet*.[37]

The 33 wounds of Caesar in Anthony's liturgical commemoration [3.1] do not only, for Shakespeare's audience, recall Christ's 33rd year and re-mark in this death the early political announcement of Christ's deferred passion, but these wounds would attest to the exemplary pseudomorphosis of Christ's passion to the politico-theological end of *Richard II*. For *Julius Caesar*, it seems, Christianity did not manage to make a difference, the *Divine Right of Kings* remaining a Roman rhetorical guise. We do not have to convert to Oswald Spengler's *Decline of the Western World*, whose echo we hear in Carl Schmitt's *Political Theology*, but we might reconsider the cunning of Hans Jonas, who made use of Spengler's *pseudo-morphosis* in his analysis of the developing Gnostic text milieu of the later Roman Empire.[38] As a generalized figure for the fusion of horizons, the historical pseudomorphosis on display in *Julius Caesar* contains more than meets the eye of an allegorical or typological interpretation. It may seem too much to expect more than fragments of the brutish idiom in *Julius Caesar*, foreshadowing the emerging post-republican speech situation that has found its most refined representation in Tacitus.[39] Still, a most remarkable achievement of Shakespeare's account of Caesar's tragic *exemplum* may be his portrait of the language that governed the last days of the republic and became a hallmark of the new administrative order: the linguistic dimension of a "political hypocrisy," which drastically surmounted the ideologies embedded in the Elizabethan format of sovereignty.[40]

Strangely, if not tragically, Caesar's ostentatious "parade" of *clementia* as the most ambiguous achievement of his power had superseded the redefining force of a new sense of *libertas* that was on his mind and would emerge in the century after Augustus; it would replace, instead of revive, the old conception of aristocratic liberties.[41] Brutus's desperate effort to emulate in action Cato's fatalistic farewell to the lost case of a deluded republic is decomposed, if ever so intuitively, in Shakespeare's farcical mime of the liberators' bewailing old values. It may indeed have been Cato's suicide that stole Caesar's show of *clementia* and turned it backwards into the questionable prerogative of the once and future kings. Sallust's account of Catiline had set a stage early on.[42] In addition, Shakespeare and his time had read Seneca's deeply ambivalent evaluation of Caesar's practice of clemency in *De ira* and *De clementia*, texts ironically written – in the irony History amounts to in Tacitus's rewriting of history – for the uses of a certain Nero.[43] Clemency is a question of history, it turns out in Seneca, a question of credibility to be established in years of political practice, and in the aftermath of Caesar's death, this credit history of Caesar's project, precariously unstable as it was, was destined to be destroyed; it remained almost unreadable up to now, Shakespeare's brilliant intuition notwithstanding.

The new type of an *exemplum*, thus, was to be taken as a decidedly post-Caesarian one: After Caesar, History had taken on a new meaning, grounding the advent of the Christian era. In the aftermath of the *Divine*

Right of Kings, tragic history was to continue in spite of the fact that its foundation was over and, in the process, turn into something in which Foucault became interested, and of which Kantorowicz had already been mindful. In old Rome, on the contrary, there was a tragedy to be registered that had outrun its course, but remained latently in place, threatening with a return neither Foucault nor Kantorowicz would recognize in that period, except for the symptoms – deferred representation – of the revolution to come. Constancy of the mind became the maxim of a stage and an age in need of self-historicizing distance. The *caesura* – in itself a providential pun on Caesar the stage had to offer and the age could not but meditate in melancholy reflection – was no thing to hold on to constantly. Another irony, the irony of history, whose preservation in the histories of Shakespeare amounts to the actuality of history itself, began to impose itself: neither the bygone "senses of an ending" in the histories of salvation, nor the "counter-histories" of war, against which the philosophers of history from Augustine to Foucault have expressed their dismay. Deeply divided from their fatalistic giving in to the reign of history, built on nothing but the occasional premises of the theater, a skepticism (which shared the dismay, no doubt) arose and began to ask for another sense of the political, which was to include a different sense of the historical to begin with. In the Rome where it began, this new sense of politics includes the classical example of exemplarity: of a history of distance from, and resistance to, the histories of power like those of Jupiter's, the God name's, position.

Seen from the distance, the distance of advanced history, the Jupiterian history that found its definitive sense of an ending in the terror of the French Revolution seems as dead an affair as it could ever be. According to *Julius Caesar*, the "Roman Revolution" – a term coined after the French Revolution in the century of Mommsen and in the rediscovered Renaissance of Burckhardt and Pater – proves still to be an entirely open-ended affair.[44]

CHAPTER 6

The Future of Violence: Machiavelli and Macbeth

The future in the instant
Lady Macbeth (1.5.58)

The future of violence is nothing that could be prophesied.[1] I do not mean to say that violence would have a future, but rather that a tendency towards the future dwells in it, an unlimited futurity that from the beginning of the modern age advanced as a momentum inherent to modernity and that momentum has become a new, and in the meantime total, type of unlimited violence. Lady Macbeth is not the discoverer of this new violence but its most eloquent agent and theoretician, and Machiavelli, who places the name of her husband in the proper light, is its first and most significant informant. Although the resonance of the names, Mac-lavellus and Mac-beth, could not have been wasted on Shakespeare's pun-obsessed public, it has not incited much significant attention, and the similarities noted between the two, Machiavelli and Macbeth, seem hardly to exceed the commonplace that Macbeth was a theatrical villain for whom the Elizabethan theater had the character-name of "Machiavel."[2] For the role of the unscrupulous prince, Richard III appeared as the more typical example, whereas Macbeth, in his Scottish Highland version of atavism, full of witches and auguries, appears rather to bear the pre-rational features of a bygone prehistory.

A satirical pamphlet from the middle of the seventeenth century,

Machiavel as he lately appeared to his dear Sons, the Modern Projectors, a pamphlet from the quill of the dramatist and publicist Thomas Heywood (1574–1641), has as a theme a modernistic orientation towards the future, which seems to have no purchase in *Macbeth*.[3] There are few heroes with so little future as Macbeth, who for Shakespeare was anything other than a modern projector. Consequently, the bulk of enlightened Macbeth critics up to the present day have taken pleasure in the attribution of the piece to the possible commissioner, the theologico-politically retrograde James VI of Scotland, who at the beginning of his succession of the great Elizabeth is said to have had occasion to play at overcoming the primal Scottish conditions of a Macbeth. Shakespeare did not make it so easy for himself; nor was James in fact such a simple soul. On the contrary, it is exactly this simplicity with which until today we make it too easy for ourselves whenever we construe violence and the increase of violence as an enigmatic, ever-returning reminder of a prehistory that we, just as the age of Macbeth, consider to be behind us – although this violence actually increasingly governs modernity, or more pointedly, is nothing other than a phenomenon of the modern. Therefore, the moral of the story of *Macbeth*, which Shakespeare took from Holinshed's chronicle and its predecessors and cut to match the present of James I of England, is not the vanquished past of the wild Scotland of clans, but rather the confrontation of his time with the ghostly present of a violence which, in a barbaric after-image celebrating grim primal circumstances, can in no way be limited to a gloriously overcome past (this too corresponds to James's assessment).

The New Historicism enjoyed the tendency of considering the atavistic present of gunpowder plots and Jesuit-executions, of witch-hunts and high-treason trials, as the contemporary horizon of expectation, in which the past of old conditions of violence raises and keeps virulent the problems of legitimation associated with the dynastic and hereditary doctrine of *Divine Right*.[4] Violence hence is evaluated as the typical disgrace of monarchy, as the unsheddable "shadow," which reigns as a metaphor up to now and is to be found in its more recent, modern shadings from Heidegger and Foucault to Luhmann and Robert Cover. It would actually be more like the shadow that the judge of the world forecasts on the clouds of the sky in the form of its terrestrial caretaker. The scandal of Jesuit persecution and witch-phobia notwithstanding, the shadow of violence and its increasing unsheddability is not this king's ownmost problem, but that of a modernity with which he did not come to grips – a failure that, it must be said, numbers rather as one of his merits. Rather than as an embarrassedly outdated means of a stagnant form as yet uneducated in the separation of powers, I see the violence that we are talking of and that is thematized by

Shakespeare in *Macbeth* not as a residue but as a catalyst and medium of a progress whose victims would become James and Macbeth alike; the play *Macbeth* therefore an augury from witches to a witch-obsessed monarch, whose offspring – *success*, in the equivocal language of the drama *Macbeth* – already in the next generation would have to suffer its consequences. The poet Milton, a Shakespeare-adept of the highest degree, still wrote the Shakespeare-reading into his indictment of the ill-fated Carolus Stuardus, James's unhappy son. The circumstantial accuracy of this interpretation is not my object here as much as its specific mediality: the futuristic violence of the new state-forming powers.

One remembers the content of *Macbeth* to a reasonable degree not only because of a series of well-known film versions but even more so because it is a short play with barely any content, whose consistency and pace would almost be overstrained by precise knowledge of film and theater interpretations. This makes the shortest by far of Shakespeare's pieces the perfect counter-piece to the longest, the barely older and three times longer *Hamlet*. Whereas in *Hamlet* there is endless reflection and deferred action, in *Macbeth* the events precipitate one another in an unstoppable fury from the witches' prophecy to its speedy fulfillment; from the sudden ascent of the hero to kingship and his just as rapid fall – "a tale/ Told by an idiot, full of sound and fury/ Signifying Nothing" – in short: history in the face of whose prospective, even all but apocalyptic, rage the present sinks into nothingness. The "medium of reflection," which through Hamlet's mask of melancholy engenders the excessive running time of the play, in the case of Macbeth's rise and fall, is violence. There is no piece of literature (not even Schiller's *Robbers* touches it) that would take violence so clearly and exclusively as its theme, object and plot, impetus and tendency, as *Macbeth*. There is no other play whose verbal force would have expended such a forceful eloquence on violence. That there is no bigger contrast than that between language and violence; that the violence of language can never touch the speechlessness imposed by violence; that language in the hyperbolic gesture of violence only proves that it is everything other than violence, and that it has nothing under its force but itself (and us as well) – this is what *Macbeth* presents as a riddle of the medium. The most violent language (the most formed by violence) proves, demonstrates to the eye and ear, that it is *not* violence, is nothing less than the violence that it re-presents; proves that its representation has to do with nothing less than the violence that it destroys in its own unconditional lack of violence.

Taken for itself, the violence of speech is violence-annihilation; in speech by itself violence is not sown. He who sows violence does not do so by means of language alone but through mediated, staged, functionally "de-languaged" speech. In this regard, the staging of violence-speech in *Macbeth* is a de-staging of violence, whose cathartic overcoming through tragedy has remained the false phantasm of the theater. In this sense, *Macbeth* (like *Hamlet*) is decidedly an anti-theater, and this is not a question of more or less pure, action-distanced reflections, which are the masque of Hamlet, but of that which Antonin Artaud at the end of a theatrical tradition (within which, however, Artaud counted Shakespeare as first in line) called "cruelty": called it the "necessity" and "implacability," which (as Derrida has put it) restore the "force" of the "classical forgetting of the stage" and "the triumph of a pure mise-en-scène" – a force that it, as "mere reflection," lacks in effectivity.[5] Benjamin's rediscovery of the theatricality of the Baroque *Trauerspiel* shares with Artaud's theater of cruelty the theorization of the medial conditions not only of its origin, but also of the origin of a wider-reaching setting, in which violence is the most progressive, progress-producing medium.

Interestingly but not surprisingly, the mediatization of violence into a medium of progress is connected to the crisis in which this medium slips out of the control of the sovereign and overwhelms him, behind his back, in the manner of a dangerous supplement that should be in his hands. In a manner distinct from the theatricalization of the German *Trauerspiel*, Shakespeare in *Hamlet* aimed at this sudden change of the medial-supplementary role of violence. What is unfortunately missing in Benjamin is Machiavelli's primal scene of the new Princes, who were James's ideal as little as they were Carl Schmitt's. Claude Lefort recognized the necessity of learning how to read Machiavelli anew and underlined the peculiar value of his theory as a source of political praxis. In the role of the theatrical villain it became unreadable; and to read it as an allegory of the political theory that engages with this villain, as Leo Strauss advocated with decisiveness, can only end again with the pre-decisiveness of the original prejudice, if not to affirm it even apotropaically.[6] Shakespeare is the best occasion to read Machiavelli anew, just as, conversely, Shakespeare's politics cannot be fully comprehended without a closer reading of Machiavelli in the sense of Lefort.

There is a key place in the *Principe*, in which the new role of violence, that of its mediatization through theatricality, is presented *in nuce*. It is located in Chapter VII of the *Principe*, which deals with the new category of principalities purchased through foreign weapons and the fortune of war. Cesare Borgia embodies this new type of a prince, who formed the lasting image of Machiavellianism. From the start, Machiavelli underlines the exemplary role of Borgia for his analytic purposes; he wouldn't know "better precepts to give a new prince than ones derived from [his] actions."

Unfortunately, he must admit: "if what he instituted was of no avail" [because Borgia in fact failed almost immediately], then "this was not his fault but arose from the extraordinary inordinate malice of fortune."[7] A paradoxical exemplarity (Lefort speaks of the "double jeu de l'écriture") in a chapter that pertains to incalculable *fortuna*: to declare a prince as worthy of imitation to whom – and be it through "estraordinaria ed estrema malignità di fortuna" – *no* lasting success was granted. The reason for an extreme adversity in a business, which depends on nothing but success, baldly jumps out, even without the author specifically bringing it forth. Granted, the rupture with the genre of the mirror for princes serves the education of a specific "modern political sensibility" at the price of the old concept of political norms.[8] But Machiavelli not only publicizes this achievement (and in any case not as an achievement) – he presents at once its subsequent costs. This proverbial mythic intractability of the Goddess Fortuna does not let itself be domesticated by the *raison* of the new princes as an inherent, self-destructive moment of their projects (including bourgeois projects in the sense of a Thomas Heywood or a Daniel Defoe).

The episode still belongs to the fortunate, ascendant portion of Borgia's unfortunate career and recommends itself almost innocently for imitation by the new princes: that of "Messer Remirro de Orco, a cruel, efficient man," as Machiavelli writes, whom in 1501 Borgia made the governor of the Romagna and equipped with what Machiavelli calls, tongue in cheek, "plenissima potestà" (30/31).[9] The expression is by no means only descriptive, although it is this, too, in respect of what Messer Remirro does and undoes. It is the definitive quotation of definitive authority, of the *plenitudo potestatis* of the Pope, which Boniface VIII had proclaimed with the *Unam sanctam* bull, and this is why Machiavelli's model Dante stuck him in the deepest *Inferno*.[10] To give it in the hands of the son of the Borgia-Pope, epitome of illegitimate descent, is no mere irony of history (in the rhetorical countersense of irony); it discloses a trickery of reason, which Machiavelli publicizes as a Machiavellian competence:

> So he placed there Messer Remirro de Orco [...] to whom he entrusted the fullest powers (*plenissima potestà*). In a short time this Remirro pacified and unified the Romagna, winning great credit for himself. Then the duke decided that there was no need for this excessive authority, which might grow intolerable [...]
>
> Knowing also that the severities of the past had earned him a certain amount of hatred, to purge the minds of the people and to

win them over completely he determined to show that if cruelties had been inflicted they were not his doing but prompted by the harsh nature of his minister. This gave Cesare a pretext; then, one morning, Remirro's body was found cut in two pieces on the piazza at Cesena, with a block of wood and a bloody knife beside it [*con uno pezzo di legne e uno coltello sanguinoso accanto*]: the brutality of the spectacle kept the people of the Romagna at once appeased and stupefied [*la ferocità del quale spettaculo fece quelli popoli in uno tempo rimanere satisfatti e stupidi*].

The effect is doubled, as is that of the problem into which it successfully blends – whose causality [*non causata da lui*] it on occasion overplays [*presa occasione*]. Justice appears on the scene out of the blue as that which has been already enforced. The sheer violence of the state of exception, even though handled with the utmost skill and success, falls prey to its own means and is perverted into a moralistic *tableau*, whose eye-catcher is the miraculously enforced yet not staged enforcement: the corpse that is torn in two pieces, with the instruments of the execution at its side. The achieved gratification is that of an ironic catharsis; the purifying intention [*per purgare li animi*] leaves behind empty heads [*rimanere satisfatti e stupidi*].

The opposition of *mantenere* und *ruinare*, observed by Roland Barthes in Machiavelli, emerges as the double point of view of the catastrophe continued in the state of exception.[11] The act of positing is finalized in the ostentatious crossing out of the moment of violence in itself. The astonishment of the public arises from the slaughter of the slaughterer, which through the violence produced experiences satisfaction against the most obvious appearance. Borgia's theatricality is effective insofar as it redefines the moment of violence. As a "representation well used," Victoria Kahn adduces a public moral, which conforms to the logic of a Habermasian "representative publicity" [*repräsentative Öffentlichkeit*].[12] Machiavelli's representation is more refined than this moral of the story. True, the transvaluation, which Machiavelli undertakes, is that of a "rhetorical redescription," yet this is more than merely, as Quentin Skinner suggests, "a means of depreciating and undermining the so-called 'princely' virtues of clemency and liberality,"[13] because this would again be only a theory of evil, not a theory of violence and its provenance. Machiavelli's redescription goes deeper; it includes with it a new disposition of rhetorical foundations, a new "consideration of representability" in Freud's sense [*Rücksicht auf Darstellbarkeit*].[14] Just as the *plenitudo potestatis* of the Pope's offspring, Borgia, is a borrowed one, so too is the enforcement that he puts into scene, of the theological miracle that Carl Schmitt declared as the criterion of political theology without achieving anything better than a vague analogy of "theological concepts."[15] Borgia does not emerge in the hypo-critical role of the judge who restitutes the injured right; on the contrary, he avoids this role and that he avoids it is the critical point. Quite homogeneously and totally demonstratively, the second violence prolongs the first: no self-healing catharsis but an incurable self-destruction is its form of appearance in the *raison* of the new princes.

In the restaging of this image, whose theatrical gesture achieves here an exemplary novelistic emphasis, Machiavelli underlines a destructiveness of the moment of violence that is deeply embedded, at the level of its theological–political presuppositions, in the ostentation of positing [*Setzung*]. This has direct significance for the liberation of Italian politics from foreign powers (Ramiro de Lorqua was a Spaniard), including the Pope's manipulative use of the *plenitudo potestatis*. In this, too, Machiavelli follows Dante. In another context, Shakespeare will start out from this constellation. Machiavelli presents himself as prudently as possible, austerely even. He left out from this episode, to which he was an eyewitness (as proven in a letter from Cesena of the 26th of December 1502), the date, Christmas 1502, birthday of the Son of Man and the designated crucified, from whose *potestas* the papal placeholders derive the *plenitudo* of their *plenissima potestà*, from the model, that is, and example of imitation of the natural son from the house of Borgia with the telling name of Cesare.[16] Machiavelli excluded – held at a distance – from his presentation this theological pre-figuration of the calendar, with which the Pope's son was accustomed to having free reign. The juridical terminology and juridico-political diction of *causa* and *occasio* takes its place, whose "a-rational" perversion Carl Schmitt calls "political romanticism."[17]

"In the *Trauerspiel* of the seventeenth century the corpse becomes the emblematic *requisite* as such," Benjamin writes under the heading *The Corpse as Emblem*. "The apotheoses are barely conceivable without it. *They are resplendent with pale corpses* and it is the function of the tyrant to provide the *Trauerspiel* with them."[18] The corpses become emblematic not only physically but as the result and proof of execution, meaningful only in the dismemberment whose gesture is the object of *Trauerspiel*: "The drama" brings this out by "endowing the ruler with the gesture of execution as characteristic of his power" (69). Earlier Benjamin had emphasized that "this view is by no means a privilege of the dramatists" (65). What is it that Shakespeare adds and the German Baroque would not have delivered, which did not comply to the melancholy of the conditions, and in itself deeply split representational politics of the time? Machiavelli's achievement in thematization is just as acute as it is consequential a set-up; alongside *Hamlet* and even more than *Richard III*, *Macbeth* is the case that wins from it the sharpest profile.

The crux in *Macbeth* is just as distinct as the surrounding environment is alienating. The wild Scottish scene of clans does not harmonize with the Upper Italian cities, it submerges it in a barbaric light; that, however, is the lighting effect that Machiavelli himself supported in his Florentine setting, and that up until the present is not without an effect: that political avant-gardes cannot act without regression into "barbarism" (barely anyone is ever concerned with the reputation of the poor barbarians). Thus, the Scottish scene in a certain way naturalizes what happened on the piazza of Cesena in Macbeth's savage will to "bloody execution" (1.2.18). What leaves the Cesenati speechless sets free a hidden sadism, whose masochistic front side it satisfies. What leaves the Scotsmen speechless, after the initially unchecked, sadistic cheer for the bloodthirsty hero Macbeth, is the encroachment of his "destructive fury" upon the authorizing power of the king, a primitive encroachment, whose statute along with his own bloodthirsty disposition it flushes down to the same level, on which the rule of Royal blood, which authorizes the *Divine Right of Kings* treasured by James I, bleeds out just like every other "bare life."[19]

Out of the overflow of sheer linguistic cruelty, in which this play remains unrivaled, a theater of cruelty *avant la lettre*, but down to the final letter, the monstrosity of the deposition of the kingly blood that Lady Macbeth spells out in her delusion still sticks out: "who would have thought, the old man had so much blood in him" (5.1.37–38).[20] This is not a question of the character of the two heroes, of the "butcher and his fiend-like queen," as viewed by the victor Macduff after his "execution" is performed (5.9.35). It shows that something is "rotten" in the state of Scotland, unsound [*morsch*] from the bottom up, as Benjamin cites this condition in a silent *Hamlet* quotation of the "Critique of Violence."[21] Like Hamlet's Denmark, the Scotland of Macbeth finds itself in a "war-like state," an enduring state of exception without a dynastic base. It only looks as if the murdered king Duncan (just as the old king Hamlet) had been an undisputed ruler; he was most likely a hero in the manner of Macbeth, whose savage violence he underwrites and facilitates with open admiration: "O valiant cousin! worthy gentleman!" he bursts out in raw enthusiasm over the bloodthirsty report of an officer who, reveling in his own wounds, captures Macbeth's latest heroic deed in one of the most disgusting descriptions of "bloody execution" ever delivered (1.2.7–24).[22]

The point of this report is not the soldier's bravery of the established histories – in *Macbeth*, for instance, that of the young Siward fallen in battle at the end of the play, a scene that serves as a silent commentary on the death of Macbeth.[23] It is, rather, sheer violence-obsessed fury as it in unfettered brutality rapes the rebel-whore Fortuna who, "like Valor's minion" (not Goethe's Mignon), is devoted to violence.

> Disdaining Fortune, with his brandish'd steel,
> Which smoked with bloody execution,
> Like Valor's minion, carv'd out his passage,
> Till he fac'd the slave;
> Which ne'er shook hand, nor bade farewell to him,
> Till he unseam'd him from the nave to th' chops,
> And fix'd his head upon our battlement.

Duncan thereupon:

> O valiant cousin! worthy gentlemen!
> (1.2.17–24)

It is easy to lose sight of the constitutive crux of positing [*Setzung*]. Due to the emptying effect of speechless stupidity, which in Machiavelli as in Shakespeare is achieved by means of most powerfully eloquent gestures, one remains stupefied by the same semantic butchery, the same emblematic wrath of dismemberment, in short, the same horror. The historical Macbeth, however, but also the mythic Macbeth whom Shakespeare puts on stage, was a juridically effective law-maker [*Setzer* as in *Gesetz*], with a much bigger legal reputation than a Borgia could ever acquire; and even James I, who would take delight in Macbeth's ruin, preached loyalty towards even the most disreputable tyrant inasmuch as "except where his lusts or passions are involved, he will generally favour justice."[24] What James did not understand, and what hardly should be understood as an adaptation of his conception, is the new "fury" that is mobilized in the new princes' state of the exception, and whose "sound" *Macbeth* – ear-splittingly rather than eye-catchingly like Machiavelli – intensifies and elaborates in its medial modeling. In this time, conspiracy and betrayal, fear of witches and the rage for execution are only the most well-known phantasms of the theater-place that is the public, and they are "everything but," as Benjamin is right to say, "a privilege of the dramatists." But neither the strengths of the play, nor of Shakespeare in general, lie in faithful depiction, whose trope of contextualization is so gratifying for the old and new Shakespeare-historicists.

Machiavelli, no – Borgia already – had brilliantly brought before the eyes the mechanics of positing and its continuation [*Setzung und Fort-Setzung*], which Shakespeare transposed. In the standing and bringing to a stance of an image, the spectacle of Cesena exposed the caesura of positing. The standing image shows the strategic displacement of the invested violence, whose furious continuation drives Macbeth mad. In this dislocation, violence appears on the scene as an overwhelming medium and perpetuates itself as a futuristic, future-generating momentum, "the future in the instant" as Lady Macbeth says (1.5.58).[25] It reproduces itself without the distinction of having legitimate offspring. This is the problem of the ever prepared, futuristic woman who is totally beyond children; this is also Hamlet's moralistic, world-historical insight, whose legacy lies in the ghostly darkness of history: "In that sense, the rest was not silence."[26] The Caesar from the house of Borgia, an enlightened Hamlet without maternal burden, might have seen with irony the dynastic interest to which he owed his career; the decisionistic aspect of positing and order-founding thus becomes more apparent in him than in the other occasionalist princes of the new kind. James might have liked to find in the overcoming of Macbeth a dynastic opportunity that he could turn to his own use: to transform the contingency of positing into the victory of a successful dynasty: with Macbeth as the primal picture of Messer de Orco, and history as a generalized primal picture of what was to come.

Precisely here is where Shakespeare's theater had something to add without, however, having to add much: what hardly could have slipped the attention of the interested James but otherwise would have remained easy to ignore. Claudius, who in Hamlet's dumb show was put to the test, knew how to handle this (we cannot be sure to the present day).[27] In the dramatic totalization that in *Macbeth* drives Shakespeare's theater to its bitter end, quite other than in the exemplary novelistics of Machiavelli, which puts it at an analytic distance, the rolling stone cannot be stopped in any market square, cannot be captured by any other fixated snapshot than that of the overcome "usurper's head" (5.9.21). In *Romeo and Juliet* it still came to a more peaceful prospect, but these were the earlier days of the Scaligieri from around 1300, and the medium was that of love overcoming violence. The battle of the new princes rages on into the foreseeable future, and to be nothing other than the master of the moment must be uppermost on James's mind. Machiavelli's mirror for princes says there must be something to learn from Borgia's fate – regardless of the outcome: Just like the corpse of the emblem, Borgia's *exemplum*, the life of the princes, is torn in two.[28]

In its sought destruction and conscious renunciation, *Hamlet*'s ending comes close to the Machiavellian emblem. His end amounts to a monumental memorial, whose heroism is anything other than that of the melancholic masques of the hero. As far as heroism is concerned, Macbeth does not linger behind. In contrast to the beastly Richard III stabbed to death behind the scenes, Macbeth delivers himself over to his successor. In this the ending of Hamlet is a significant counterpart: the hero, who by the command of Fortinbras is laid out, missed his succession but handed it over. Macbeth, driven into a corner and set up by Macduff, is slain in a duel on the public scene and the victor presents to the audience the head of the king's murderer, which the revenge of Hamlet had spared them (could spare and had to spare). It may thus be correct that whoever wins in *Macbeth* consolidates the hereditary kingship from which James himself descended, while Hamlet relinquishes it (and more specifically, must relinquish it).[29] But the mortgage, worthy of neglect as it might have seemed to James who was successful in succession, nonetheless remains: *success* in the double meaning of descent and accomplishment is a leitmotif that is written on the body of the offspring in the line of succession. The reversal in the order of success, from successfulness to mere successivity, is characterized by an ongoing state of latency, wherein *fortuna* can only be mastered through permanent rape. It is not the baseness of violence, but rather its futurity that takes her – Fortuna – as its source-goddess, whose role Machiavelli's *Principe* at once determines anew and finds as pre-determined from time immemorial. The witches, who embody the dominant media design and without fail know the future better than does Macbeth, are a quiet quotation from antiquity in the fashion of Fortuna: "the weird sisters," in the contemporary Virgil translation by Garvin Douglas, are the Roman *parcae*, "having the power to control the fate and destiny of men" ("the wayward sisters" in Onions' *Glossary*). The relapse was clear to Hegel when he referred to Macbeth's witches in the *Phenomenology* as "the ambiguous sisters of fate" and recognized in them "nothing other" than the ancient "priestess through whom the beautiful God speaks."[30] The fateful medium of Macbeth's witches is for Hegel "nothing other" than the "deceptive" dark side of the "light side" of the Apollonian oracle, and the scandal of Jesuit equivocation which historians detect in the background of *Macbeth* is itself nothing other than its contemporary variant.

With the inevitability of a quotation from antiquity, the *ananke* of ancient tragedy, the fate of the new princes befalls Macbeth; he delivers himself over to it in the theatrical pose of the death on the cross from the passion plays and thereby points to an unaccounted for mortgage. From the *translatio imperii* of antique rulers, which had merged into the *plenitudo potestatis* as a parody of god-loaned power, all that remained for the kings is the passion of the Son of Man on the cross. Though they might, like James, reassure themselves through the doctrine of Divine Right, all that is assured them is passion. A wide-reaching, unabatedly persistent, self-radicalizing Christian burden is propagated by the antique cast of characters, the Fates in the clothing of the "weird sisters," as if Christianity were haunted by a primeval form of violence that pins onto the *dramatis personae* the Christian world-picture under the cross of the savior and declares the English reformation a popish relapse of the Renaissance; Machiavelli's Borgia is the debunking example. The prophecy of the "weird sisters" comes from far away and reaches far.[31] Carolus Stuardus, James' unfortunate son, will in the place of success bear the crown of the martyr, but he will not lack for success. Yet the procreation through blood, if one takes Lady Macbeth at her word – that is, according to the Machiavellian appearance assigned by Hegel to its definitive place – is no longer a matter of descent.

In contrast to the illustrative motif of procreation sustained through violence, the medial principle that follows it is that of an endlessly ongoing theatrical inscription. Its emergence in the text is remarkable; it appears in the first major monolog, which is held by the lady and interrupted by Macbeth's return from the witches. She greets her spouse with an echo of the witch-sisterly prophecy "Great Glamis! Worthy Cawdor!" (1.5.54), the success become-effective of the "all-haile hereafter!" (55) as if she had heard these words herself. Its sudden becoming-true has overtaken the hereditary problem of succession. Shakespeare's stage trick is a near-anachronism: the witches' prophecy encroaches upon the letter, a mythical medium on its way from the fates to the postal services, which has itself become sheer witchcraft:

> Thy letters have transported me beyond
> This ignorant present, and I feel now
> The future in the instant. . . .
> (1.5.56–57)

Macbeth's affirmation follows on the foot of the same verse:

> . . . My dearest love,
> Duncan comes here to-night.
> (1.5.57–58)

The letter conveys success – "They met me in the day of success," reads Lady Macbeth aloud, starting the monologue in which the message becomes the medium of bloodshed and the kingly victim, following inexorably, becomes the effect, whose risk-managers Machiavelli recognized and publicized in the new princes. In this regard as well, Shakespeare does not miss the medial double-plot: the mariological framing of the good news, which the Lady is reading, leaves little doubt: "Lay it into thy heart," recommends the spouse at the end of the letter, which allows her to conceive the message of near-success (1.5.13–14). She conceived, but the seed is the violence by which her savior, marked by his end, awaits a travesty of the Christian myth of sacrificial death. His blood comes over him and his successors. No king can be resurrected from these dead.

Lady Macbeth's prompt doubt about the fitness of her husband turns the doctrine of *Divine Right* on its head: he is too timid in his human nature – "too full o'th'milk of human-kindness" (1.5.17) At the place of the grace of the *Divine Right of Kings* he lacks the sense for evil, the "illness" that would fundamentally exceed the demonstrated brutality and could prove in the negative the transcendence that counts as recognized in the right bloodlines. The un-sexedness, which the Lady conjures, not her sex, shall fill in – "Come you Spirits [. . .], unsex me here" (1.5.40) – and shall redeploy the missing, kingly bloodline, which she does not have and cannot propagate for herself. Childless and pointedly insensible to children as such, she goes for procreation through the blood, which sticks to her hands like a futuristic prophecy: his, the dead king's blood, shall come over her and her children.[32]

Modernity is horribly Christian, Christianity horribly modern – "oh horrible, most horrible" in old Hamlet's infernal irony – and Shakespeare is tragic in an unprecedentedly modern sense; nihilism is only one of the trite expressions with which *Macbeth* criticism takes the easier way out.[33] Heidegger's reading of Nietzsche's "will to power" as the *telos* of "European nihilism" seems an unavoidable challenge here. The relapse into violence is a pre-lapse, a prolepsis of the becoming-true of a prophecy, whose mise-en-scène appears as pre-modern but whose logic is by contrast futuristic, thus reducing history to the caesurizing moment between prehistory and future. From the consequence of Hegel – "to let tragic conflicts appear as something definitely passed" – no reconciliation is "construable" but that of an incalculable, hovering "tragic" that exceeds the old name.[34] By contrast, the much-cited decision represents a hopelessly regressive solution, and the medium of blood, reserved for the case of redemption and established on its basis as if for proof, is singled out as a symbol with a fatal latency. In Benjamin's "Critique of Violence" it is treated as explicitly mythical.[35] The intuitions of the two Macbeths have experienced an unforeseeable political affirmation in the biopolitical success of blood. One cannot account for either the intentions of the period or of

Shakespeare's own; but this anticipation nonetheless makes his theater, just like Machiavelli's politics, the prototype of the following, still ongoing development of the medial phantasmata of modernity. Already in *Macbeth* these phantasms appear no longer as the teleological remnants of a bedeviled purposive rationality, but rather as the ideal of a purity that in the purity of blood serves as a model of functional equivalence and medial immediacy.

The princes did not become leaders, nor the politicians villains, but they became managers of risk-politics; the Fates are no longer witches but instead go by the name of the media. For the media, the blood secretly congealed into semen; for the politicians the end of salvation-expectation was frozen in torture. In the post-World War I paradigm shift from John Dover Wilson's *Hamlet* to Maynard Keynes' *Macbeth*, "the Economist Prince dethrones Plato's Philosopher King" (whose deconstruction Hamlet had performed), but even this was to remain a faint hope of the neo-pragmatist kind.[36] In the meantime, one reads once more Montaigne, inasmuch as "he (the risk-theorist knows) cushioned his life with doubts while around him the world fell into ruin."[37] Montaigne in hand, the theorist of risk-management meditates upon statistical codes, which fail before the baroque landscape of melancholia just as the German *Trauerspiel* did before Shakespeare's political challenge. Certainly, "the individual does not justify narration," one has famously remarked, but *this* – that it does *not* – does not justify narration either. "The individual is" *not* "the transcendence of every code," but it is transcendental in relation to every code.[38] A beyond of the statistics of genocides and democides, for which an "over-extension of transcendence" could be argued in the manner that agitated Benjamin's *Trauerspiel* can be hoped for neither from the singularity of the individual nor, as it once seemed, from the collectivity of salvation.

CHAPTER 7

A Whispering of Nothing: *The Winter's Tale*

Tragic Humor to Follow: The Post-Romantic Present of Tragedy

It was Heinrich Heine who first sensed the subterranean political attraction and affinities of Shakespeare's *Winter's Tale* in his cycle *Deutschland – Ein Wintermärchen*, which he wrote under the eyes of Karl Marx in Paris 1843–44. Here he proposed an attitude of "tragic humor" that might be able "to strike political-romantically a fatal blow against the prosaic-bombastic poetry" of his time.[1] Even though Heine never elaborated on his use of Shakespeare in this remark, the idea of tragic humor provides a first handhold for a political interest in that play, even if we leave the late- or post-Hegelian coloration of Heine's intuition aside.[2] In Marx's contention, expressed about a decade later, of the supra-historical interest of literary works like Homer's and Shakespeare's, some new sense of the political comes to the fore that distances itself from the melancholia of tragic irony that had been the Romantics' last word and Hamlet's last reading. Against the "heroic melancholy" of a tightening "dialectics of the Enlightenment" – a melancholy vis-à-vis the inescapable irony of the tragic as tragedy's ineluctable past – there is now another, a new aesthetic present and new actuality of tragedy that would announce itself in Late Shakespeare; an actuality that the shift from tragic irony to tragic humor sensibly registers.[3] The politics of *The Winter's Tale* may not be what a Marxist expects, but it foreshadows a sense of politics which a reader of the later nineteenth century may recognize – even though this all too long century's many insights, like Shakespeare's intuitions, seem to have barely become apparent and fully reflected before the turn to the twenty-first.

Instead of taking the clue from the later Romantic Shakespeare reception as a point of departure – a clue that would necessitate some major theoretical reassessments to which I will return only in the end – I will begin with a less doubtful kind of manifestation of *The Winter's Tale*: that of Shakespeare's manifest text itself as it was handed down in the First Folio edition and is hardly in need of editorial work, displaying only minor differences with the text that Heine and Hegel have read. The rare case of an unequivocal Shakespeare text like *The Winter's Tale* makes it appropriate for some fundamental genre-theoretical and poetological considerations of dramatic form, independent of the historical performance conditions to which we otherwise take resort. The last half dozen of Shakespeare plays, among them *The Tempest* and *The Winter's Tale*, experiments with a new blend somewhere between tragedy and comedy, for which the predicate "Late Shakespeare" became a trade mark. This is less a solution than the first shadowy indication of a question for which we now have, thanks to Hegel, Nietzsche, Benjamin and Artaud (even though they have in their references to Shakespeare remained unimpressed by the late plays) some almost classical terms and criteria. The substantial, anything but ephemeral role of Shakespeare for Hegel, Nietzsche and Benjamin, all the way to Heiner Müller, remains to be supplemented and completed with regard to Shakespeare's late theater. To do this, it is necessary to break with a predicament that has remained a commonplace of a still largely puzzled scholarship: Despite the characteristic unity of the late plays that is always acknowledged, they are in the end judged as remaining tentative in search and experimentation, open-ended sketches of an old man who has become weary, indecisive about his art.

The one illuminating moment in this indecision is the fact that late works are rarely ever a linear extension of earlier efforts, but instead they are marked by processes of self-historicization, in which the double crux of mimesis that is traditionally to be faced anyway – the imitation, that is, of nature, and the emulation of previous efforts – experiences an abyssal deepening of its own. Not only do Shakespeare's last plays stand out by their remarkable interconnections, at the same time they recursively refer back to the work that has preceded them, producing a unique kind of intra-textuality that has occasionally been commented on, but needs to be analyzed as a systematic working through of materials and conceptions: conceptions of the tragic, the comic and the historical (if we take the divisions of the First Folio). The genre of Late Shakespeare answers the problem situation of the tragical histories or *Trauerspiele*, in which the techniques of comedy played no minor role. With regard to *The Winter's Tale*, the references to *Othello, Hamlet, Lear* are unmistakable, but also to the early comedies they are fairly obvious. There is no need to bring out their reply-character in a more explicit way, before I come back to the question of tragic humor that is to connect them in the end.

Instead I begin with a state of affairs that has been negotiated since the nineteenth century under the heading of "romance."[4] Ever since Northrop Frye consolidated the commonplace, things have stagnated: "*The Winter's Tale* (he decided) is a diptych, in which the first part is the 'winter's tale' proper, the story of the jealousy of Leontes, the slandering of Hermione, and the perilous exposure of Perdita. The second part, the last two acts, is the story of Florizel's love, Perdita's recognition, and the revival of Hermione. Shakespeare's main source [the novella *Pandosto* by Robert Greene] is almost entirely confined to the first part; for the rest, Shakespeare appears to be on his own."[5] Shakespeare is supposed to have taken up the tragic novella material and ornamented it with a comedy-like supplement, in order to force the tragic orientation of the narrative substrate, inherent in the novella of his colleague Greene, to some novel consequence called romance. By splitting off the structure called tragedy – "tragedy is the name of a structure," Frye asserted on the occasion – Shakespeare had added to the tragic material a second, meta-tragic part, which seems to follow the tragedy like the satyr-play of antiquity, and in "a tragic exhibition of death and revival" its untamed sense of an ending is said by Frye to be completed by what he calls "a natural perspective."

The structure in the case of *The Winter's Tale*, as it were, is the structure of extended tragedy – of a spectacle to become the entirety of some new type of theatrical performance – which is self-exceeding to the extent that it causes the five-act scheme to change over into the duality of a diptych.[6] Obviously, the division of acts is not simply falsely foregrounded; formally it provides everything that it, as tragic structure, must contain in order to be enacted at all. But within the sequence of the five acts a duality develops, asserts and enforces itself. A silent transposition, following the dialectical allusion of a pastoral interlude (the rescue of Perdita), resets the tone of the tale and comes into its own at the beginning of the fourth act, in the temporal jump of sixteen years that have elapsed since the tragic opening (Leontes' jealousy), leading to its post-traumatic supplement (Hermione's revival). The temporal shift speaks for itself in the allegory of an ancient chorus that is "Time" and comments upon the common theme of time on stage. The tale that Shakespeare picks up, second hand, as if by hearsay, is a winter's tale to the extent that it most fabulously turns natural time in the cycle of the seasons toward the spring that slumbers in every winter.

Appropriately, it invokes the myth of Persephone, which finds itself subjected in this tale to a rather peculiar interpretation (only faintly mindful of the common *Ovide moralisée*).[7] The coming of spring, however, remains an episode: fall recurs, and the morality becomes – turns into – a politics, the politics of tragic humor.

The Renaissance Blueprint: Botticelli's Performative

The mythical substratum, and especially the Persephone myth, provides the spectacle with the transitional energy to move from the tragic trace into a new kind of *enargeia* that shall become the bone of contention of Romantic reflection, not to mention the innumerable indices and tokens the history of ideas had in store. I will turn to some of them only after I have secured the dramatic "alteration of tones" (*Wechsel der Töne* is Hölderlin's term) according to the details of its disposition: a tonal transposition that unmistakably intones rebirth, renaissance. In Botticelli's *Primavera* there is an intriguing iconological program to be uncovered. I shall restrict my investigation to the more general, iconological level since I do not mean, at this point, to imply any kind of influence: *La Primavera* is not to be taken as an iconographic matrix on the level of possible influences. Instead it exemplifies a paradigm of change and transition or, more to the point, the logic of a strategy of reoccupation, which *The Winter's Tale* presupposes, theatrically assesses and exploits. I avoid expanding on the convoluted fate of the *Ovide moralisée* out of which Persephone eventually molts into the exemplary instance of a "vegetation myth," according to Frazer. I thereby also avoid the treacherous task of reconstructing the methods of staging in which *The Winter's Tale* may have found its first performances. As Edgar Wind's analysis makes clear, Botticelli's painting establishes a model and type of performativity, to which Shakespeare reacts as to an epochal, historical *a priori*. In the shadow of Botticelli, *The Winter's Tale* features a type of theatricality for which the pictorial turn can be taken as the symptomatic fallacy: it is not the dramatic instance of the sheer visuality presented by *La Primavera*, but the exemplary instance of a performative latency on the brink of a future "condition" of performance in Freud's understanding [of *Rücksicht auf Darstellbarkeit*], which would allow *The Winter's Tale* to be produced, understood or also misunderstood, in the performative praxis of its staging.

If we leave aside, for the moment, the philosophical argument that Botticelli presupposes in literary terms and shares with Shakespeare (Lucretius, Horace, and Ovid are the names, and always the exact same passages); and if we also skip the intellectual effect of the acutely "lyrical" (with which Wind, not contrary to the main stream of *Winter's Tale* interpretations, endows Botticelli's performative), what remains is the refined logic of the octave that the painting brings before our eyes: the famous line of a musical staff upon which a row of eight mythic figures is arranged. Divided into chords of 1+3+1+3, Amor floats above it and scans the ascent of the gods, in which he appears as the key and notorious companion of Venus, whom he identifies, and needs to identify in this case.[8] Because unlike the naked goddess on the seashell also painted by Botticelli, this Venus is resplendently clothed and returns in the drapery of a Madonna. This is not the way it is explained by Wind, but in accordance with Petrarch. The Venus here, in the dress of a Madonna, emerges into the auratic halo of a wooded clearing, stepping with a most merciful gesture of Christian *caritas* into the line of pagan figures, while Cupid, everything but blind, continues to shoot his arrow at the mourning *Castitas*, who goes hand in hand with her more resolute sister *Pulchritudo* and looks *Voluptas* straight in the eye, who is devoutly submitted to the destiny of her drive. In short, the mythic program keeps running, uninterrupted by the *caritas* that is about to revise the score. The moment is decisive, of the motion frozen in a standstill; the moment of the metamorphosis of the goddess of love converted from *cupido* to *caritas*: Venus in the appearance of the Madonna. Conversion is accomplished, but shows itself completed in the figures of a pagan metamorphosis, transformed into the new *structura caritatis*.[9] Mercury, who is known to understand the course of things, protects the divine assembly from the left side, leading it over the edge of the frame to the neighboring painting. Meanwhile, the events behind him remain caught up in the accelerating natural transformation that is the subject of Botticelli's painting: The arrival of Spring, which, in light of the transfigured Venus, no longer appears in the form of the pagan *Ver*, Latin Spring itself, but arises in the opulence of *Flora* preparing the way for the Madonna. The mythic allegory of Spring recedes and appears to be folded back into an implication of the revealed apparition of Venus in the Madonna.

Before I lose myself in Botticelli and prematurely arrive at an interpretation that Shakespeare shall unlock in its theatrical potency, I will first return to the structure of the scene in which, prior to any allegorical or psychological latencies, metamorphosis is captured as a matrix of the natural order of things. Botticelli's painting is a word-for-word explication of Ovid, following step by step, in a practically cinematic sequence, the series of cuts in which, flowing from right to left, the Greek *Chloris* is pursued by Zephyr and about to be raped. In this moment she turns into Latin *Flora* (literal Ovid) whispering flowers from her mouth, the wind in pursuit, but finally falling back and fading into the shadow of myth, colorless as her suitor, the Greek god of inspiration. In short: myth saves itself through the metamorphosis into Christian Latinity. It is Flora, and not Chloris, who prepares the carpet to bloom at the feet of the Madonna, whose *caritas* cannot, however, completely rid herself of the sting of the pagan Amor. Let us leave aside Petrarch and the completion of *interpretatio christiana* (before which the neoplatonic allegory of Wind's pupils proves in the end helpless). Shakespeare's diptych duplicates the fate of tragedy in a mime resembling Botticelli's design, regardless of the individual details that may distinguish Shakespeare from Botticelli's neo-Platonic orchestration in tone and key, notation and modulation.[10] It may be fair enough to proceed with the Dantean comedia-structure that emerges in Shakespeare in the place of the lyrical ensemble of the Petrarchan Botticelli and returns in Hermione's *donna petrosa*.

The Christian Deepening of Tragedy: Saint Augustine's Primal Scene

Shakespeare's *Winter's Tale* opens with the oppressor of Myth, the Christian revision of tragedy. The part Frye talks about, "the 'winter's tale' proper, the story of the jealousy of Leontes, the slandering of Hermione," is not conclusive as in the source *Pandosto*. Following the tragic development of three acts, it opens into a pastoral fermata, Perdita's rescue, whose name, the "abandoned," is thus not fulfilled. Contrary to the fate of Leontes' desire in Shakespeare's adaptation, Greene saw Leontes able to get a hold of his wife only in the figure of their daughter with whom he inevitably falls in love, leading to his inescapable suicide – not a classical fate, though certainly an Oedipal one that Shakespeare averts with Ovidian means. The tragic elements from Greene's set-up cannot define the predisposition of the first part of *The Winter's Tale*. But already Greene, it is important to see, experiments with tragic irony: "to close up the comedy with a tragical stratagem," he laconically explains the death of Leontes, in an irony, which he thematized in narrative alienation rather than on the stage.[11] *The Winter's Tale*, in turn, brings the alienating effect (anti-Aristotelian for Brecht) back to the theater, only in order to stop it there, in the middle of the act, and leaving the catastrophe hanging in midair, between heathen tragedy and Christian desire for redemption.

Everything seems to depend here on the compensatory rubric of "conversion" (whereby the Latin *conversio* translates the Greek *catastrophe*), a compensation that proved elementary for salvation since Dante's poetics of conversion made its entrance and thereby also entered into Shakespeare's *Trauerspiel* as a kind of mortgage on the Christian tradition. Obviously enough, this constellation reveals the opponent to Ovid's *Metamorphoses*, Augustine's *Confessions*. Although to my knowledge it has strangely enough never been realized or subjected to commentary, the first and basic reference-point for the tragic nexus of *The Winter's Tale*, the sudden intrusion of jealousy that befalls King Leontes out of nowhere – and certainly not from Cupid's arrow (he seems above all stupid cupidities for the moment) – conjures up a tragedy of ancient proportions while simultaneously invoking the, Saint Augustine's of all people, standard refutation of tragedy. The Christian intervention is used, in the first part of *The Winter's Tale*, for the sake of an intensification and deepening of a tragedy that had long since been pacified in its cathartic potency and blunted by the idea of salvation history.[12]

Thus the tendency has been, not entirely incorrectly, to take Leontes' jealousy as a more or less (rather less) plausible variant of Elizabethan maladies, for which melancholy served as the more general term, as listed in Robert Burton's compendium.[13] Benjamin has found this without Burton in *Hamlet*. But *The Winter's Tale* is more precise and in its wording leaves no doubt that *Confessiones* I.7 is its source and point of departure. In Greene's novella, the older commonplace of the envy of the gods is being spun out: "Fortune envious of such happy success" is his classical way of putting it – success here in the meaning that haunts also Macbeth, in the sense of succession. Shakespeare's unhappy Leontes, who does not lack in this respect, instead finds himself psychically confused, though he is evidently not less successful for it, as the numerous psychological and psychoanalytic elaborations dedicated to him were eager to show (even though their real origin remained in the dark all the way up to Freud). No matter how we may want to assess the interaction between Shakespeare and Augustine, whether anticipatory of psychoanalysis or in terms of everyday psychology, the patristic aspects, institutional aspects of church formation, remain comprehensively invoked and constitutive of Shakespeare's text. The full justification of this would require a kind of philological investment I refrain from here. Instead, in the mere interest of reconstructing the plot, I will pare it down to an abbreviated version of what happens to Leontes.

King Leontes of Sicily has just put the much-desired visit of his childhood friend, King Polixenes of Bohemia, behind him, because the friend, his milk-brother, in fact (literally his *conlactaneus* in Augustine), is about to unexpectedly break off his stay. Polixenes wishes to leave the very next day, following nine harmonious months, and a comedy develops in which the friend must be convinced, and Leontes' irreproachable wife Hermione is recruited to accomplish the task that her husband unhesitatingly forces upon her, and shall later turn against her: She must move the guest to stay. Leontes asks for, and indeed provokes, some excessively gallant overtures for which he is himself to blame, and which a talented, congenial and paranoid sympathizer can, if willing, find sufficient reasons to distrust (although modern audiences mostly aren't really willing, because of their distance from the Elizabethan senses of the games people play). The task Leontes gives to his wife is in any event the trigger that causes jealousy to intrude out of nowhere, and in quick succession costs the King his wife, his son, his daughter, his friend and his counselor. Even a Delphic oracle – word for word taken from Greene's historicist imagination – cannot slow it down, but instead suspends the catastrophe at full speed and turns it into a catastrophe at a standstill (to vary Benjamin) that Leontes is to make permanent. Granted, the oracle that brings the resolution is suspiciously univocal, "the most plain-spoken and un-Delphic Delphic oracle."[14] So much so that the hero is almost forced to interpret it as the totalizing challenge of his own paranoia: "There is no truth at all i'the'Oracle," he senses with the logical reaction to the fact that there was never, ever an un-ambivalent oracle: "The session [consequently] shall proceed" (3.2.140–41). And so the years go by.

The counselor pleads with the friend instead of getting rid of him; the Queen, absolved by the oracle, vanishes with her confidante, whose husband saves the disinherited newborn; only the minor son does not survive his mother's shame. And the daughter's loyal rescuer must put his life on the line in an overly burlesque fashion, but the full scope of all of this wrenching involvement in the catastrophe becomes fully apparent only after the fact and after the chain of events has been frozen to become a mere spectacle of tragic gestures and pathos-laden formulas of theatricality. The nail of Greene's subtitle, "The Triumph of Time," seems to be hit right on the head, transforming the catastrophic nexus of events into a masquerade of passions, distant descendants of Botticelli's pagan gods under the regime of Cupid. Under his guidance it cannot be otherwise that after nine months – "Nine changes of the watery star" to begin with (1.2.1) – the guest takes his leave in carefully chosen verses, leaving the pregnant hostess, whose husband realizes it like scales falling from his eyes, while the audience, in the psychological spelling out of the mythic plot for which it is prepared, accepts the ancient *ananke* of a fatal disposition as it awaits the coming of spring. The first acts culminate in the third with the breakdown of poor Hermione upon the news of the death of her son, and reach the high point of a tragic farce when the poor rescuer of the endangered baby falls prey to nothing less than a bear that takes the stage before the events come to repose in an unresolved tragic-comic middle position. No tragedy runs its course here; instead, tragedy experiences its tragic decomposition into mere and sheer theatrical spectacle – mimicking the bear-garden next door.

This makes all the more pressing the question of the imputed Augustinian primal scene: the intensification of the tragic in the instance of its Christian interpretation that separates Shakespeare from Greene's outcome and undermines the mythic plot with a double plot of the Empson variety: The jealousy of the milk-brother leads the way behind the foreground scenery of the melancholic play of courtly jealousy and revenge, the dominant maladies of the age. Stanley Cavell was able (without Augustine) to make a start in this direction, in that he placed importance on the role of little Mamillius, the six-year-old Prince, sound of mind and body and much admired. His name designates him as breastfed, indeed, a son right out of a picture-book, the spitting image of his father, in whom Leontes takes great joy, and upon whom his attack of jealousy, mnemonically consequent, promptly crystallizes: "as if it was brought on, with Mamillius sitting on his mother's lap and whispering in her ear" – as if the vision of his son on the mother's lap had brought him back to what he had experienced with his milk-brother Polixenes and yet could scarcely remember: Cavell is able to see this much without reference to Augustine and without the *Confession*'s theory of memory that is of striking pertinence in Shakespeare's adaptation of the scene.[15] The reference Cavell lacks reads as follows (in the almost contemporary translation of the *Confessions* from 1624/31).[16]

> So that it is not the mind of infants that is harmless, but the weakness of their childish members. I myself [Augustine] have seen and observed a little baby to be already jealous; and before it could speak, what an angry and bitter look it would cast at another child – his *conlactaneus* – that sucked away its milk from it.

Children are by no means as harmless, according to the more harmless words of the translator, as their physical weakness makes them appear; they are instead, as their jealousy proves, marked by original sin from the beginning, a factor of great importance for the *character crucis* of baptism. It is therefore not necessary to describe Leontes' jealousy as "psychologically derivative," as Cavell does. It is rather the primal trace of the Fall:

> seeing that in regard of the darkness of my forgetfulness of it, it is like that part [of my life] which I passed in my mother's womb. Now if I were shapen in iniquity and in sin conceived by my

mother; where, I beseech thee, O my God, in what place, Lord, was I thy servant, where or when was I innocent? But behold, I now pass-by that age; for what have I to do with it, whereof I can nothing at all call to memory – *nulla vestigia recolo*?

(I.vii)

Before Leontes is set upon by original guilt, and the whispering of his son on the lap of his wife inexplicably helps him figure it out – the murmuring of latency – his friend and brother Polixenes recalled himself to be innocent upon Hermione's questioning and boldly proclaimed – "as twinn'ed lambs that did frisk i'th'sun" – the innocence of the little lambs that they once were: "what we chang'd was innocence for innocence: we knew not the doctrine of ill-doing," something he knows all the better now (1.2.67–70). Augustine had confessed to the rhetorical question of where and when he had ever been free of guilt – *Ubi aut quando innocens fui?* – and covered over the clubfoot of the performative that he invented, that of confessing, which is the first and primal instance of a mis-recognition, a repression: *ecce omitto illud tempus* – look how ostentatiously I omit this time. "By this we gather/ You have tripp'd since," Hermione replies (1.2.75–66), and not without a coquettish note, which Polixenes attempts to quickly extinguish in the same verse: "O my most sacred lady" (76), he declaims, but only in order to finally pass the buck completely over to her: Hermione and his own wife were the decisive temptations in the life of those little lambs that they robbed of their innocence. As women they were and remain the instruments of the original sin that they had caused.

Leontes, who stands to the side, loses the thread of this exchange at exactly the moment when Hermione starts to make the guilt, to which she bravely acquiesces, into the *felix culpa* of the prevailing situations: "The offences we have made you do, we'll answer: If you first sinn'd with us, and that with us/ You did continue fault and that you slipp'd not/ With any but with us" (1.2.83–86). Even if the double entendre of the two pairs for whom Hermione speaks is not taken as an intentional misspeak – Leontes does not perceive it this way here – the exchange of words in which he entangles Hermione in the following conversation and with which he cuts her off – "Is he won yet" (86) – extends in the direction of this consequence: Leontes, now led by paranoid cunning, calls the effort to convince the guest to remain, his wife's second best act, second only to her consent to his own marriage proposal; and in so saying he intensifies the ambiguous talk of "faults." Hermione has her hands completely full – although she now can no longer successfully accomplish it – trying to summon the only fall that the childhood friend will confess to, back into the state of matrimony as (sacramental) grace: "O, would her name [the name of the older sister-promise, of marriage] were Grace" (99). This is no favor in the sense of courtly discourse, though this is the sense immediately governing the conversation, which had provoked in Leontes an abrupt attack of heart tremor (1.2.110), *tremor cordis* in the medical terminology of the time and love's symptom up to Proust's *Recherche*. Not favor, but the Augustinian concept of grace is at stake here, the mercy granted to the child, who is bad by nature and embodies the trace of the Fall in its jealousy and carries this flaw into fraternal relations. Politically, the problem of brotherhood is the crux, which has composed the unholy historical prototype for the *civitas terrena* ever since Cain slew Abel, up to the Republican fraternity that is meant to overcome this rotten state and govern society after a revolution of this worldly state of affairs.

I will not pursue this hunch in the particulars of Shakespeare's text (although this would be rewarding), because the Augustinian radicalization of jealousy, invoked as the ineradicable trace of fallenness in *The Winter's Tale*, is not further explicated or expanded upon but is to the contrary thwarted and suspended. No "natural perspective" is presented as an antidote that Late Shakespeare is supposed to have come up with; again to the contrary, he turns toward a renewal of *conversio:* no return to nature, which remains just as bad as ever, but a return to the point at which myth functions as a refound enlightenment and intercedes for the relapse of Christian Revelation in the form of Ovid's Metamorphosis. This relapse is, according to Benjamin's formatting, precisely what Shakespeare had already played out in his great tragedies, and was later to be extensively diagnosed by Hegel, Nietzsche and Freud. Cavell, who worked through *The Winter's Tale* with a similar intuition, recognizing the jealousy of Othello and Leontes as allegories of skepticism, summarizes the status of his insights in *The Winter's Tale* as follows: "to be given a portrait of the sceptic at the moment of the world's withdrawal from this grasp (. . .) in comparison with which the philosopher's portrait of the sceptic as not knowing something, in the sense of being uncertain of something, shows as an intellectualization of some prior imitation" (206). The suspicion that the literary may function as the first inkling of a philosophical elaboration intersects in Cavell's passage with the inkling – "my initial approach to the 'Is whispering nothing?' speech" – that both philosophy and literature, as forms of skepticism, find themselves caught up in parallel attempts at articulations, of which the whispering of nothing provides the philosophical concept with its first clue. This *Winter's Tale* is a whisper of the change of season – Spring slumbering in Winter – and prepares it according to a mythic analog. That which lurks in myth seeks its way onto the stage as a whisper: of the castration behind the "nothing" promised by, and in anxiety expected from, the female sex (according to Freud and Cavell).

"The triumph of time," with which Greene outlines the mythic horizon, is something that Shakespeare assiduously avoids adopting. The latency of myth, which the whispering of his stage articulates, is no triumph of time and it is also – even more decidedly – not the passing of time or mere temporal elapse. He rather economizes, negotiates and makes a business out of the myth that he stages, and *The Winter's Tale* is, like the Late Shakespeare in general, the balance sheet of his scenic economy as a preservation of the latent. "Time," which takes the stage as the chorus at the beginning of act IV, parodying the theatrical tradition of the ancients, presents itself as an allegory of the stage, makes itself recognizable as staged Time, installed as a mask in the shape of nature and emerging from it as if presenting "a natural perspective." The narrated time, figured as historical – "that wide gap" (6.1.7) – that the theater is able to jump over in the fourth act, makes space for the time of stage in the polyphonic chorus: "I that please some, try all: both joy and terror/ Of good and bad, that makes and unfolds error/ Now take upon me in the name of time to use my wings" (4.1.1–4). The formulation of World History as the World's Judgment (the Shakespearean adept Friedrich Schiller's *Die Weltgeschichte ist das Weltgericht*) is nothing but the illegitimate literalization of the theatrical self-installation of Time: the "try all" of the *Weltgericht*. In mythic "joy and terror," the "error" of fate unfolds itself, a mistake the theater takes upon itself, takes under its wing, in and under the name of time. And because the wings of a theatrical time, which borrows the general term time and takes it for itself, manifest and compensate for the time that history has stored up in the time spent within the theater: "If ever you have spent time worse ere now" (in the theater), "you never may" (1.1.30–33). The tragic scheme of the cathartic intervention (assuming that Aristotle may have been right in this construction) remains with and within the myth that has been made subservient, and it fades just like Zephyr with the Greek Chloris in Botticelli's *Primavera*. In the place of catharsis emerges the schema of a metamorphic transformation, in which the Latin Flora escapes from the violence that her Greek predecessor suffered. Chloris remains behind, murmuring flowers, like the lost and unredeemed Augustinian babe Mamillius, for whom Hermione mourns so as not to lose faith in his sister, Perdita, thought lost, but she has come to Polixenes' son, the Flora-endowed Florizel: "[I] preserv'd/ Myself to see the issue" are the words that Paulina, the aide of her transformation, takes from her mouth in the same line: "There's time enough for that" (5.3.127/28).

The whisper of the latent transforms itself in the process of its theatrical preservation, in the "try all," that is, of a democratic proceduralism to come.[17] I share Cavell's concern about the whispering of the lost son, the child devoted to its mother: "Here is what becomes, at the final stage, of the great Shakespearean problematic of legitimate succession: 'recognizing one's child,' Cavell writes, and let me add, not just any child, but the one caught up in the gender-political whispering of a son, who is bound to the mother like the oedipal Hamlet, who will find himself betrayed by this same whisper. What becomes of the problem of succession "now appears as a matter essential to individual sanity, a discovery begun perhaps in Hamlet and developed in Lear," Cavell concludes (204). The winter's tale that little Mamillius whispers in his mother's ear, "told in a whisper, having the effect of drawing on the vengeance of a husband and father who, therefore, has interpreted the tale as revealing something (. . .) to do with the fact that his wife has or has not been faithful to him, where her faithfulness" – Augustine is unavoidable here – "would be at least as bad as her faithlessness would be" (198/99). This according to a closing scene, whose undecidability – Hamlet's "to be or not to be" born – can never be conclusive. Just as the tragedy of Oedipus helped Freud to name the mythic latency of the Oedipus-complex, *The Winter's Tale* manifests within the mythically latent a gender-political latency in the whispering of the son. Leontes does not succumb to it like old Hamlet; instead he mercilessly removes the princely stone of contention: "Bear the boy hence, he shall not come about her" (2.1.59). He is naturally unredeemed according to the mythic rationality that re-originates from the madness of Christian re-mythologization.

"Nothing" is a lot in the Shakespeare lexicon, even though it is not always already equivalent to Freud's threat of castration.[18] For Leontes, who has fallen into a regression to early childhood, wallowing in grandiosity, "nothing" is the triumphant ob-scenity, not to say the ob-scenery of the female sex, of the missing member of generation that provokes his tirade of nothings – "nothings/ If this be nothing" – out of nowhere – *ex nihilo* – out of which his ongoing self-assertion makes much ado (1.2.296). A child's whispering demolishes the resonating board of the stage. When, in view of the happy ending, Hermione has eyes left only for Perdita and hardly at all for Leontes, who is in the best process of sentimentally reconquering her, she addresses, looking past him, the audience about her sole endurance to "see the issue" (5.3.127): the fruit that will blossom forth in the female lineage, in the sign of the twin who has been cured of his envy. While the cured king meanwhile takes all the time for himself, burning impatiently at his heels, and – "hastily lead away" (5.3.155) – flees the stage with a haste that lacks, and concedes nothing in comparison to that of his guest at the beginning of the play.

The pastoral fermata preceding the temporal leap possesses, in addition to its rhythmic function, also that of the double plot structure discovered by Empson, even if it were only in the form of an ornamental accompaniment for which Botticelli had provided the illustration.[19] Perdita takes the stage as Flora, and the Prince Florizel, of course, has eyes for nothing other than for her: "These your unusual weeds" – a breath of irony in light of her attire – "Do give life: No shepherdess, but Flora/ Peering in April's front (4.4.1–3). The switch to Latin Flora, which Florizel puts into words, is the very moment brought to a standstill in Botticelli's *Primavera*. In *The Winter's Tale* it takes only a short scene, outside of Time. As important as the scenes from Bohemia are for the reconfiguration of the plot, they remain emblematic and transitional at the same time. The Spring of Flora introduces the Autumn of life for the protagonists, who have grown old in separation, but shall be consoled, pacified by Paulina's art. Thus and to this extent, leaving aside the support lent by the Renaissance pictorial, the tale that is this *Winter's Tale* generically centers around a timeless middle stage.

Resistance to Augustine: A New Ovid's *Metamorphoses*

"What remains" is the healing magic, anticipating in Nietzsche's account of Hamlet as the Dionysian *par excellence* the "saving sorceress of the healing arts," that is, art itself and at its best.[20] It is this art that Paulina practices on Hermione and names as both "holy" and "lawful" (5.3.104/5). Leontes does not mistake its artistic character for a second: "If this is magic, let it be an art" he famously proclaims, "Lawful as eating" (5.3.110/11). *Ars adeo latet arte sua*, Ovid's recorded commentary on the metamorphosis of Pygmalion (10.253), is an accurate motto for Hermione's metamorphosis. With the artistic means of self-concealment it leads into a region of animation that was already a borderline in Pygmalion's case. Pygmalion's desire, important to note, raises Venus according to the measure of his art and not according to his desire alone or as such: the animation of the object of desire is extended by an art that is able to hide itself within life, and thanks to means that are all its own – *arte sua* – it reaches its effect out of latency – *latet* – like the nature that it imitates and completes.[21] "Lawful as eating" may be another tiny splinter from Augustine's metaphorics of memory, which for Leontes' unconscious recalls the infant's coveting of its sustenance (and that was precisely Augustine's point), thus evidencing the naturalness of natural law while parodying it at the same time in its rotten state (Benjamin's complaint). Hermione's metamorphosis is deceptive just like Pygmalion's metamorphosis; it is a metamorphosis that is, as a matter of fact, no metamorphosis at all in Hermione's case, but already Pygmalion's transformation, art-centered and unnatural as Ovid makes evident, was no metamorphosis like the others. Jonathan Bate, whose thesis it is that "in accordance with the demands of theater," Shakespeare's theater had – either literally or metaphorically – naturalized myth, claims that this process is suspended in *The Winter's Tale*: "the nature of the events is left ambiguous: the cause of Mamillius' death is not given, and the nature of Hermione's collapse is not explained. We cannot be sure whether or not the gods have acted directly."[22] This, however, is not our problem exactly but only that of Leontes, who – despite the authority of an overly unambiguous oracle – was not to be helped in his delusion.

How quickly one forgets and cannot resolve one's self to it in the theater – performance history constantly illustrates this effect – that the metamorphosis in *The Winter's Tale* does not follow and conform to the Pygmalion citation as expected. The staging proceeds according to a metamorphosis where there is no need of one: Hermione was not dead, after all, and her animation only makes a scene on stage. Announced as harmless magic – art, in short – Hermione's metamorphosis brings the return of someone repressed, upon whom the traces of repression have not passed away. Sixteen years is a long time, and Leontes' conversion is only one, because he proves able to recognize, "at time's full cost," the one whom he thought was dead. More strictly spoken, the metamorphosis of the column called Hermione is no metamorphosis, but the citation of a bygone metamorphosis: of an irony, indeed, of masculine desire that Ovid both represents and lays bare – a desire for which the self-made statue meant more than the faithful companion of enduring age could have been. As *donna petrosa* Hermione adds a touch of Dante to the petrification from which Paulina pretends to wake her – although this literary quality seems to amount to nothing but whitewash.[23] When Leontes, stormily re-awakened by his old love, wants to kiss her on the spot, Paulina's presence of mind is able to restrain him, because the color of restoration, true to nature, is not yet dry, that is, not yet kiss-resistant: "The ruddiness upon her lip is wet/ You'll mar it if you kiss it, stain your own" (5.3.81–82). The art of Dante's *petrosa* called up in passing turns out to be in the service of the art of the stage – *ars adeo latet* – which is able to mask both arts. Whereby the point of the cover-up is different and of a completely opposite kind of latency than it had in the case of the metaphorical petrification: Despite the years passed, Leontes is able to recognize Hermione and finds himself magically attracted to her. What transpires with him is precisely what did not happen with his pendant in *Pandosto*, who no longer recognized the wife he had cast off, except in the daughter's resemblance. Paulina's art does not transform Hermione, it changes Leontes.

The king, who had needlessly sacrificed the male line to fraternal strife, owes both the reconciliation and the resolution of the succession to the female line. In the Crown Prince of the competing brother he acquires (and learns to bear) that which he has lost and what he had sought to avoid in one person. Barely gone, he appears to seek salvation of the historical compromise beyond the bounds of the theater; a compromise that, in the world – the year is 1611 – was as yet unable to be addressed. In the following year, 1612, however, James would in fact lose his own twelve-year-old Crown Prince Henry to a childhood fever, and in the next year, 1613, the marriage of his daughter Elizabeth to the – strange coincidence – later Bohemian heir took place, a sequence of events which, in the fitting words of Stephen Orgel, took on an "eerie topicality." The Tragical History of Old Hamlet – a father killed by his brother, and of a son who, unreconciled, gives up paternal power along with the mother, as if damned to destruction by Kafka's *Judgment* – arrives in *The Winter's Tale* at its virtually opposite limit: that of a father who, before things reach Danish proportions, destroys both wife and son in order to maintain his power, while the daughter who is doubted – that dubious child of the new moon – saves the succession upon which his indestructible Queen had placed her bets. A *Hamlet* without Hamlet admonishes Paulina, as she names the conditions for the success of her mousetrap for King Leontes, that is, Hermione's metamorphosis: "Do not shun her" – she seems to remind him of Claudius's fate – "Until you see her die again; for then/ You kill her double" (5.3.105–7). Hamlet's dumb show had the Player Queen say: "A second time I kill my husband dead/ When second husband kisses me in bed" (3.2.179–80). The art that had failed in vengeance does not refuse itself reconciliation: A winter's tale of tragic humor?

Admittedly, there is an identifiable "political geography" in *The Winter's Tale*, which is supported, according to convention, by the pastoral alienation of events: Thus, Perdita could well pass as a missionary figure, who returns from Protestant Bohemia to Catholic Sicily and there draws attention to herself with traitorous words, such as "to make proselytes" (5.1.108).[24] Her mother Hermione, whose enlightened competence in her dealings with the Bohemian King has been striking, would provide the model for an enlightened femininity, secure in the reformed performance of its role. Just as she is significant for the reformed conversion of the ruling Sicilian couple (the conclusion can be read as if it were taken right from James' mouth), she is also free from Gertrude's tragic aporia, while in the near future, on Shakespeare's and his contemporaries' horizon, the fraternal republican hordes are about to take the stage and deeply inscribe the milk-strife of antagonistic brothers within the constitution of an early bourgeois self-understanding. Is it gender-political consolidation that opens up and seems illuminated by a Paulina, whose name extends the Augustinian charge in the direction of its Paulinian origin?[25] Or is *The Winter's Tale* a false cadence (the "de-cadence" Nietzsche has sensed as the weakness of Renaissances), a backward-looking "political-romantic" conclusion (in Heine's sense)? Almost at the same time as *The Winter's Tale*, Shakespeare wrote his play on *Henry VIII*, who famously played with Anne Boleyn, the mother of Great Elizabeth, in the way Leontes does with Hermione. Henry, however, ended without reconciliation, and birth and baptism of the glorious daughter – still on the horizon of this play – serve as the teleology for which Shakespeare's work was intended, all under the title "All is True."

Appearance deceives. Shakespeare extracted a tragedy of jealousy from Greene's novel, so as to anchor it even more deeply in the Augustinian fates of inheritance, desire and inherited desire, and in the spectacular return of Hermione he found an ending equivalent to tragic catharsis, which may have corresponded, on top of it, to the syncretistic fantasy of the ruling monarch. Thus the fairytale design does not in fact correspond to any kind of ideology that would be anti-tragic or neutral to tragedy. *The Tempest*, interestingly enough, that sees Prospero returning to his dukedom on the occasion of its happy ending, can hardly – cannot at all – be the final tempest, since the usurper-brother, pardoned, has in no way disavowed his ambition: he will try again.[26] Time, which speaks in *The Winter's Tale* as an allegorical *veritas filia temporis*, will indeed bring the truth to light, but its magic is limited to the island, where Prospero has left it with Ariel, the guardian spirit. Such is the price for his re-entry into political reality.[27] Similarly, the temporal island of *The Winter's Tale* leaves no time for any utopia. "Hastily led away," the comical effect cannot be dismissed, which takes it that the knowledge of life, as practical as it may appear, is not the same thing as the knowledge of fate.[28]

The comic aspect of the tragic predisposition, which Late Shakespeare brings to the fore after having made it abundantly manifest in tragedy (where it was no less present, just differently, latently in the case of tragedy), shows "that the tragic experience of the theater is not the end" and cannot be the end.[29] But it can be moved across time as tragic humor (giving the honor to Heine). The grace that Hermione brings about may be that of art, the art that had saved her for the time being and according to the conditions of the theater: "O would her name were Grace!" Her plea looks down now, at the end of the play, at her daughter, without having much of an eye for the husband that was restored to her. Thus, the humor of this *Winter's Tale* is not without bitterness. It may not be without its own horrors and does not, in any case, spare what it has mortgaged from tragedy as its own immemorial inheritance.[30]

The Actuality of Tragedy: Benjamin on Fate and Character

In one of Benjamin's early elaborations of the *Trauerspiel*-material, the short article on "Fate and Character," a broader spectacular horizon that comprises both tragedy and *Trauerspiel*, is stated, marking and incorporating both with utmost pregnancy: "The complete elucidation of these matters (of fate) depends upon determining the fixation of its particular time," Benjamin writes, in the peculiar density of abbreviation that makes his sentences particularly suited to being ripped out of their contexts.[31] The dramatic interpretation of fate represents the time of the stage as its "complete elucidation" on the basis of the fabrication of its own "concept of time as a fabric of guilt," which is, however, "improperly temporal." Benjamin adds that this kind of a time is "parasitic" in its improper distortion, referring to "the time of a higher and less natural life," for which reason it only knows of "past and future" in "peculiar derivations and modifications" – in metamorphoses, let's say, like *The Winter's Tale*'s. The play of mutations ("derivations and modifications" – I am abbreviating again) is for Benjamin the play of a time that "can at all times be made contemporaneous with another time" and which therefore "cannot be present." In short, it is mythic latency at a standstill, with which the "order of law" (as Benjamin had previously explained) as a "remnant of man's demonic stage of existence" ends up in the wrong more than on the right side of things. The play of time in shades of times becomes spectacular through the manifold resonance of the boards that signify the world, the stage: a resonance of pre-performative quality. The present of tragedy in this sense is the immemorial futurity of its past: a winter's tale that carries on through spring in the shape, or even the epiphany, of a "dialectical image" (in Benjamin's later terminology).

The impressive emblem and example of this carrying through is the metamorphosis, which brings about, and is in the process called, the Renaissance. In Shakespeare's text it hides and reveals itself in the self-thematization of the theater in the theater. It includes a meta-political point about which I will say just a few words more to answer the question in Marx's *Grundrissen*, which may help to comprehend Heine's conception of tragic humor as the enigma of literary influence and effect: "the relation of Greek art to the present, and then of that of Shakespeare, is not to be understood such that Greek art and epic are tied to specific forms of societal development. The difficulty lies in the fact that we still enjoy them as art and that they count in certain contexts as both norm and unachievable model."[32] In *The Winter's Tale*, the "certain contexts" represent the latency of Greek myth, which Shakespeare among the moderns (like Marx, Nietzsche and Freud) is said to have brought to life and continual effectivity. They are contexts that make it possible to speak of "validity, norm and unachievable model," as if there was implied in the present of the theater a continuation of myth – a myth, whose effectivity is presented in *The Winter's Tale*, more precisely, as the latent Latinity of Ovid's resistance to Augustine's Christian interpretation.

What Heine was able to add here, beyond the strong resistance that is all too easily read in his tale of German winters, may be a strong sense of the latencies lingering below the ancient proportions of violence, a latent threat of the law thematized in the most exemplary and far-reaching manner in *The Merchant of Venice*, whose impact Heine had discussed most movingly in his portrait of Shylock's daughter Jessica. This remained to be read against the grain of his usual irony in coffee-table matters; Heine's tragic humor does not fail to do justice to the tragedy within the comedy of *The Jew of Venice*.[33] Adorno was in serious doubt, in his famous essay "Heine the Wound," that Heine "had such a strong influence on early Marx as many young sociologists would like to think," and even less that "one could count on him" politically. "But" (Adorno continued, approaching the realm of tragic humor) "he held fast to the idea of uncurtailed happiness in the image of a just society."[34] Tragic humor in tales of winters, as Heine perceived them and reconceived of them, does not fall for the political springs to come; it remains mortgaged to tragedy, remains possessed and repossessed by tragedy as its own immemorial inheritance – including, in the case of *Merchant* and *Jew*, the comedy of law and justice.

Like the early modern princes – and even more afraid – the republican fraternity of brothers shall find itself threatened by the ghost of such a theater, written on the wall from Plato to Rousseau. In their anxiety, the new fraternity has proven only too right.[35] The theater does not merely hold up some mirror to real relations and illustrate them in the garb of ancient gods. A whispering as of nothing extends beyond the frames. Within the fatal constitution of the fraternal horde it exposes the generational role of mothers and daughters; it clothes the beguiling beauty of the mythic objects of desire with the fashion of *caritas* and mercy. After the dramatic double plot of the mourning plays had run out and the Christian intensification of tragedy knew nothing else to achieve except the bloody series of

Machiavellian Princes (as in Macbeth's vision), the later Shakespeare discovers a gender-political whisper in a masquerade of literalized metaphorical appearances, tokens and props; fragments of a much older, ancient enlightenment. Empson described the effect as semantic "ambiguity" and hit upon the ambivalence of emotional impulses operative in it, an ambivalence that prescribed for Benjamin a "heroic melancholy" to the triumph of time, in the face of the *civitas terrena* with its history of fratricide and revenge.[36] In this, the presence of tragedy in the *The Winter's Tale* – its tragic *energeia* and spectacular *enargeia* – betrays a constitutive gender-political inscription, whose suspicion is made transparent by Paulina's cunning, non-tragic art: a historical mortgage that, flowing out of art's past, erodes the political concepts of a heroic, all too heroic modernism. It erodes a modernism that has expanded its melancholia, as it had "overextended [its] transcendence" (Benjamin again) – overextended beyond recognition and beyond love's measure: something unbearable and hard to take ever since Shakespeare's last plays gave a first, unquiet warning: in a theater bordering, though not without grace, the rough and the cruel of the times to come.

Tailpieces

CHAPTER 8

But Mercy is Above: Shylock's Pun of a Pound

Shylock's scandalous payment – we find this obliquely noted in Hegel's *Philosophy of Right* – quotes a problematic remnant of the ancient Law of the Twelve Tables in Rome, a remnant which – like the by now notorious *Homo Sacer* excavated by Giorgio Agamben – serves as the index-fossil for a whole legal-historical formation.[1] Its attraction stems from the exposure of a historical latency in legal practice, into the historical site of which the Augustan turn, into which Christianity entered, is marked by Agamben's source Pompeius Festus as a constellation without which the success of the new religion and its means of binding, *religio*, would barely be thinkable.[2] Hegel's suggestion, which opposes itself to an all too flat enlightenment of legal history, draws attention to a latent virulence one has to look for in Shakespeare's London if one wants to illuminate Shylock's scandal in detail; it may suffice to note here the existence of that historical crux in Roman law as well as the fact that Hegel still saw reason to cope with it.[3] Crucial patterns of latency maintenance in politico-theological semantics rest on a Roman crypt, which – in itself definitely not Christian – hides a legal-historical core that rests in the dark of hidden binds and relations.

Hegel refers in this part of his lectures to a debate, going back to Cicero, concerning the Twelve Tables: "Take the horrible law which permitted a creditor, after the lapse of a fixed term of respite, to kill a debtor or sell him into slavery. Nay, further, if there were several creditors (he goes into detail), they were permitted to cut pieces off the debtor, and thus divide him amongst them, with the proviso that if any one of them should cut off too much or too little, no action should be taken against him" ("a clause" – Hegel adds in a parenthesis – "which was credited to Shakespeare's Shylock in *The Merchant of Venice* and" – disclosing his detailed knowledge of the text – "would have been gratefully accepted by him").[4] The addition reveals how much more the digression meant to the Shakespeare reader Hegel – he knew him by heart – than did the abomination as a whole.[5] For the more or less of the cut is Shylock's sole problem – a problem not without a certain irony in regard to the scales of justice, on which precisely this one pound shall come to rest. The irony carries all the more weight insofar as a "pound" is as much as a "pun" in the English of the time and appears in Shakespeare's vocabulary in this way also on other occasions. Although the meaning of this metaphor for a pointed use of words is still in flux, it wins its particular wit from dramatically abyssal situations such as this one.[6] Hegelians present themselves as being generally immune to such bad jokes – about Hegel himself I am not so sure – whereas Shakespeare is full with verbal usury of this kind. In Shylock's case the pun is constitutive: this is what distinguishes Shakespeare from his sources in this matter, the variants of the graphic tale of the "Jew from Venice" that spread in his day. The subtitle, or even alternative title of the play, *Otherwise Called the Jew of Venice*, betrays the dangerous undercurrent of the *Merchant of Venice*.[7] The anti-Semitic intensification of business life in one of the most enlightened urban centers of its time – already in Aristotle's *Poetics* "witty" means "urban" – falls back on atavistic patterns whose juridical genealogy and plausibility Shakespeare stages down to the letter. Hegel had localized these patterns effortlessly – in distinction from the morally anxious theatrics that hypocritically fall for it, including its designation as a "moral institution" in a Schiller's sense.

The meta-historical clarification is inevitable if one turns towards Shylock's later fate of reading in a reception, which burdens Shakespeare's representation with a very specific and far-reaching latency: that of the holocaust – a latency that hovers in the clichés of *The Merchant of Venice*'s manifest anti-Semitism, a latency that no reading can circumvent and whose appearance at the surface of the thinkable was seized by the poet Heinrich Heine long before its becoming true. It is a disturbance that is absolutely crucial in that it speaks of a deeper literary latency, the trace of a pre-history of the inconceivable deep in the heart of the canon. Whatever Shakespeare's intention and whatever the effect of his play in his time may have been, they have been overwhelmed by the vehemence of the deferred reaction formation.[8] The legal historian Anton Schütz used the occasion of a Legendre-Festschrift to exacerbate this embarrassment to the point of sharpest acuity. He intervenes in this scenario of surging belatedness [*Nachträglichkeit*] in the most pregnant moment passed on by Heine.[9] No coincidence, because Romanticism, which Heine is about to leave behind, was the modern site where Shakespeare's latency experienced its first exemplary exposure and a reflection that persists into the present and finds itself immeasurably bound up with Heine. No wonder that of the Romantic voices, which Heine interiorized, it is that of Rahel Varnhagen (whom Schütz overlooks) which is the most striking.[10]

Splendid, even persuasive, apologies for the author won't do, and – this shall be of more interest here – they do not serve the problematic circumstances. The prompt hint of none other than John Dover Wilson from the year 1938, "he merely exposes the situation," lacks precisely an understanding of that situation.[11] It may certainly be the case that Shylock "is the inevitable product of centuries of racial persecution," but "Mercy, mercy in the widest sense, which embraces understanding and forgiveness," as Dover Wilson hastily concludes, is just as certainly not "the only possible solution of our racial hatreds and enmities" – not to mention that it is not what Shakespeare had actually to offer in the play. In the last act, Belmont, the place of pleasure, delivers no happy ending – neither in the broader, ordinary sense nor in the special sense that is pressing here. One would like to say (should wish and would have to postulate) that the intemperate and extreme overextension of the reception, the radical historical raising of the threshold of reception, brings forth a new point and punch-line of its own in the heart of the situation on display – it compels it to the same extent that it was compelled to latency in the dramatic representation.

Stanley Cavell's profound insight into the belatedness of Shakespeare's dramatic representation – the "deferred" mode of representation [*Darstellung*], which in *Hamlet* becomes explicit – would have experienced in Shylock's Venice what, for our times, would turn into the deepest possible representational distortion [*Ent-stellung*].[12] The pun of the one pound, which already in the transmission of the Twelve Tables of ancient Rome had endangered the balance of Iustitia, delivered the judiciary, just as in the proverbial *clementia Caesaris*, to an unweighable ruse of reason – and this must have been as much fun for the students of law in the audience as the logical textbook crux of "to be, or not to be." Juridical casuistry is the continuous trait in the transmitted variants of the story, which drastically indulge the unweighability – the impossible measuring – of the contentious pound and thus force the drama into the farce of a juridical decision: a piece of mock-justice with a wink, which can be answered for at the end only by the Doge himself and just in time brought to order and into the necessary equilibrium of state justice – just right for law students – but which Shakespeare himself takes apart entirely. However apt Portia's proclamation of mercy (4.1.193) presents itself to be – "But Mercy is above" – it sounds just as "hollow and void" as Austin's dismissal of staged speech acts describes them.[13] As if spoken on a stage, it leads right into the illusory world of the *Jeunesse dorée* of Belmont, whose continuing blindness can only affirm the tragic constellation that is set up for an uncertain duration and which, with a fatal sense of the comical, alleviates nothing.

Julia Lupton has devoted herself to the groundbreaking work of determining the type of *Shakespearean Negotiation* that, in the figure of Shylock, brought forth a new and staggering founding saint for modern civil societies: "Shylock undergoes not so much a forced conversion as a procedural one, pointing to forms of naturalization that might be nominal rather than national, driving a wedge between 'demos' and 'ethnos', between political and cultural forms of belonging."[14] This, finally no longer in the one-sided, notoriously flattened version of a René Girard, who presented Shylock's case as the comedy of Christianity which, by means of Judaism, is convicted of its own hypocrisy, but thereby brought to itself all the same.[15] For Lupton, the comical side of Shylock's "discontented contentment" must lie buried more deeply, far beneath the involuntary ironies of Venice's limited negotiability:

> When Portia strips Shylock of his corporate privileges and Antonio offers naturalization in its place, the play begins not only to imagine the foundations of Jewish emancipation, but also to calculate its costs. Emancipation, too, can be framed as a loss of sorts – another scene of death into citizenship – but, like Shylock's life story, it, too, is not simply a tragedy.
>
> (101)

Comedy as "not simply a tragedy" asks for the theatrical retraction into a latency, whose mythical pressure it successfully defies – for the price of some "cheaply available" (as Lessing's *Nathan* has it) concept of the tragic. Heine in his "tragic humor" saw this clearly enough when he added to his portrait of Jessica that of Portia, but finished the portrait of Portia nevertheless with the "sobbing" of Shylock's exhaustion, "which could have moved a stone to pity." A voice wrests itself from this sobbing, which "only the poet" (as Benjamin claimed) was ever able to pursue, "as if I had heard it once, when it wailed despairingly: 'Jessica, my child!' " (IV: 401).

The founding saint of bourgeois market-morality who, in heart-rending humor, is pulled out of the crypt (let us put aside for a moment the analytical subtleties in the history of liberalism that, for this purpose, is always and for good reason troubled anew),[16] is a figure of great art between moral allegory and dramatic character, who in the crossed-out mise-en-scène of the performance of an implementation that does not take place – collapsing as the grotesquely thematized latency that it was meant to embody – falls back from drama into the allegorical traits of an unredeemed, crudely comical and ill-humored character. Subjected, *nolens volens*, to the *character crucis* of baptism, Shylock must lastingly bear its cross; under this cross he rests in the crypt of the founding-saint of market-modernity. Instead of the sign of the cross, in its place remains the pun of the unweighable, signum and trace of unsubdued latency whose cipher it cites as a juridically blind inclusion, resting in old Roman law. The unbelievable circumstances, in defiance of every historical plausibility, on which Hegel, citing it extensively enough, does not want to dwell further, namely: how this unprecedented example of a primordial legal binding, as un-proven in practice as it is un-overcome, began to turn into and function as an anti-Semitic cliché – this pre-historical riddle is convicted by Shakespeare, dramatically and mimetically, step by legal-procedural step, of its overloaded significance. Late echoes of the negotiated circumstance – "The discontentment in Shylock's content is emphasized; he becomes the model for the liberal complaint against liberalism" – in the best case weakly put the rule to the test, for example in results like these:

> What emerges out of the specifics is a picture of a thoroughly vulgar modernity in which Venice and Belmont are not at all at odds: the former represents economic reality and the latter its sit-com fantasy.[17]

Shakespeare's point lies thoroughly ahead of such presentisms; he does not do things by half-measures, does not subject any partially enlightened state of things to an arrangement that could be retroactively rounded up or that would have to be rounded off in hindsight. Of the many puns for whose thoroughgoing effects he is notorious, none has a point that is as precise as that of Shylock; his dramatization establishes and stages the genre of the pun as an exemplary quantum of paradoxical non-exemplarity. This is no vague, approximate paradoxy, it is a pointed *literary* affair and Shylock's pun is the paradigmatic instance and place of its negotiation – even and particularly in its legal aspect. It is of a calculated singularity that allows the merchant in the figure of Shylock to tend towards a staged, acted-out emblematic, which, with a fine post-allegorical fermata, finally suspends the drama within the play. The moral of this emblematics is a latency, which in the form of the pun is linguistically marked rather than theatrically realized. Within its demarcation of the Venetian scene emerges from the depth of Roman Law the aporetic figure that takes on the traits of the Jew. In the end, this figure does not know what else to say other than to ask for dispensation from the allegory in which he finds himself together with his audience – *nolens volens* – entangled, though *not* – Lupton is right – banned: "I pray you give me leave to go from hence, I am not well" (4.1.391/92).

The precise capacity of a re-occupation of Christian exegesis full of the most fitting ironies is to be witnessed in every word of this text; in recent times it has been discerned in many illuminating treatments. At the end, which results from this intricate semantic profiling, there stands the carefully staged fallacy offered by Portia as a fictitious judge: her jurisdiction explicitly implements itself – a theater in the theater – *as* a dramatic fiction: "Enter Portia, dressed like a doctor of laws" (4.1.163).[18] In this fiction the art of the "point," which renders Shylock's scandal a pun, proves it a pun and proves it in the form of a pun, unfolds itself completely. And Portia, in spite of her upper-class charm, in spite of all her procedural cunning – a pure pleasure, as I said, for the proficient audience – does not measure up to this pointed art; she cannot, for this art is playing games with her behind her back, just as she is playing games with the Jew. Such is the theatricality of mimesis putting the mimesis of judging on trial.[19] For the sake of brevity, I quote from a summary, which, at the level of the most recent research, leads from Shakespeare's virtuoso performance of an exegetic casuistry to the crucial decision:

> Despite Gratiano's continued comic cheerleading (4.1.331–32) at this point, we must admit that there is a dramatic instant when Shylock might go ahead and follow the Law and kill Antonio even if this means enacting his own death sentence. This possibility, in fact, creates much of the dramatic energy of the scene. Indeed, Gratiano's words can be read as breaking the dramatic tension, a realization on his part at least that Shylock will resist the call of the law and not kill Antonio. Perhaps Shylock lowers his knife and this cues Gratiano's taunting about "A second Daniel." Perhaps even Portia has been holding her breath, waiting to see what Shylock will actually do, before calling attention to Shylock's "pause" (4.1.333). But we must acknowledge that it is at this instant that the comedic passes closest to the tragic, not later on when the Duke intervenes with his sovereign gesture and "pardons" Shylock (4.1.366). Of course, after a reasonable period of stage time Shylock must try to walk away, this time on substantially reduced

terms: "Give me my principal, and let me go" (4.1.333). But we must attend to the instant when he pauses.[20]

The dramatic dead-end out of which the reversal into the mock-judgment occurs – occurs in the becoming apparent of the caesura – is that of a counterfactual threat; a threat in which the pun reveals itself as such and lets the forced realism of the scene, which had until this moment developed and maintained itself behind the back of the allegorical construction, tip back over into a stationary emblematic image. "Dialectics at a standstill" was Benjamin's unsurpassed expression for this moment of historical truth [*Dialektik im Stillstand*].[21] Here it is the pun that fulfills the linguistic structure of latency that Benjamin names "dialectics." In the case of Shylock – as often in Shakespeare, and constitutive for a modernity that is rooted in his state of language – the structure, in which the pun becomes dramatically constitutive, congeals off-stage into a scandal, whereby the ancient Roman index-fossil crosses the threshold of latency and betrays the "illatency" of motives. Not by chance did Johannes Lohmann, Heidegger's historian of language, link this "stepping-out of the 'latency' into the 'illatency' of actual self-consciousness" to a number of grammatical achievements of the Latin language, in a kind of linguistic analogon to the development of the law that, after all, is already apparent in the title of Festus' *De verborum significatione* used by Agamben.[22]

Thus, Shylock's pun is exemplary in a calculatedly paradoxical way. For in an example that is in fact unprecedented and, that is, *without example* – a case for which there was no example before it came to the crassest anti-Semitic actualization – the pun of the pound presents implementation by way of the latent threat that inheres in it, so as to not be able to carry it out seriously, indeed even to thwart it in the performative thrust of the threat itself.[23] The point of the pun, which in this single case functions smoothly and proves that *pun* means *point* is successful in its dramatic performance, without having to be successful in the presented case, indeed not being allowed to be successful in this case – for in the latter scenario, it would have to fail in the implementation of the performance and thus sink into the platitudes of what is bound to happen. The dramatic fiction of the judgment that adapts the dubiously immemorial act of its ancient Roman institution – Portia bears the name of Cato's daughter, whose ancient Roman aspect *Julius Caesar* will put on stage – supports (just as she does in *Julius Caesar*) the political givens, whose ideological blindness is endlessly exposed in the last act, in which the breaking off of the story is completed and pulled towards an abyss of the comical.

To put it simply, Shylock is an allegory of latency, though in the form of a self-destructive installation that presents itself in the performative implementation of self-representation as a mis-presentation and consequently remains stuck within the process of its implementation. It interrupts itself in the implementation, intermittently. The dramatic reflection, whose technical achievement is Cavell's "deferred representation," is broken by a latency which in the belatedness of its effects succeeds cunningly and without mercy. The tragic necessity, however, which brings history about and mis-presents it in naked, merciless inevitability, does not find its fulfillment on stage; it proliferates beyond the theater. This proliferation in latency, always and ever anew, follows on the heels of tragic necessity. What remains on the stage itself is the dead residue of the distortion, ideology.

Pun – Lexical addendum: among the entries of the O.E.D. there is an unusual conjectural footnote added on the older history of the word *pun*, according to which – though this is not proven – *pun* as a "clipped word" would have come from the Italian *puntilio*, meaning "a small or fine point."[24] Documented "soon after 1660," it appears in Shakespeare only in the unfinished state of an emerging pun that in the *Merchant of Venice* takes on a first tentative form. Onion's glossary derives the metaphorized meaning of the *punto* from the lexicon of fencing: as a "stroke or thrust with the point of the sword," whereby – lexically still unconnected and therefore eminently pregnant for the development of a pun – the phonetic equivalence of *pun* and *pound* is apprehended.[25] Shylock's "pound" hence is a phonetically appropriate, self-reflexive pun on the force – indeed, the "punch" – of all puns that enhances the "point" of the sword, the *punto*. The specifically juridical point of Portia's "just pound," which doubles the pun (4.1.323–24), is a "just" one in the sense of a precise pound, at which the tip of the sword aims in the rhetorical exchange before Portia the judge – fully in tune with Quintilian's metaphor of the fencer (taken up by Benjamin from Baudelaire): "nor cut thou less, nor more/ But just a pound of flesh" (4.1.323–24). By means of the prejudice towards the unredeemed literality of the Old Testament, Portia parodies the brutal latency of ancient Roman sacrality, which she threatens to take at its word. The Latin *punctum*, which the point of the sword assumes as cause and goal – "a small hole made by pricking or piercing" – is a wound with which the text threatens and whose threatening character the text leaves to the afterworld.[26]

CHAPTER 9

Habeas Corpus: The Law's Desire to Have the Body

> But mercy is above this sceptred sway,
> It is enthronéd in the hearts of kings,
> It is an attribute to God himself.
> – Portia (4.1.193–95)

The point has been made more than once, and runs through the debate on violence like a leitmotif, that the progress of legal procedures is embarrassed by the shadow of violence that keeps following the law and cannot be shrugged off. The pathos of the force of law's shadow haunts analytical descriptions by Benjamin and Heidegger, by Foucault and Lyotard, by Luhmann and Robert Cover.[1] It reminds us of something that is wrong, "something rotten," as Benjamin has put it, in law's rule and empire.[2] Something has been overlooked in the various histories of progress, whose pride and prejudice it invariably is and was to have overcome the cruelty of darker ages. By contrast, Robert Cover ended his famous article on *Violence and the Word* with "the overwhelming reality of the pain and fear that is suffered," again and again, by those subjected to the law's procedures now as ever. He concludes thus his analysis of "what all would agree is an unredeemed reality" with law's inescapable shadow: "Between the idea and the reality of common meaning (...) falls the shadow of the violence of law, itself."[3] Whose shadow, then, is it? The law's "itself"?

Cover's observation that in "an unredeemed reality" the shadow of violence belongs to the law itself; that, in other words, this shadow is not the removable after-effect of legal acts, whose pure words would be overshadowed by the circumstances of their execution, but rather part of the law's ways of coming into being and being real (its "phenomenology," so to speak) contradicts, not to say refutes, any faith in the law's possible purification, or any final epiphany of justice as such. It may not completely contradict the notion of some so-called progress in the domestication of violence. But it puts the question first of how to account for the violence implied by, and administered through, legal acts. Where, actually, does the performative force of a sentence reside, and what is its extension? How literally does a judge act in sentencing, and how figuratively, if the sentence is to be taken literally, is the act to be taken? For a "sentence" to be literal, the act that produces it would have to be metaphorical in the first place.[4]

We shall leave the answer to this rather complicated technical question open (technical in the sense of the rhetorical *techne* to be applied), while implicitly pursuing the issue in a different register, on the descriptive level of history. The focus of the description, however, will be the same, systematical issue: What is the law's part in violence? Is it the law's "itself"? And, if violence is bound to come with the law, as part of the law's own performance rather than with the social or representational functioning of this performance, what part of the "illocutionary force" of sentencing would violence play with respect to the "perlocutionary effect" called execution? Is it possible to conceive of the legal sphere apart from the inflicting of violence as the mere result or outcome of the law's force (or "illocutionary potential")?[5] Do we indeed have to go beyond the law, do we have to leave the legal sphere behind, in order to avoid the violence involved both in the making of law and its administration?

To answer these questions, we have to face the contingencies of a particular legal history, for example the set of procedures, devices and circumstances which amount to the "legal fiction" that is the English Common Law well into the nineteenth century; it "permeates," according to Owen Barfield's fitting description, "the whole of our jurisprudence, which most certainly is law, and not merely procedural."[6] Full of inconsistencies, the history of *Habeas corpus* provides us, nevertheless, with a starting point: the topology, namely, of what belongs to the law's taking place. Moreover, the *Habeas corpus* writ and act together exemplify the technical, procedural interaction of sentence and execution; in the transfer of due process (qua "metaphor"), it also exposes the displacement ("metonymy") of its taking place, i.e. the sentence's taking place *in* the execution, and the execution's taking the place of the sentence: the topology, in short, of due process.

There is no act, it seems, without the presence of the body in question, and no process without act. As we shall see, *Habeas corpus* the writ is to guarantee *Habeas corpus* the act in that it produces the body, if only to interrupt and delay the process by the very same token. Or, to put it in the idiom of speech-act philosophy, the exemplary instance of the act performed *in saying*, the juridical act, participates silently in the writing of an underlying, fundamental writ.[7] It is this essential participation more than any other, moral obligation that carries the institutional pathos of the *Habeas Corpus Act*. Already the primordial act of jurisdiction is dependent on this transfer, and it is the mode of translation, which asks for further translation, displacement and delay, rather than for speedy execution.

After exile – the local solution which made the trial superfluous – had become impossible, the temporal solution of delay and its substitutes like bail became imperative. Do we read this problematic correctly or, that is, do we do justice to the underlying legal crux, if we take the measures of displacement and delay as merely practical responses to otherwise unmanageable situations and, vice versa, the means of speedy execution as the logic and the rule of the law "itself"? Or is it, maybe, otherwise, and the law is first of all an institution of citation rather than execution, the sentence a means of interruption rather than implementation? It all depends, we submit, on the law's desire to have the body cited rather than executed.

Having the Body
The coincidence of body and law begins with a command, the king's command addressed to a sheriff: "Have [i.e. produce] the body of the defendant on a given day before the court."[8] The beginning of the order – "Have the body" – lends its initials to the fact of *actually having it*, of how to have and, that is, produce the (living) body. The *Habeas corpus writ*, later the *Habeas Corpus Act* of 1679, names what is at stake and owes no small part of its notoriety to the intricacy of the named, the law's desire for the body. It is an institutional desire, a desire produced by an institution and manifest in writing, a desire whose reference, or extension, is re-enforced through the institutionalization of what became notorious at the time as "the rule of law."[9] It is the institutionalization of the warrant that "the writ," the written request for the body, brings the body before the law, produces, seizes it for the law. *Capias*, as the formula at first had been, captures the body in order to secure the defendant's appearance in court and enable the trial literally to take place.

It follows thus almost by "definition" – i.e. locating the trial in time and space – that body and law are to coincide in court and not in prison.

Remarkably enough, every body involved in a trial should gather there, in the courtroom, since the *Habeas corpus* served as a summons for the jurors as well as the defendant. They all were equally commanded by a single writ. At first they were simply summoned by a call, a crier's voice or a bell comparable to the *vocatio* in Roman Law.[10] The scene invoked, however, is the king's; it is the theater of his sovereignty, where jurors and defendant are called upon as *dramatis personae*. For the instant of the trial they belong to the one *corpus juris*, which embodies the king's power over his subjects – or so it seems until the "rule of law" came to contest the king's jurisdictional power and to limit his involvement. Most notoriously, in 1608, Chief Justice Edward Coke went so far as to tell James I that he had no authority to participate in the judicial decisions of his own courts. *Habeas corpus* clearly belongs to that "steady stream of medieval statutes from Magna Charta onwards" insisting on "due process of law" against royal prerogatives, as in arbitrary deprivation of life, liberty or property.[11]

From the thirteenth century onwards the trial-body including jurors and defendant embodies the king's power, his power to produce and dispose of bodies; it incorporates the king's power. After the trial, the *ad hoc* body produced by the "interlocutory mandate" of a *Habeas corpus* is released into bodylessness. The one and decisive function of the *Habeas*, it seems, is to secure the scene, not to secure or enforce the punishment. The desire for the body in question is satisfied by the scene, satisfied with the performance, itself. Afterwards, the corporate body of the trial falls apart; outside the topos of the court, it cannot be located or defined. It can neither be fixed nor defined within the coordinates of writing or geography. Naturally, because the body is fugitive, the defendant can evade or evoke the trial; he or she can either escape from the king's realm or throw him or herself on the king's mercy and thus evade trial. These are the two options, but they come with two different types of risks.

Evading the trial is rather easy as long as the sheriff summons without searching; and a summons, though hardly distinguishable from a warrant of arrest yet, is anything but the elaborate search-net of a police-apparatus in those days. But the consequence of evading trial and escaping from liability would mean to become an outlaw, whereas to go for the king's mercy would be the opposite, of recognizing the law and having a probable chance for every body standing trial. In some sense, the exception through mercy resembles evasion in that it suspends the law. Precisely for that reason, the law is eager to have the body before the court, and its principal rationale is to secure the trial scene. Its most impressive mise-en-scène was that of Frederick the Second. As *Stupor mundi* he became notorious for the stupendous display of kingship with respect to the law, of "law-centered kingship" in Kantorowicz's study.[12] Whether we speak of *Iustitia mediatrix* or *lex animata* (in Frederick's own terms), the motif of clemency, traditionally taken from Seneca's *De clementia*, adds to the intricacies of these concepts of mediation an indispensable ingredient easily overlooked and systematically forgotten.[13] Clemency makes manifest the king's position *above* the law, but *with respect* to the law. Both aspects together are decisive for this moment of representation in the strictest sense. That the king is bound to a law never to be applied against his will is not a simple but a double bind; it is not to be dissolved by the logic of due execution.

Thus the trial opens the space for the ceremony of clemency; it exposes the king's power over life and death. Mercy is the king's prerogative despite and beyond the law, a monopoly with respect to the law's formal existence as well as its fulfillment, justice – of "that within which passes show," in Hamlet's words, that is; we have to twist them just slightly (*Hamlet* 1.2.85).[14] The king needs the convicted body in order to perform above the law what is the law's innermost self. The historically far-reaching formula "Master over Life and Death" – Frederick's maxim from Seneca – has to be read as He who has the power to pardon is the master over producing and dismissing bodies through both judgment and mercy. As a warrant of arrest *Habeas corpus* is one of the devices that demands and remands bodies according to the *voluntas regis*, that is, it demonstrates the king's power over the law in producing an interlocutory body: it performs, creates and annihilates, in the double act of summoning and discharging, calling and pardoning.[15]

English law distinguishes pardon *de cursu* and *de gratia*; only the latter is due to the king's sovereignty. While the first is jurisdictional, that is, concerned with questions of excuse, the second depends entirely upon the king's grace. Obviously, the royal decision was often enough influenced by all kinds of advantages taken in return like service or payment.[16] That pardon was granted in the majority of cases recorded from the thirteenth century onwards, may not be surprising and quite in line with the later decline of pardon to a symptom of weakness. The royal prerogative as such, however, in its balancing rather than executing function, attests to a different economics of the law.[17] The merely procedural economy was able to absorb, to a certain extent, the *gratia* part and to neutralize the instrument that was to produce the body with respect to the law; and the king's superior exercise of mercy turned into the very act which, in turn, individuated the body wanted into a bearer of rights. Clemency declined, and the rule of mercy took on the appearance of mere favor. Not by mere accident, then, the execution of Charles I in 1649 preceded the celebrated *Habeas Corpus Act* of 1679.

Foucault's juxtaposition of the monarchical body politic and "the least body of the condemned man" presupposes this tendency and tries to make sense of it.[18] But against the grain of Foucault's homage to Kantorowicz in this point, it is the same king's body politic that is constituted by the king's court and claimed by the law's rule. Thus Coke's (rather unlucky) successor Mountagu was still able to take a middle position and explain *Habeas corpus* as "a prerogative writ, which concerns the king's justice to be administered to his subjects; for the king ought to have an account why any of his subjects are imprisoned."[19] The formulation is telling, because it manages, if only for the moment, to reformulate the king's position above the law in terms of a responsibility for his subjects.

It is not by accident that the decline of pardon coincides with a functional change of *Habeas corpus* into the crucial device for determining the lawfulness of detention. There was a tendency to use the *Habeas* in order to contest the validity of imprisonment even before. But the bearer of rights, of Human Rights after all, produced and invested by the *Act* of 1679 is no longer the body produced by the older writ as the subject to the king's grace. Edward Jenks, the most thorough historiographer of *Habeas corpus* at the beginning of this, by now last century, was highly doubtful of the progress produced; he put it precisely the other way round in that *Habeas*, in fact, "created no new remedy, but merely strengthened and perfected an engine which had been used with effect in the great struggle between Crown and Parliament" (64). The King's clemency, in other words, became superfluous because the Law found a parliamentary device against itself; not against the king's arbitrary execution of mercy, but against the law's own jurisdictional errors.

The tedious system of control instituted in 1679 bound legal agencies up to the Lord Chancellor, to whom the sheriff was to "bring or cause to be brought the body of the party so committed or restrained," in order to "certify the true causes of his detainer or imprisonment."[20] In order to guarantee such certification, money may be substituted for the body in question, as explained by the same introductory section of the *Habeas Corpus Act*: "many of the king's subjects have been and hereafter may be long detained in prison, in such cases where by law they are bailable, to their great charges and vexation." Since detention in the seventeenth century has the purpose of custody and was not yet a means of punishment, bail is a placeholder for the time before the trial takes place and before "the true causes" could be certified. Or, as Maitland in his classical work puts it: "When a person is said to be bailed this means that he and some sureties have entered into recognizance, have been bound over, for his appearance at the trial."[21] Not the physical presence of the body, not the body of tortures emerges, but this body's freedom of movement. From now on, imprisonment, the deprivation of personal liberty, will turn into a punishment of withdrawn freedom.

The way in which bail from now on is to translate the topology of the law into money is even more evident in the second case provided by the *Act* of 1679: "security is given by his [the defendant's] own bond to pay the charges of carrying [himself] back," we find in Stubbs (518). Although the text is somewhat unclear about who is to cover the cost, it is perfectly precise in calculating most of the details: the sum to be deposited by the prisoner should not exceed 12 pence per mile for his journey back to the prison, and even the deadlines are defined in most precise terms: within 20 miles 3 days, beyond 20 to 100 miles a "space" of 10 days, beyond 100 miles 20 days. The trade includes the body's transportation, the costs of the journey or alternatively the escape. Whereas the older *Habeas corpus writ* was concerned with the topography, the *Habeas Corpus Act* finds an exact calculation of costs in terms of transportation. The local fixation of guilt is translated into a permanent, virtually ubiquitous debt. Indebtedness through surety, tender or bail, are the prescribed bond between body and law; they redefine the law's desire to have the body and to keep it within reach.

The new money-body transaction happens on the back of a writ. The connection between body and law through indebtedness continues the scriptural process; the deposit is "endorsed on the writ." The writing perpetuates and de-corporates the body at the same time; the body is dissolved within an economical order, while the law's desire to have the body seems suspended by this order. From the seventeenth century onwards, the time gained by the procedure is used for preliminary investigations. The law no longer takes an interest in the body as such, it focuses on the surrounding network of environment, contact and movement. Written deposits allow for the deposition of witnesses before the actual trial; they are taken down in writing in order to perpetuate testimony: those "who have to frame the indictment have the advantage of seeing the whole of the evidence of the depositions [and] if a witness dies, or is too ill to attend, his testimony is perpetuated," Maitland says (132). Whatever there is to be put in depositions serves to make them independent from the witnesses' actual performance in court. Thus the depositions function in the same way as the deposits; they conserve the body wanted by written or pecuniary surrogates. The alternative of "jail or bail" opens up a zone of discretion functionally analogous to the clemency of the king. It is an administrative zone, to be sure, which lends itself to police-like actions without proper legal grounds; like the king's favor, it borders on terror.

Social control, it turns out, is to contain a similar zoning as the king's, a violence structural rather than intentional, and the question is how to read its representational *ratio*.

First, of course, it remains to be seen how discretion, the king's prerogative at first, was discredited in favor of public control. The principal point in this development still tends to be overlooked, the dialectic of Punish and Pardon. It seems that Foucault, in featuring discipline and control as major forces in the shaping of the modern subject's "subjectivity," is forced to confuse law and sovereignty on the same grounds as the legal positivists against whose conception of progress his work is directed; he leaves untouched or, moreover, gives in to the fiction of the juridico-discursive formation, whose ideology he so effectively criticizes.[22] It may suffice to quote the highly significant account given in Baker's handbook. There, the "little" irony, as Baker perceives it, that the "original purpose [of the *Habeas corpus*] was not to release people from prison but to secure their presence in custody," is deepened by another, no lesser irony, namely that of pardon: "Ironically, the existence of this merciful prerogative served to perpetuate a procedure which was far out of line with prevailing notions of criminal responsibility, so that what ought to have been a plain question of law remained for centuries at least nominally a question of favour" (589).

Ironically, "what ought to have been a plain question of law" seems to have escaped and transcended the law's rule; or, as it were, in a more recent version, the law's wish "to have a formal existence."[23] Above all, what it seems to have needed once is representation from "above," and the question is to what extent there resides in this "above" a consideration of representability, which escapes not only the law's representation of itself in its formal existence but transcends the understanding of itself with respect to justice. Derrida's "force of law," for example, aims to transcend what is due in the process (and fair in Rawls' sense) in that it always already transcends itself.[24] What could be said about, and in favor of, that mode of self-transcendence that is to be represented in the presentation of the law as itself?

In iudicium stare

The *Habeas Corpus Act* is celebrated as a major success against the king's rule, although the *Habeas corpus writ* had previously been a prerogative of the king. The transition and translation from the king's order to "produce" the body to the liberty of "having the body" are significant, the false understanding of the original Latin notwithstanding. Shifting from "having" in the one sense to "having" in the second sense, the Latin idiom of *Habeas* provides a suggestive bridge and documents a displacement easily overlooked, the literal displacement of the *corpus* in question – it may go as far as "freedom of movement." To whom belongs this body? The king's, the law's, the subject's? And whose subject? To whom is this body subject?

While a most important landmark in constitutional history, the act of *Habeas corpus* "in no sense creates any right to personal freedom, but is essentially a procedure act for improving the legal mechanism by means of which that acknowledged right may be enforced." As the *Encyclopedia Britannica* of 1910 puts it, "It declares no principles and defines no rights, but is for practical purposes worth a hundred articles guaranteeing constitutional liberty" (Habeas Corpus, 784–85). An obvious triumph of legalism, *Habeas corpus* belongs to a set of "legal powers" guarding the application of law.[25] But as Foucault has shown, the consequent turn to control – to "social control over precept" in terms of the particularly British debate on "secondary rules" and "legal powers" – no longer focuses on the body, but on the soul: "Puisque ce n'est plus le corps, c'est l'âme" (22). This turn to the soul, the conversion from body to soul, subjecting the body to the soul, is embarrassed by the violence inflicted, and more precisely, by the traces betraying the violence that remains part of the law's rule, its exercise of power, in spite of the law's explicit disengagement from the body and its pains.

Thus we may have to reconsider a paradoxical side-issue of Foucault's story: that the discipline imposed in the new era of punishment denies the body under control, in order to control. Against the denial of the body as the object of violence, the story of *Habeas corpus* reads as the reminder of some other, perhaps more fundamental setting, which was superseded by the later function of social control, just as the older, representational function of the law seems to have been superseded by that same controlling function. In the case of *Habeas corpus* this perhaps more fundamental setting adds to the picture of the law's bygone representational function to the extent that it contradicts the structure of representation as such, at least in the way we are used to this feature as a primordial mode of world maintenance and interpretation. The understanding of *Nomos* as world picture may be nothing but a belated, metaphorical projection of enlightened times. In other words, the *Habeas corpus* motif may be conclusive when it comes to redefine legal progress through an alternative prehistory of what made this progress an ambivalent affair from the beginning.[26]

There is, above all, the scene of the writ as invoked by the writ, the court. This topos, as any topos, is everything but universal; it is limited (as the writ is limited to the particular grievances at hand, or in view). It needs the presence of the defendant in order to act (as it needs the presence of others, officials). The fact that in Rome exile was equivalent to execution, while the king's body throughout the Middle Ages embodied the equivalence of pardon and execution, shows that the court was able to represent itself in giving presence to itself, just as the law was to be re-enacted as "itself." The performance rested entirely in itself without serving any other end – except for the king, but likewise the king was nothing but the embodying principle of the body assembled. To a certain extent, the Hegelian monarch resuscitates this principle; and one could be tempted (as we are, in fact) to see Hegel keep or, rather, reintroduce the monarch for the very reason discussed here, namely, the "right to pardon [arising] from the sovereignty of the monarch (. . .) one of the highest recognitions of the majesty of mind."[27] The perlocutionary effect did not simply add to the performative power; rather, when the king's performance was weakened and its force vanished, violence had to be brought in to compensate for what was missing in terms of representational value and, therefore, had to be re-presented.

In Hegel, the concept of positing [*Setzung*], presupposed by legal positivists and taken for granted in the pragmatics of the day, i.e. "history," finds itself rationally deduced from the *Logic* that is the framework of Hegel's *Philosophy of Right*.[28] In this deduction, a logic of representation is revealed and brought into terms [*auf den Begriff*] with the law itself. According to the nineteenth-century jurist John Austin's conception, such "principle" was plainly derived, as of old, from God's positioning power.[29] The representation of this power cannot but present and exhibit the law's own logic as independent of any worldly interest. Already the emblematic scale of *Iustitia* had its point not alone in measuring the unmeasurable, but in deciding the undecidable; and the now forgotten *corda* of *misericordia*, memorable inscription in her name, was meant to remind her of the crucial possibility of justice as *clementia* (thus the famous mural of *Iustitia* and *Buon Governo* in the Palazzo Publico in Siena).[30]

Quite differently, but still in the same tradition, Chief Justice Coke's "Lady of the Common Law" showed mercy, or the pretense of it, by way of *Habeas corpus*, the writ which ordered a body to court and brought it into place, before justice. This picture has changed; after centuries of shifting meanings, *Habeas corpus* has turned into the awkward name of a petition, which in the continuing rush to execution in U.S. capital cases has become synonymous with the possibility of successive attempts to delay execution. The function of mere delay is recognizable even in the rough statistics of Shakespeare's England as calculated by Francis Barker, where an incredibly rapid rise of the execution rate was still balanced by between a third and a quarter of pardons.[31] Where there is no longer any unconditional pardon possible, the conditional delay becomes imperative for the death row in waiting.

The Benjaminian analysis of "overextended transcendence" had quite naturally taken for granted what he, Benjamin, saw exposed, in the very same century of Justice Coke and the *Habeas Corpus Act*, as the "rotten" state of "the law itself." "For in the exercise of violence over life and death more than in any other legal act, law reaffirms itself," Benjamin finds, and this reaffirmation of "itself," of its own positional power, makes the law the most effective agent of representation itself, and of its power to make present what is not.[32] This, however, may not be, and may not have been, the law's point all along, nor was it the point of the law's acts. Nor was it any more the law's point, what Foucault described as the law's crucial new function of discipline and control from the age of reason onwards. Foucault offers a significant insight when he explains the law's need for supporting evidence that, from now on, the legal sphere was no longer interested in the body and its pain, but in the soul and its improvement. A dangerous supplement, one is tempted to call it, because it takes over what it is meant to support, the law's office of judgment. But while "it," the supplement this time, displaces, even replaces, the functional *ratio* of representation, it also effaces, disperses, disseminates the topos and the scene of writing the sentence, including the law's own performative force, the force of law, itself.

Against this effacement, the writ and the act of *Habeas corpus* cite and re-cite the law's condition of being effective, its performativity. What else but its desire for the body could make its performance effective? While the law's execution seems to give up the body and ask for the soul instead, the sentence whose execution is thus excused with respect to the soul's improvement and final salvation, still needs a referent and, as Foucault is able to explain, both transcendentalizes and literalizes this referent *as* the body; it identifies the body in question, the body "to be had," as the referent needed. The body, whose surface was the target of punishment and served its representational function as a vehicle of symbolism in the manifold modes of torture, evaporates, vanishes into the "Ding an sich" of execution, hit by the Guillotine in but one decisive point and moment. After the event, this coming true of the sentence is embalmed in a multitude of interpretive acts of compensation, repairing for the sake of the surviving world what cannot be repaired for the victim, whose being cut off is nothing but the literal consequence of his or her being expelled from this *Nomos* and its narrative.[33] Thus, the ideology of interpretive communities was consoled by the thought of law and order as merely or mainly the outcome and merit of interpretive acts.

Calling for the body in order to establish the scene of law's acts, *Habeas corpus* rearranges the procedural connection between judgment and execution (in speech-act terms, between illocution and perlocution as effect). It is the very point of the *Habeas corpus* regulation to take care of the transfers and displacements necessary to guard the topos of the law's own economy, the conditions of judgment in changing social configurations. Without the body there is no act, although the desire for the body is *not* to have the act executed and the power exemplified through violence. Rather the body is to focus the decision, while the decision itself remains undecided between grace and execution, discretion and representation. It is, however, to be taken. The casuistry of substitutions, of cash and delay, rather than the incessant and monotonous shame of executions, keeps the force of law forceful. How if the law had been calling and citing, invoking and delaying, including and excluding, before it came to institutionalized prosecution and enforcement, punishment and execution? An economy of its discourse rather than a sociology of its effects may be needed.

Hegel's insistence on the subject's standing in court on his or her own feet – "im Gerichte leiblich, mit den Füßen, zugegen zu sein" – discarded, displaced but also replaced, the old topics of jurisprudence, the "*in iudicio stare*" quoted by Hegel as an outdated feudal metaphor for the subject's *Leibeigenschaft* (literally, the subject's bodily submission to a feudal lord). In his consequence, the Habeas corpus motif enables and produces a new, precarious space called freedom of expression, which is structured according to a new procedural logic, asking for a new rhetoric of self-presentation.[34] The subject's mental identity [*Geist*], its own know-how of life [*Lebenswissen*], has to take the sentence, and put up with it – but cannot take it, and cannot put up with it, except for some utopian moment, or anticipation, in Hegel's understanding, of an "absolute" knowledge. How can an economy of grace and discretion, of mercy in the face of what we do not know, or avoid to know, deal with the displaced desire for truth that is not genuinely the law's? Is that, in fact, philosophy's one and only way to come to terms with what it perceives as the law's guise of a philosophical truth and comfortably translates into a "discourse of truth"?[35] Would not such discourse deny the law's positional logic and encrypt it instead as the secret of its own desire to know, or avoidance, at that, of "knowing what it cannot just not know."[36]

Notes

1 *Perpetuum Mobile:* Shakespeare's Perpetual Renaissance

1   Heiner Müller, "Shakespeare eine Differenz" (Shakespeare-Tage Weimar, 1988), *Shakespeare Factory* 2 (Berlin: Wagenbach, 1994), 227–30. The exemplary *Hamletmaschine* of 1977 begins with the Hamlet scenario from Paul Valéry's "De la crise de l'esprit" (1919), which figures prominently in the post-war statements of Harry Levin, *The Question of Hamlet* (New York: Oxford University Press, 1959), as well as in Jacques Derrida's *De l'esprit* (Paris: Galilée, 1987) and in the title of *L'autre cap* (1991). Hamlet at Elsinore, on the edge of Europe: "I was Hamlet. I stood at the coast and spoke to the surf BLABLA, the ruins of Europe at my back. The bells rang in the state funeral, murderer and widow a couple, goosestepping behind the coffin of the High Cadaver the councilmen, wailing in badly paid mourning."

2   This is the flipside, or side-effect, of the "bifurcation of nature" in Alfred North Whitehead's *Concept of Nature* (Cambridge: Cambridge University Press [1920] 1964), Chapter II. See more recently Isabelle Stengers, *Penser avec Whitehead* (Paris: Seuil, 2005), 24 ff., 52 ff.

3   Harold Bloom, *Shakespeare: The Invention of the Human* (New York: Penguin Putnam, 1998), 12, whose saying I use here against the grain. See in the meantime (and not without implicit reference) the revisionary supplement by the same author, *Hamlet: Poem Unlimited* (New York: Riverhead Books, 2003).

4   Stephen Greenblatt, *Shakespearian Negotiations: The Circulation of Social Energy in Renaissance England* (Berkeley, CA: University of California Press,

1987), 191. For the crucial Aristotelian connection of *energeia* and *enargeia* in the Renaissance, see Kathy Eden, *Poetic and Legal Fiction in the Aristotelian Tradition* (Princeton, NJ: Princeton University Press, 1986), 71 ff. The relevant Renaissance places have been discussed by Rosmond Tuve, *Elizabethan and Metaphysical Imagery: Renaissance Poetic and Twentieth Century Critics* (Chicago: University of Chicago Press, 1947, 1961), 29 ff. For the most recent actuality of the concept, see Jacques Derrida, *Voyous* (Paris: Galilée, 2003), Chapter 1; Jacques Derrida, *Rogues* (Stanford, CA: Stanford University Press, 2005), 15.

5   In the sense of Jürgen Habermas, *Strukturwandel der Öffentlichkeit* (Newied: Luchterhand, 1962), 24 ff., 38 ff. *The Structural Transformation of the Public Sphere*, trans. Thomas Burger (Cambridge, MA: MIT Press, 1989), 14 ff., 27 ff. Not untypical (and in spite of Lessing), Habermas underestimates the role of the theater (Shakespeare) and prefers the rise of the novel (Richardson, Goethe) in his search for thematic rather than structural (aesthetical) evidence in the literary sphere.

6   In his seminal essay *The Empty Space* (New York: Atheneum, 1968, 1978), Peter Brook developed the thesis that Shakespeare's "rough theatre" – not far from Antonin Artaud's "theatre of cruelty," where Shakespeare also serves as both the negative starting point and the vantage point of dramatic fulfillment – is a "model" that "contains Brecht and Beckett, but goes beyond both" and produces the "need in the post-Brecht theatre to find a way forwards, back to Shakespeare" (85/86). With *Hamlet-Machine* of 1977, Heiner Müller and his Berlin Ensemble followed the same agenda from Brecht to Shakespeare, though in a different key. After the 7-hour-long production of *Hamlet-Maschine* in 1989, which was directly involved in the fall of the Berlin Wall, Müller's last *mise-en-scène* in 1995 of Brecht's *Arturo Ui* was the most memorable highlight of this effort and came to an additional head, when Marianne Hoppe, idol of Hitler's Thirties, served as replacement for her sick colleague, the old Bernhard Minetti. Matthias Langhoff's Paris production of *Richard III* in 1995 formed part of the same school's post-Brechtian venture, bringing the machine up to date (Langhoff had collaborated with Müller on a Hamlet production in 1976). For the 1989 production of *Hamlet-Maschine*, see Christoph Rüter, *Die Zeit ist aus den Fugen* (Frankfurt/M: Filmedition Suhrkamp, 2009), including the Garath Dialogue between Alexander Kluge and Heiner Müller in 1990. Nota bene: The Hamlet of *Hamletmaschine* in 1977 as well as in 1989, Ulrich Mühe, famous for this role, was also the hero of *Das Leben der Anderen*, Academy Award-winning best foreign film in 2008. Again, it seems, Hamlet was Germany.

7   *Gloucester Time: Matériau Shakespeare/Richard III*, dir. Matthias Langhoff, Chapelle des Pénitents Blancs, Avignon, July 1995. For General Schwarzkopf's German-American notoriety, see QRT (Markus Konradin Leiner), *Schlachtfelder der elektronischen Wüste: Schwarzkopf, Schwarzenegger, Black Magic Johnson* (Berlin: Merve, 1999), 18 ff. See also Avital Ronell, *Finitude's Score:*

Essays for the End of the Millennium (Lincoln, NB: University of Nebraska Press, 1994), 269 ff.
8 Stanley Cavell, *Disowning Knowledge in Six Plays of Shakespeare* (Cambridge: Cambridge University Press, 1987), 191.
9 Stephen Greenblatt, *Will in the World: How Shakespeare Became Shakespeare* (New York: Norton, 2004), 324. For a particularly striking account, see most recently, Margreta de Grazia, *Hamlet without Hamlet* (Cambridge: Cambridge University Press, 2007).

2 The Ghost of History: Hamlet and the Politics of Paternity

1 Friedrich Hölderlin, "Pläne und Bruchstücke," *Sämtliche Werke*, ed. Friedrich Beissner (Stuttgart: Kohlhammer, 1946–85), II.1: 317. Cited by Heiner Müller, *Hamletmaschine*, sect. 5, as well as in "Shakespeare eine Differenz" (1988), *Shakespeare Factory* 2 (Berlin: Rotbuch Verlag, 1994), II: 228.
2 Paul Valéry, "De la crise de l'esprit" (1919), in *Œuvres*, éd. Jean Hytier (Paris: Gallimard, 1957), I: 994. Jacques Derrida, *De l'esprit* (Paris: Galilée, 1987), 98. Harry Levin, *The Question of Hamlet* (New York: Oxford University Press, 1959), 106 f.
3 Hans Blumenberg, *Die Genesis der kopernikanischen Welt* (Frankfurt/M: Suhrkamp, 1975), esp. 691 ff. *The Genesis of the Copernican World*, trans. Robert M. Wallace (Cambridge, MA: MIT Press, 1989). Anselm Haverkamp, "Paradigma Metapher/Metapher Paradigma" (1987), in *Die paradoxe Metapher* (Frankfurt/M: Suhrkamp, 1998), 268–86: 269 f.
4 This is an abbreviation of Walter Benjamin's more complicated argument in *Ursprung des deutschen Trauerspiels* (1928) in *Gesammelte Schriften* I (Frankfurt/M: Suhrkamp, 1974); *The Origin of German Tragic Drama*, trans. John Osborne (London: Verso, 1977), the closing section of the first part of which displays the title "Hamlet." The intricacies of Benjamin's argument remain to be developed in the following. For the Benjaminian context of the concept of history, see Samuel Weber, "Genealogy of Modernity: History, Myth, and Allegory in Benjamin's Origin of the German Mourning Play" (1991), *Benjamin's – abilities* (Cambridge, MA: Harvard University Press, 2008), 131–63.
5 Friedrich Nietzsche, *Die Geburt der Tragödie* (1872), the central passage is at the end of sect. 7. Sigmund Freud's footnote, introducing the Oedipus Complex in *Die Traumdeutung* (1900), appeared for the first time in the 4th edition, which supplements the mere citation of the Oedipus myth that had been previously illustrated with a comparison between Sophocles and Shakespeare and the history of repression that connects them. For Jacques Lacan, see "Desire and the Interpretation of Desire in Hamlet," *Yale French Studies* 55–6 (1977): 11–52; repr. in *Literature and Psychoanalysis: The Question of Reading: Otherwise*, ed. Shoshana Felman (Baltimore, MD: The Johns Hopkins University Press, 1982); this is the "cursed spite," with *Hamlet* "possibly illustrating a decadent form of the Oedipal situation, its, decline" (45).

6 The text of *Hamlet* is cited according to Harold Jenkins' edition, *Arden Shakespeare*, Second Series (London: Methuen, 1982/Routledge, 1989), and supplemented by John Dover Wilson's edition, *New Cambridge Shakespeare* (Cambridge: Cambridge University Press, [1934] 1968). The decision of the editors Ann Thompson and Neil Taylor in the new *Arden Shakespeare*'s Third Series (London: Thomson, 2006) to separate the 2nd Quarto of 1604/5 of *Hamlet* from the texts of 1603 and the First Folio of 1623 is both illuminating and useful, but it ruins literally and on purpose the network of lacunas and latencies operative in the vicissitudes of the historical reception to which Jenkins' commentary did justice. In this respect, Jenkins' edition is irreplaceable – as the new edition freely admits (I: xix).

7 Sigmund Freud, *Die Traumdeutung*, last edition (1930), *Freud-Studienausgabe*, ed. Alexander Mitscherlich, Angela Richards, James Strachey (Frankfurt/M: Fischer, 1969–75), II: 269 (my translation). See here, again, Lacan's commentary, "Desire and the Interpretation of Desire in Hamlet," 25 ff.

8 Johann Wolfgang von Goethe, *Wilhelm Meisters Lehrjahre* (1796), Hamburg edition of *Goethes Werke*, ed. Erich Trunz (Hamburg: Wegener, 1948–60), VII: 245/46 (my translation). The notorious passage occurs in Book IV, Chapter 13. Thus also Book IV, Chapter 14, "the hero has no plan, but the play is carefully designed" (254), a point which is taken up again later in Meister's adaptation of *Hamlet* in Book V, Chapter 4, with emphasis on "the unity of this work, in which the hero in particular has no plan" (296). A closer reading of this influential commonplace from *Wilhelm Meister* will have to wait, but it might well show how much awareness Goethe himself invested, even in Meister's adaptation, in the difference between the "external conditions" and the decisive motif that allows these "external, isolated, disparate and dissipating motives" to become the object of "substitution for a single motive" (296). Goethe's ability to stage himself in the solution to this problem that he brought into the world is equally noteworthy, but has gone largely unnoticed. I am tempted to see in it the beginnings of an anamorphotic reading like the one I am advocating, whereby, however, Goethe's insight remains especially significant: The anamorphosis lies in the lee of the melancholic predisposition, and consequently Goethe's own deciphering must also remain entirely in the shadow of the prefiguration that he expounds.

9 This aspect of the play has been developed by Lee Sheridan Cox, *Figurative Design in Hamlet: The Significance of the Dumb Show* (Columbus, OH: Ohio State University Press, 1974). Stephen Greenblatt has further explained, on the occasion of his *Shakespearean Negotiations* (Berkeley, CA: University of California Press, 1988), how the scenes of the self-representation of theater through the theater become the center of the "symbolic acquisition" that transpires in Shakespeare's re-institutionalization of the institution that became the theater.

10 J.W. Lever *The Tragedy of State: A Study of Jacobean Drama* (London: Methuen, 1971, 1987) correspondingly finds: "the typical situation of the revenge play is

unrelated to the operation of the feud or the possibilities of recourse to law" (12). Eleanor Prosser's *Hamlet and Revenge* (Stanford, CA: Stanford University Press, 1967, 1971) still offers the most detailed discussion of the sources (133 ff.), tracing the origin of the revenge motif to the allegorical personification of "Vice" in the moralities and makes the revenge's lack of concrete motivation palpable through a large number of examples. As the contemporary motto puts it: "Revenge now rules as sovereign of my blood." The reasons for revenge are, like those of the contemporaneous melancholy, entirely without reason: "several [in *The Revenger's Tragedy*] are immediately forgotten and at least five have no motivation whatsoever" (38). Revenge is, in other words, like melancholy, a chronic Elizabethan malady, the flipside of the manic-depressive disposition. Hamlet reacts in his melancholic mask to the imposition of the ghost, which for its part covers up another motive beneath the mask of revenge.

11 Benjamin's *Trauerspielbuch* characterizes the figure of the intriguer, in its later, Baroque dimensions, as if he had Polonius in mind as an early prototype (I: 274 f.). Only recently, following Tom Stoppard's *Rosencrantz and Guildenstern Are Dead* (1967), did Patricia Parker show, in a series of texts, the full extent of spying and discovery, secret intelligence and secret intents in *Hamlet* and *Othello* and thereby uncovered an entirely forgotten layer of semantic latencies. Comparable to the microscopic readings of William Empson, Parker's analyses in *Shakespeare from the Margins* (Chicago: University of Chicago Press, 1996) show how indispensable rhetorical reading is for the discovery of these layers.

12 Hegel's intuition at the end of his *Phänomenologie des Geistes*, ed. Hans-Friedrich Wessels, and Heinrich Clairmont (Hamburg: Meiner, 1988), 481, is already impressive and worth mentioning: "Thus the consciousness [Hamlet], which is purer than the last one that believes in ghosts [Macbeth], and possessed of greater presence of mind, and more systematic ... hesitates to commit revenge and seeks to orchestrate other proofs – for the reason, apparently, that this ghost, who reveals the plot to him, might also be the devil" (my attempt at a translation for the purpose at hand). I shall come back to this crucial passage in the course of the next chapter.

13 The comparison with Dante has been made effective by Roy W. Battenhouse in a classic article with the title "The Ghost in Hamlet: A Catholic Linchpin?" *Studies in Philology* 48 (1951), 161–92, with the result that the ghost cannot have come from Dante's *Purgatorio* (164). To the contrary, as I am underscoring, he must be from the *Inferno*. The discussion following Battenhouse unfortunately fails to draw this conclusion, due to a misrecognition of the status of rhetorical corruption in the *Inferno*. As such, it is not only decisive for Dante, but following him also for Machiavelli, as has been exemplarily shown by John Freccero, "Medusa and the Madonna of Forli," in *Machiavelli and the Discourse of Literature*, ed. Albert Russell Ascoli, and Viktoria Kahn (Ithaca, NY: Cornell University Press, 1993), 161–78. See in the following

Freccero's key concept of "Infernal Irony: The Gates of Hell" (1983), in *Dante: The Poetics of Conversion* (Cambridge, MA: Harvard University Press, 1986), 93–109.

14 Bill Readings, "Hamlet's Thing," in *New Essays on Hamlet*, ed. Mark Thornton Burnett, and John Manning (New York: Palgrave, 1994), 52, makes this rare point: "The ghost cannot tell, cannot unfold, but unfolds the picture of one in torment." That does not mean, however, as Readings continues, that "What cannot be told, it seems, can be seen" and comes to be seen, as it were, in this scene; it remains to be heard within that "which passes show" (Hamlet's maxim) in the untold of the falsely proposed. For the impressive repetition of this – again – Dantean figure, see Barbara Vinken, "Encore – Francesca da Rimini," *Deutsche Vierteljahrsschrift für Literaturwissenschaft und Geistesgeschichte* 62 (1988), 395–415.

15 Stephen Greenblatt, *Hamlet in Purgatory* (Princeton, NJ: Princeton University Press, 2001), takes another and more refined view, thereby offering and exposing nevertheless, as it seems to me, the deeper underpinnings of the ghost's "infernal irony" (Freccero's *Dante*, 108). What Greenblatt does indeed add to the "long-standing critical game" (239) is the "young man from Wittenberg, with a distinctly Protestant temperament, [who] is haunted by a distinctly Catholic ghost" (240). *Hamlet* is a drama of secularization that, far from completing itself, was bound, in the historical double bind that *is* History, to fall back into being possessed, or repossessed, by what it is about to leave, prematurely, behind: a mortgage that betrays our "desire to speak to the dead" (as in *Shakespearean Negotiations*, first sentence) through the lies of History, the pursuit of revenge the biggest among them.

16 This is, among others, an extension of William Empson's bold study "Hamlet When New" (1953), collected in his *Essays on Shakespeare* (Cambridge: Cambridge University Press, 1986), 79–136. Empson conceives the theatrical collusion of specter and protagonist, of revenge and melancholy, in the pointed sentence: "Hamlet was the rage" (94). See Martin Harries, *Scare Quotes from Shakespeare: Marx, Keynes, and the Language of Reenchantment* (Stanford, CA: Stanford University Press, 2000), 108 ff.

17 Despite all efforts of textual criticism, the fact is hardly ever made sense of – and if it is, its significance is left unexplained – that the *Hamlet* of the Restoration (in the version that Sir William D'Avenant produced from the last prewar quarto of 1637 and which first appeared in 1676) parenthetically excises – cuts – all the Fortinbras material in the final scene, because it, as the preface explicitly indicates, is the easiest to do without (as "least prejudicial to the Plot or Sense") of the staged events in a play that is in any case far too long. Hazelton Spencer was the first to observe this in "Hamlet under the Restoration," *PMLA* 38 (1923), 770–91: 777. Cf. Simon Jarvis, *Scholars and Gentlemen: Shakespearean Textual Criticism and Representation of Scholarly Labor, 1725–1765* (Oxford: Oxford University Press, 1995), 57.

18 See Ernest B. Gilman, *The Curious Perspective: Literary and Pictorial Wit in the Seventeenth Century* (New Haven, CT: Yale University Press, 1978). Gilman demonstrates a highly complicated arrangement, projected across an entire series of countervailing structural symmetries, which oscillate between "right" and "wry" points of view when they are properly reflected toward each other (126). Instead of thematizing the device, *Hamlet*'s anamorphosis privileges an exclusively ego-centered perspective at the expense of the crassly de-centered outside perspective. The result, more importantly, which is to be gained only against the grain of Gilman's useful explanation and is also not to be confused with similar "symbolic" uses like Christopher Pye, *The Regal Phantasm: Shakespeare and the Politics of Spectacle* (London: Methuen, 1990), is of a plot-organizing, rather than meaning-producing, nature; this was already Goethe's insight, whose *Wilhelm Meister* uses this insight for bringing *Hamlet* to the stage.

19 The legal-constitutional interpretation, which brings the events of *Hamlet* into a more precise focus, has been developed thanks to John Dover Wilson, summarized in his edition of the *New Cambridge Shakespeare*. Interestingly, Rosencrantz speaks of "the late innovations" (2.2.330), which according to Horst Breuer, *Notes and Queries 232.2* (1987), 212–15: 213, cast a politically ironic light on the transfer of power to Claudius. In Harry Levin's "Shakespearean Overplot," *Renaissance Drama* 8 (1965), 62–71, the general heading for this observation, the "overplot," is a means of dramatic irony, as in William Empson's "double plots" in *Some Versions of Pastoral* (London: Chatto & Windus, 1935).

20 Dover Wilson's commentary conceives the act in the formula: "Hamlet, in full council, receives 'the voice of the king himself for his succession.' It is a bid for acquiescence in the fait accompli" (150/151, ad 1.2.108/9). "The voice" – which in Wilson is a citation taken from the mouth of Rosencrantz (3.2.343) – is the equivalent of the dying voice, which Hamlet explicitly passes on to Fortinbras and which he can only transfer to him on the assumption of this legal basis: "He has my dying voice" (5.2.354).

21 G. Wilson Knight, praised by T.S. Eliot, comes first to mind, "The Embassy of Death," from *The Wheel of Fire* (Oxford: Oxford University Press, 1930/ London: Routledge, 1989), 17–49, but here the opposite is meant to follow from the fact, since character analysis of the melancholy man is the priority: "Hamlet's soul is sick" (with William James's *Varieties of Religious Experience* on the side). More remarkable, and entirely unconnected to the character question, seems to me C.S. Lewis' insistence, in his famous address "Hamlet: The Prince and the Poem" (1942), in *Selected Literary Essays* (Cambridge: Cambridge University Press, 1969), 88–105, on the death obsession underneath the character masks: the latency of death (*nocte tacentia late* – *Aeneid* 6.246, by the way), "but," more to the point, "a fear of *being* dead" (Lewis, 1942: 98/99, emphasis added).

22 For the advanced state of a "subjective solution," to be localized "in the

characterization of Hamlet himself" – a solution most prominent through its neo-Hegelian rationale – see Peter Alexander, *Hamlet, Father and Son* (Oxford: Clarendon Press, 1955), reviewed by Harry Levin, *The Question of Hamlet* (New York: Oxford University Press, 1959), 134 f.

23 Nicolas Abraham, "Le fantôme d'Hamlet ou le VIe acte," *L'écorce et le noyau* (Paris: Aubier-Flammarion, 1978), 449. For myself, I mainly share Abraham's starting presuppositions: "Si un fantôme revient hanter c'est pour mentir: ses prétendues 'révélations' sont mensongères par nature" (449). Hamlet's intermediate situation "entre une 'vérité' fallacieuse et imposée et une vérité 'vrai' que de longtemps l'Inconscient avait devinée" shows itself ineluctably in the first act, when he anticipates the ghost in his own reflections on the cold plates of the marriage feast and the manliness of the dead King, his father – reflections which follow according to the Freudian family plot. The latency of this highly comedic exchange between Hamlet and Horatio – from Hamlet's sudden intuition "methinks I see my father" to the affirmation "A was a man" (1.2.183, 187) – has been analyzed in greater detail by William Empson, *The Structure of Complex Words* (London: Chatto & Windus, 1951), 321–5. The latency ("pregnancy") is confirmed as something that Hamlet thinks he has always known and which, as an inkling, he systematically elaborates in this scene: "O my prophetic soul! My uncle!" (1.5.41).

24 Georg Friedrich Wilhelm Hegel, *Ästhetik*, ed. Friedrich Bassenge (Berlin: Aufbau Verlag, 1955, 1966), II: 581. Continuing Hegel's argument, Lacan puts specific emphasis on the semantics of the "foil" ("Desire and the Interpretation of Desire in Hamlet," *Yale French Studies* 55–6 (1977): 33). For the technical details of the plot, see James L. Jackson, "They Catch One Another's Rapiers," *Shakespeare Quarterly* 41 (1990), 281–98: 285. In Benjamin's analysis, the "vehement externality" of this ending has become specifically "characteristic of the *Trauerspiel*" as opposed to classical tragedy (I: 315; Engl. 137, trans. modified).

25 Stanley Cavell, "Hamlet's Burden of Proof" (1984), in *Disowning Knowledge in Six Plays of Shakespeare* (Cambridge: Cambridge University Press, 1987), 179–91, develops the *mise-en-abîme* of the dumb show to this conclusion. What spectrally haunts the play under the name of revenge is in the end revealed as the "destroyer of individual identity" (188).

26 The term lends itself almost immediately after its introduction to figurative uses: most generally, "to establish a claim in advance upon" and "hence *pass.* to be attached or pledged to something" (first use, according to the OED, 1530, first fig. use 1588). Shakespeare's own *Sonnet* 134 – "And I myself am mortgag'd to thy will" – includes in the many meanings of "will" not just the legal testament but, as in Joel Fineman's conclusion about the metaphorized negotiation involved: being "thus possessed, or repossessed." See *Shakespeare's Perjured Eye: The Invention of Poetic Subjectivity in the Sonnets* (Berkeley, CA: University of California Press, 1986), 284. What matters most, is the spectral implication within the figurative use of the term, which reinforces, like all

associations with the financial sphere, especially usury, a devilish touch that comes to bear even in the most cunning defenses like Francis Bacon's "Of Usury," with respect to "mortgaging," in *Essayes or Counsels, Civil and Moral*, ed. Michael Kiernan (Cambridge, MA: Harvard University Press, 1986), 126.

27 The point is missed in thematic discussions like Ewan Fernie, *Shame in Shakespeare* (London: Routledge, 2002), where the semantics of shame are taken for (psychologically) self-descriptive. No "instinctive Christian perspective" (112) is at stake and responsible for the delay; the shame is a sham, a masquerade that turns into an epistemological means. Thus Hamlet's pantomimed inscription of the ghost's command on the tables of his memory – "My tables. Meet it is I set it down" (1.5.107) – is ambivalent from the start, and Cavell is right in his assertion, made under the especially fitting title *Disowning Knowledge*, when he claims that Hamlet in this scene does anything but merely mime a obedient carrying out of the order: "[he] seems to go out of [his] way to show that the line [...] containing the line 'remember me' is *not* what he sets down in his tables" (184). I come to this in the next chapter.

28 So goes the complicated complex of suspicions that undoubtedly lasted for quite some time among those contemporary to the situation – something which becomes all the more apparent when read from the perspective of *Hamlet*. Far from reaching a satisfactory resolution, J.J. Scarisbrick's classic monograph on *Henry VIII* (Berkeley, CA: University of California Press, 1968) works through the various suspicions with admirable perceptiveness, even if he does not pursue the birth of Elizabeth – "probably the most unwelcome royal daughter and most celebrated woman in English history" (323) – into all of the convoluted details of succession regulations. The double annihilation of Anne Boleyn, in the annulment of her marriage simultaneous with her execution, points in the direction of the neuralgic moment through which Elizabeth remained consciously bound to her mother (350). Wherein it is more than interesting, and has rightly been the object of Scarisbrick's special emphasis, that also Elizabeth's half-sister and predecessor Mary was able to successfully establish herself in the succession through identification with her mother, thereby "with a terrible logic" driving her dead father like an evil spirit from the rest of his grave and destroying him literally in flames (497) – a kind of precedence that deserves to be pursued in *Hamlet*'s historical mortgage. Ironically, old Hamlet's ghost is like Henry returning from hell, where Elizabeth's sister and predecessor had brought him not by chance.

29 It was Helm Stierlin who named "delegation" the basis for any Oedipal framework, under the explicit title of *Delegation und Familie* (Frankfurt/M: Suhrkamp, 1978), and not without reference to Shakespeare (28). The older apparitions of the dead and the tasks they impose upon the living, secured the image of the father and along with it the patrimonial structure of the *familia*, studied by Jean-Claude Schmitt, *Les revenants: Les vivants et les morts dans la société médiévale* (Paris: Gallimard, 1994), 214 ff. As the father

leaves behind and commands the family, in *Hamlet* the "name of the father" forbids the mother. This is something Lacan made productive in a different way than Abraham, to the extent that the father, with the structure of the law behind him (which Lacan calls the "name of the father," embodying the incest-taboo), leaves behind a mortgage that is nothing other than the inheritance of his sins.

30 Nietzsche, *Die Geburt der Tragödie*, Neue Ausgabe (1886), in *Werke*, ed. Karl Schlechta (Munich: Hanser, 1966), I: 29, 30, 31, 33, 48, 130. Nietzsche introduces the motif of the "wise Silen" by way of King Midas (29), intensifies it in the complaint of Homer's Achilles (31) and then varies it throughout the entire text, with Hamlet as its culmination (30, 34, with Nietzsche's special emphases). Janet Adelman, *Suffocating Mothers* (New York: Routledge, 1992), adds the infantile fantasy that Shakespeare recapitulates (35), while the genealogy of a collective spectrality in which Nietzsche senses a primal scene is the theme of Jacques Derrida, *Spectres de Marx* (Paris: Galilée, 1993), among whose specters Marx's reading of *Hamlet* stands in first place (50), and whose underpinnings have been cleared up by Harries, *Scare Quotes from Shakespeare: Marx, Keynes, and the Language of Reenchantment* (Stanford, CA: Stanford University Press, 2000), 93 ff.

31 Nietzsche's Silen cites *Oedipus at Colonus*, where the sentence is not spoken by a Silen but by the chorus. And in Sophocles the sentence does not occur as a sudden insight but rather appears to be some popular, quasi-Dionysian wisdom (*Oedipus at Colonus* at 1224). The methodologically difficult question is to what extent this citation may have already been on Shakespeare's mind (whose education in classics is often underestimated for no good reason). Nietzsche could at least have been under this impression on the grounds of Hamlet's "Hyperion to a Satyr" comparison (1.2.40), in which Claudius figures as the satyr. The accent in Sophocles' choral song lies, however, entirely on the negation and not on the being of Oedipus. Freud, who may have had this in mind, turns Hamlet's insight back toward Sophocles to the extent that "Hamlet knows *that* he knows but not *what* he knows," as it has been superbly put by Julia Reinhard Lupton and Kenneth Reinhard, *After Oedipus: Shakespeare in Psycho-Analysis* (Ithaca, NY: Cornell University Press, 1993), 111. I can only briefly indicate here the importance of the fact that, on top of all of this, Hamlet utters the sentence in question to Ophelia. Whatever the case may be, Freud's Hamlet-thesis found its foothold in this passage, which went far beyond that which he found in it in his fixation on Oedipus: a quasi-Dionysian pretext for the whole Oedipus Complex, which Sophocles' choir attested, Nietzsche perceived, and, between the two of them, Shakespeare restaged. The complementary question is asked by Margareta de Grazia on the general occasion of "Soliloquies and wages in the age of emergent consciousness," *Textual Practice* 9 (1995), 67–92, where she emphasizes the complicated genre of multiple addressing that ties this monologue to the ghost. In both scenes, Hamlet seems to use the same kind of a *vademecum*, memorizing some logical *quodlibet* (74, 77). The rhetorical

refinement in the use of this *quodlibet* (particularly in Q2 compared to Q1), meticulously exposed by Marion Trousdale, *Shakespeare and the Rhetoricians* (London: Scholar Press, 1982), 58 ff. sharpens the fun for the experienced scholars in the audience. This amusement of the "richly varied" (60) would supply, along with the scholastic milieu, a humorous subtext of the reformed mentality of melancholy and motivate the quasi-Dionysian, "satiric" layer – Claudius as "satyr" – of *Hamlet* references to antiquity, a structure sustained in the canon-shaping capacity of Robert Burton's *Anatomy of Melancholy*.

32 Thus Lacan begins his investigation of "Desire and the Interpretation of Desire in Hamlet" with the "one shift" that would "distinguish [the plot] from previous treatments," namely, "the character Ophelia" (11) – a complication, which I put into brackets in this chapter, since – interestingly enough – Hamlet does not include his insight in Ophelia's role in his experiment. See Björn Quiring's treatment of the intricate, aporetic structure of speech-acting in that most exemplary case of the mousetrap, *Shakespeares Fluch: Die Aporien ritueller Exklusion im Königsdrama der englischen Renaissance* (Munich: Fink, 2009), 92 f.

33 A.C. Bradley, *Shakespearean Tragedy* (London: Macmillan, 1904, 1956): "This is surely," he underlines, "the most natural interpretation of the words of the ghost" (134) – by which forbidden jointure the ghost also and inversely forbids, and no less so, that "she was not privy to the murder of her husband." Following Bradley without going beyond him is John Dover Wilson, *What Happens in Hamlet* (Cambridge: Cambridge University Press, 1935, 1951), 292–4, and with the same qualification Jenkins' "Long Note" ad 1.5.42 (*Arden*, 455/56). Marc Shell approaches the question more radically in *Children of the Earth* (Cambridge, MA: Harvard University Press, 1993), 100: "Might Hamlet be the offspring of that incestuous union?" but for him the question remains a purely rhetorical one in the investigation of the motif of incest at the time, a generalization which leads him to see it as a conventional aspect of the Oedipal drama rather than, as I am claiming, the cancellation of this aspect. Cavell, as already indicated, had generalized Bradley's suspicion in the direction of Nietzsche: "that his father experienced Gertrude's annihilating power before him" (185).

34 This is the point where Claudius' name becomes captivating, less as a reminiscence of Seneca, but in view of Agrippina's role as a jointress for Nero, most prominently in the *Annals* of Tacitus (for the first time in English translation in 1598). After the model of Nero, Shell, in *Children of the Earth*, makes the incest-provocation in the bedroom-scene plastic, and reaches the following consequence worked out of Tacitus: "Gertrude in *Hamlet* may understand that her continued existence bars Hamlet from succeeding to the throne in chaste and non-murderous fashion, that is, that only her death would free Hamlet to succeed to the throne without incest" (108). For my own proposal of the anamorphosis of the plot, the relevant point is: "Hamlet identifies with his father *and* his uncle" (109). Hamlet is bound to identify with his uncle through the spirit of his father.

35 This is the by now almost proverbial dictum, with which Carl Schmitt began his *Politische Theologie* (Berlin: Duncker & Humblot, 1922, 1934, 1990), 11. It found its master in Benjamin's *Trauerspielbuch*, where Benjamin begins the chapter "Theory of Sovereignty" with the precise opposite gesture, that is: "The Sovereign represents history" (I: 245). For the Benjaminian context, compare the *Hamlet* essay of Samuel Weber, "Ibi et ubique: The Incontinent Plot," in *Theatricality as Medium* (New York: Fordham University Press, 2004), 181–99: 190 ff. Benjamin, though (and even less so Schmitt), did not have the jointress Gertrude in mind, to whom the sentence applies in a much deeper sense: The resulting product called History, which the sovereign represents, is made present and upheld by her; and through her it remains representable.

36 Marie Axton, *The Queen's Two Bodies: Drama and the Elizabethan Succession* (London: The Royal Historical Society, 1977), 29. Axton directs her theme against the scheme of Ernst Kantorowicz, whose *The King's Two Bodies* (Princeton, NJ: Princeton University Press, 1957) had used Shakespeare's *Richard II* to illustrate its thesis. We come to this a few chapters later. For the case at hand, Axton's problem is interestingly highlighted by Adriana Cavarero, *Corpo in figure: Filosofia e politica della corporeita* (Milano: Feltrinelli, 1995), who makes free use of Schmitt and Kantorowicz in order to show the gender-political symptomatics of the role of Ophelia in the figure of the "grotesque" body. This, however, cannot very well be the point, since Elizabeth provided the precise counter-image to a "body natural" distorted by "gender anxiety." It would be worthwhile to show that Ophelia, a failed Elizabeth before her assumption of the throne (that is, Elizabeth beneath her brother Edward, if Polonius and Laertes had succeeded), was fully aware of this.

37 The constant pressure that Elizabeth withstood over the years of the succession found historical expression, according to the excellent reading of Marie Axton, in Shakespeare's poem "The Phoenix and the Turtle," published in 1601 simultaneously with *Hamlet* in a collection with the telling title *Love's Martyr*. The pressure of succession has been impressively documented by John E. Neale, *Elizabeth I and her Parliaments* (London: Norton, 1953–57). Ever since she declared to her first parliament in 1559 that in the end it is "for me sufficient that a marble stone shall declare that a Queen, having reigned such time, lived and died a virgin," and the longer she held this improbable demand through the years, the more she and her loyal public became exposed to the torture that is called a martyrdom in *Love's Martyr* and is justified in Shakespeare's poem by recourse to higher reason. "Could a Sovereign," asks Sir Neale, impressed by the continual deepening of the problem, "have been in a more harassing situation? virtually isolated and under remorseless, if loyal pressure" (I: 49, 111)?

38 Alvin Kernan, *Shakespeare, the King's Playwright* (New Haven, CT: Yale University Press, 1995), has taken this speculation to the furthest extreme, but unfortunately only the fact of the performance and not the names of the plays

performed have come down to us (31). Kernan's procedure of starting with actual performances and their occasions is extremely illuminating, but it illuminates not least of all the Janus-face of newer historicisms, whose attentiveness to the conditions of first performances is accompanied by a negligence with respect to the status of the textual evidence – often with the crassest misunderstanding of their actual words. The fact that the postulated performance of *Hamlet* on Christmas Eve of 1603 would have been "one of the great moments in Western theater, a true coup de théâtre" (32) does not really prove that it took place; it instead proves the interest of a reading that literally bypasses the entire text, which in turn is historically surpassed in the reading imagined. Kernan proposes interestingly that the text could only have come into its own in a constellation like the one of 1603. The self-thematization of the "theater within a theater" would have come to the greatest conceivable historical effect in a confrontation of King Claudius with a real King (instead of the real Queen Elizabeth): "but what did James, watching from the other side of the stage, see in *Hamlet*?" Kernan asks, rightly at a loss as to the result of his experiment with which he seems to intend to complete Hamlet's experiment. The continuation is useful, if only in the negative: to the extent, that James would have seen as much (that is, as little) as Claudius saw, and it is precisely this little – no theatrical coup, but historical irony – which may illuminate Claudius' reaction in retrospect.

39 Kernan's book is a rather simplistic but nonetheless characteristic product of this trend, which culminates in his interpretation of *Macbeth*. Kernan has no aversion to declaring Shakespeare to be entirely dependent upon the aims of his patron: "he differed little from his fellow artists in his basic patronage work" (1995: 79). In *Hamlet*, Shakespeare is said to have come so close to the Stuarts that James would have felt himself truly understood by the play (I have no idea, and do not learn from him, how). Carl Schmitt's essay, *Hamlet oder Hekuba: Der Einbruch der Zeit in das Spiel* (Düsseldorf: Diederichs, 1956; Stuttgart: Klett-Cotta, 1985), had propagated an influential variant of this thesis. He essentially wrote an extension of Dover Wilson's commentary, in order to take the latter's preference for Essex (as a model for Hamlet) as a pretext for seeing *Hamlet* implied within James' preparation for the takeover of power and for finding the drama of Maria Stuart encrypted in *Hamlet*. The "Intrusion of Time" (Schmitt's title) cannot be had so easily. Heiner Müller, in a Shakespeare-lecture from 1988 in *Shakespeare Factory* 2 (Berlin: Wagenbach, 1994), states laconically: "The intrusion of time within the play is what constitutes myth" (229). Although it is easy to see why Schmitt would like to be able to pin down a premonition of "political theology" in *Hamlet*, James would in this view rather appear as its belated coda. In the meantime, Victoria Kahn has in an all-too-generous extension of Schmitt's reading, "Hamlet or Hecuba: Carl Schmitt's Decision," *Representations* 83 (2003), 67–96, indicated a consequence that also illuminates Heiner Müller's apt reaction, namely, that Hamlet in Schmitt's intervention "rises to the stature of tragic myth" (85). The

outcome, however, as clearly recognized by Kahn, "the necessity of a genuinely tragic decision in the face of a state of emergency" (85), betrays the – in the strictest sense of an Adorno as well as, in this case, Müller – ideological replacement of myth in the figure of a re-politicized "mythic analogue," as in the timely suggestion by Clemens Lugowski in his morphological study *Die Form der Individualität im Roman* (Berlin: Junker und Dünnhaupt, 1932), 10 ff.

40 In the Lacanian consequence – Lacan ends his seminar on this note ("Desire," 52) – the mother, who "does not have a penis," can – "precisely by virtue of this not-having" – "present herself as *being* the phallus;" thus "Jacques Lacan's Dislocation of Psychoanalysis" in the Benjaminian Samuel Weber's concise reformulation of a *Return to Freud* (1978), trans. Michael Levine (New York: Columbia University Press, 1991), 144. To this inkling of a "nothing," Late Shakespeare will return in *The Winter's Tale*'s "whispering of nothing."

3 Lethe's Wharf: Wild Justice, the Purgatorial Supplement

1 Hesiod, *Theogony*, ed. M.L. West (Oxford: Clarendon Press, 1966), 175 ad 55. See Pietro Pucci, *Hesiod and the Language of Poetry* (Baltimore, MD: Johns Hopkins University Press, 1977).
2 Juliana Schiesari, *The Gendering of Melancholy* (Ithaca, NY: Cornell University Press, 1992), 2, 49. See Andrew Hewitt, *Political Inversions* (Stanford, CA: Stanford University Press, 1996), 247.
3 Samuel Beckett, "Dante . . . Bruno. Vico . . . Joyce," in *Our Exagmination Round his Factification for Incamination of Work in Progress* (London: Faber and Faber, 1929, 1961, 1972), 22.
4 Ernst Kantorowicz's intuition for Hamlet's dramatic predecessor *Richard II* in *The King's Two Bodies* (Princeton, NJ: Princeton University Press, 1957), is echoed in Jacques Derrida's *Specters of Marx* (New York: Routledge, 1992).
5 Jacques Derrida, "The Time is Out of Joint," trans. Peggy Kamuf, in *Deconstruction is/in America*, ed. Anselm Haverkamp (New York: NYU Press, 1995), 14–38: 17 (in parentheses!): "I have often had the occasion to define deconstruction as that which is – [. . .] – at bottom of what happens or comes to pass [*ce qui arrive*]. It remains then to localize, determine what happens with what happens, when it happens."
6 Sir Francis Bacon, "Of Revenge," in *The Essayes or Counsels, Civill and Morall*, ed. Michael Kiernan (Cambridge, MA: Harvard University Press, 1985), 16–19, all in favor of "Publique *Revenges*" as, "for the most part, Fortunate," in the name of memory, i.e. "the Thorn, or Bryar, which prick, and scratch, because they can doe no other" (16/17).
7 Jonathan Bate, "Introduction," in *Titus Andronicus, Arden Shakespeare*, Third Series (London: Routledge, 1995), 4. See Heiner Müller's essential adaptation under the heading of "Anatomie Titus Fall of Rome: Ein Shakespeare-Kommentar" (1984), in *Shakespeare Factory* 2 (Berlin: Wagenbach, 1994),

125–225. Here, anatomy – as in *Anatomy of Melancholy* – takes the position aloft.
8 Kathy Eden, *Poetic and Legal Fiction in the Aristotelian Tradition* (Princeton, NJ: Princeton University Press, 1986), Appendix, "*Hamlet* and the Reaches of Aristotelian Tragedy," 179.
9 See here Walter Benjamin's correlation of "Allegory and Tragedy" in his *Ursprung des deutschen Trauerspiels* (1928), in *Gesammelte Schriften* I (Frankfurt/M: Suhrkamp, 1974); *The Origin of German Tragic Drama* (London: Verso, 1977), Part III.
10 Frances Yates, *The Art of Memory* (London: Routledge and Kegan Paul, 1966), 342.
11 Martin Harries, *Scare Quotes from Shakespeare: Marx, Keynes, and the Language of Reenchantment* (Stanford, CA: Stanford University Press, 2000), 18. In greater detail, Margreta de Grazia, *Hamlet without Hamlet* (Cambridge: Cambridge University Press, 2007), 41 ff.
12 Anthony D. Nuttall, *Two Concepts of Allegory: A Study of Shakespeare's The Tempest and the Logic of Allegorical Expression* (London: Routledge & Kegan Paul, 1967), 102.
13 Stanley Cavell, *Disowning Knowledge in Six Plays of Shakespeare* (Cambridge: Cambridge University Press, 1987), 184.
14 For the formula of "giving in to the Name of the Law," see Samuel Weber's memorable contribution to *Deconstruction and the Possibility of Justice*, "In the Name of the Law," *Cardozo Law Review* 11 (1990), 1515–38: 1538.
15 Georg Wilhelm Friedrich Hegel, *Phänomenologie des Geistes*, ed. Hans-Friedrich Wessels, Heinrich Clairmont (Hamburg: Meiner, 1988), 478–531; my translation or, rather, paraphrase, makes some use of J.B. Baillie's translation, G.W.F. Hegel, *The Phenomenology of Mind* (London: Macmillan, 1910 1931; New York: Harper & Row, 1967), and some of A.V. Miller's, *Phenomenology of Spirit* (Oxford: Oxford University Press, 1977).
16 Georg Wilhelm Friedrich Hegel, *Ästhetik*, ed. Friedrich Bassenge (Berlin: Aufbau Verlag, 1955, 1962), II: 581. See my essay "Melancholie und Anamorphose: Wilhelm Meister's Meisterstück," *Arcadia* 35 (2000), 137–49, Part III of *Hamlet, Hypothek der Macht* (Berlin: Kadmos, 2001, 2004), "Die Anamorphose des Subjekts."
17 See Emanuel Hirsch, "Die Beisetzung der Romantiker in Hegels Phänomenologie" (1924), reprinted in *Materialien zu Hegels Phänomenologie des Geistes*, ed. Hans Friedrich Fulda and Dieter Henrich (Frankfurt/M: Suhrkamp, 1973), 245–75.
18 In this passage, Hegel's text is extremely opaque and hyper-complex. Werner Hamacher "(The End of Art with the Mask)," in *Hegel after Derrida*, ed. Stuart Barnett (New York: Routledge, 1998), 105–30, 319–23, brings the context to the point, but he confuses Hamlet and Macbeth in the initial comparison of the *Phenomenology*, which can easily happen because Hegel uses no names, but is instead interested in the correspondence and within this,

the emergence of characterological motifs: thus the "childlike trusting" of the *Phenomenology*, in which the Orestes motif lives on – an implied reference to Herder's famous interpretation of *Hamlet* – can in view of the "Spirit of the father" only be Hamlet, whereas the ambiguous "sisters of fate" in *Macbeth*, who at the same time are brought into play, equal in their "deceitful" power the false ghost of the father, who "could just as well be the devil" (482) – and whom, as Hegel wants it, Hamlet evades at the tragic remainder-cost of his death.

4 *Richard II*, Bracton, and the End of Political Theology

1 For the difference I propose in the use of the concept of "ideology," see the classical study of the time, Karl Mannheim, *Ideologie und Utopie* (1929), 5th edn. (Frankfurt: Schulte-Bulmke, 1969), 56 ff., with ref. to Carl Schmitt, *Politische Romantik* (1919), 5th edn. (Berlin: Duncker & Humbolt, 1998). More specifically, James Q. Whitman, *The Legacy of Roman Law in the German Romantic Era* (Princeton, NJ: Princeton University Press, 1990), 66 ff.

2 Deborah Kuller Shuger, *Political Theologies in Shakespeare's England* (New York: Palgrave, 2001), 44, 131.

3 Carl Schmitt, *Politische Theologie: Vier Kapitel zur Lehre von der Souveränität* [1922, 1934], 5th ed. (Berlin: Duncker & Humblot, 1990), 49; *Political Theology: Four Chapters on the Concept of Sovereignty*, trans. George Schwab (Cambridge, MA: MIT Press, 1985), 36 (translation modified). Compare Heinrich Meier's exposition *Die Lehre Carl Schmitts: Vier Kapitel zur Unterscheidung Politischer Theologie und Politischer Philosophie* (Stuttgart: Metzler, 1994).

4 William Shakespeare, *Richard II*, ed. Peter Ure, Arden Shakespeare, Second Series (London: Methuen, 1956); but compare in the following also *King Richard II*, ed. John Dover Wilson, New Cambridge Shakespeare (Cambridge: Cambridge University Press, 1939), the edition quoted by both Kantorowicz and Carl Schmitt.

5 Ernst H. Kantorowicz, *The King's Two Bodies: A Study in Medieval Political Theology* (Princeton, NJ: Princeton University Press, 1957). The reception of this book in Shakespeare studies remained spurious and without much knowledge of the methodological debates to be discussed in the following. It has gained some momentum, however, with David Norbrook, "The Emperor's New Body: Richard II, Ernst Kantorowicz and the Politics of Shakespeare Criticism," *Textual Practice* 10 (1996), 329–57; and, more recently, Lorna Hutson, "Not the King's Two Bodies: Reading the Body Politic in Shakespeare's Henry IV," in *Rhetoric and Law in Early Modern Europe*, ed. Victoria Kahn, Lorna Hutson (New Haven, CT: Yale University Press, 2001), 166–89. Only in the context of the Agamben debate did Kantorowicz come finally into focus as well, as in Ken Jackson, "Is it God or the Sovereign Exception? Giorgio Agamben's Homo Sacer and Shakespeare's King John," *Religion and Literature* 38 (2006), 85–100.

6 Hans Blumenberg, *Die Legitimität der Neuzeit* (Frankfurt/M: Suhrkamp,

1966), as revised in a three-volume edition, whose first volume includes the Parts I–II under the title *Säkularisation und Selbstbehauptung* (Frankfurt/M: Suhrkamp, 1974), 113, 117; *The Legitimacy of the Modern World*, trans. Robert M. Wallace (Cambridge, MA: MIT Press, 1983), 98, 100 (translation modified).

7 Ernst H. Kantorowicz, "Mysteries of the State: An Absolutistic Concept and Its Late Medieval Origins" (1955), in *Selected Studies* (Locust Valley, NY: J.J. Augustin Publishers, 1965), 281–398.

8 Erik Peterson, *Der Monotheismus als politisches Problem: Ein Beitrag zur Geschichte der politischen Theologie im Imperium Romanum* (Leipzig: Hegner, 1935), repr. in *Theologische Traktate*, ed. Barbara Nichtweiß (Würzburg: Echter, 1994). See most recently Giorgio Agamben, *Le Règne et la gloire*. Homo sacer II.2 (Paris: Seuil, 2007), 37 ff.

9 Percy Ernst Schramm, "Sacerdotium und Regnum im Austausch ihrer Vorrechte," *Studi Gregoriani* 2 (1947), 403–57. See also his *Kaiser, Rom und Renovatio*, Studien der Bibliothek Warburg 17 (Leipzig: Teubner, 1929).

10 Jacob Taubes, letter to Schmitt (Paris, September 18, 1979), in Taubes, *Ad Carl Schmitt: Gegenstrebige Fügung* (Berlin: Merve, 1987), 43. See Odo Marquard's attempt at an overview of Blumenberg's position in the debate, "Aufgeklärter Polytheismus: auch eine politische Theologie?" in *Der Fürst dieser Welt*, ed. Jacob Taubes (Munich: Fink-Schöningh, 1983), 77–84: 79.

11 Carl Schmitt, *Politische Theologie II: Die Legende von der Erledigung jeder Politischen Theologie* (Berlin: Duncker & Humblot, 1970), 109; *Political Theology II*, trans. Michael Hoelzl and Graham Ward (Cambridge: Polity Press, 2008), "Postscript. On the Current Situation of the Problem: The Legitimacy of Modernity" (*nota bene*: Schmitt cites Blumenberg's precise title: *Neuzeit*).

12 Hans Blumenberg, *Ästhetische und metaphorologische Schriften*, ed. Anselm Haverkamp (Frankfurt/M: Suhrkamp, 2001), editor's afterword, "Die Technik der Rhetorik: Blumenbergs Projekt," 433–54: 446 ff.

13 Blumenberg, *Säkularisation und Selbstbehauptung*, 113; *The Legitimacy of the Modern World*, 98 (translation changed). For a more detailed account, see my essay "La sécularisation comme métaphore," *Transversalités* 87 (2003), 15–28; rewritten as "Säkularisation als Metaphor: Hans Blumenbergs Modernekritik," in *Diesseits der Oder: Frankfurter Vorlesungen* (Berlin: Kadmos, 2008), 53–64.

14 Anselm Haverkamp, "Stranger Than Paradise: Dantes irdisches Paradies als Antidot politischer Theologie," *Geschichtskörper: Zur Aktualitat von Ernst H. Kantorowicz*, ed. Wolfgang Ernst, and Cornelia Vismann (Munich: Fink, 1996), 93–103.

15 Giorgio Agamben, *Quel che resta di Auschwitz*, Homo sacer III (Torino: Bollati Boringhieri, 1998); unhappily translated as *Remnants of Auschwitz*, trans. Daniel Heller-Roazen (Stanford, CA: Stanford University Press, 1999). For the history of Hölderlin's "stiffening" of the sign and the motif of "what remains" [*quel que resta—was bleibet*] see Anselm Haverkamp, *Leaves of Mourning: Late Hölderlin*, trans. Vernon Chadwick (Albany, NY: SUNY Press, 1995), 72.

16 In Hans Kelsen's celebrated *Logos* essay, "Gott und Staat" (from *Logos* XI, 1922–23), *Staat und Naturrecht*, ed. Ernst Topitsch (Neuwied: Luchterhand, 1964/Munich: Fink, 1989), 29–55, which must be read as an explicit counter-statement against the false semantics of Carl Schmitt's *Political Theology*, notions like "Gott, Seele und Kraft" (54) belong to the older layer of "concepts of substance" [*Substanzbegriffe*], which is overcome in modernity and replaced by "concepts of function" [*Funktionsbegriffe*] – according to (and implicitly referring to) Ernst Cassirer's seminal distinction of *Substanzbegriff und Funktionsbegriff* (Berlin: Cassirer, 1910).

17 Giorgio Agamben, *Homo sacer: Il potere sovrano e la nuda vita* (Torino: Einaudi, 1995), 21; *Homo Sacer: Sovereign Power and Bare Life* (Stanford, CA: Stanford University Press, 1998), 15. See meanwhile also *Stato di ecceptione*, Homo sacer II.1 (Torino: Bollati Boringhieri, 2003); *Etat d'éxception* (Paris: Seuil, 2003).

18 See here and in the following the fundamental essay by Ewart Lewis, "King Above Law? 'Quod Principi Placuit' in Bracton," *Speculum* 39 (1964), 240–69: 265.

19 Thus John Dover Wilson's notes to *Richard II*, 4.1.113 (204). Derek Traversi sees in Richard "the downfall of a natural, sanctioned conception of royalty, and its replacement," which would explain the advent of Machiavellian princes in terms of fortune's wheel: of "formidable but unsanctioned political energy," in Traversi's *Shakespeare from Richard II to Henry V* (Stanford, CA: Stanford University Press, 1957), 12. The cyclic structure of Shakespeare's histories – from E.M.W. Tillyard, *Shakespeare's History Plays* (New York: Macmillan 1944) to Wolfgang Iser, *Shakespeares Historien* (Konstanz: Universitätsverlag, 1988) – appears to be an echo-effect of *fortuna*, in *Richard II*'s case of Ovid's *Tristia*, as suggested by Jonathan Bate, *Shakespeare and Ovid* (Oxford: Clarendon Press, 1993), 167.

20 In the meantime, Jennifer R. Rust, "Political Theology and Shakespeare Studies," *Literature Compass* 5 (2008), 1–17: 7, has put my argument into a wider research context. See in the meantime, after the completion of this book, two articles in the *Representations* spring issue of 2009 by Richard Halpern, "The King's Two Buckets: Kantorowicz, Richard II, and Fiscal Trauerspiel," *Representations* 106 (2009), 67–76; and Victoria Kahn, "Political Theology and Fiction in the King's Two Bodies," *Representations* 106 (2009), 77–101; as well as Zénon Luis-Martínez, "Historical Drama as Trauerspiel," *English Literary History* 75 (2008), 673–705; they all deserve more than formal acknowledgement.

21 See for the centrality of the motif Philip Lorenz, *The Tears of Sovereignty: Perspectives of Power in Renaissance Drama* Ph.D. diss. NYU, 2004, 161 ff. (to appear New York: Fordham University Press, 2010).

22 John Hayward, *The Life and Raigne of King Henrie IIII*, ed. John J. Manning (London: Royal Historical Society, 1991), 98. Cf. Raphael Holinshed, *The Historie of England* (1586/87), reprinted in the Appendix to Ure's edition (*Arden*, 187).

23 The last initiative in this respect, to which both Norbrook and Hutson subscribe, was Donna Hamilton's magisterial study "The State of Law in Richard II," *Shakespeare Quarterly* 34 (1983), 5–17. The evidence suffers, however, from historical inferences which remain to be investigated instead of taken for evident. See the very considerate presentation of the case by Louis Montrose, *The Purpose of Playing* (Chicago: University of Chicago Press, 1996), 69 ff.

24 Kantorowicz's use of the distinction of "tenor" and "vehicle" according to I.A. Richards' *Philosophy of Rhetoric* (New York: Oxford University Press, 1936), shows the student of poetics continued interest in rhetorical matters.

25 Walter Pater, "Shakespeare's English Kings," in *Appreciations* [1889], *Walter Pater, Three Major Texts*, ed. William E. Buckler (New York: NYU Press, 1986), 514. See also Iser, *Shakespeares Historien*, 106, 113.

26 Gerhart B. Ladner, "The Concepts of 'Ecclesia' and 'Christianitas' and their Relation to the Idea of Papal 'Plenitudo Potestatis,' " in *Sacerdozio e regno da Gregorio VII a Bonifacio VIII: Miscellanea Historiae Pontificae* 18 (1954), 49–77: 66. I shall come back to this with respect to *Macbeth*.

27 See Kantorowicz's classical presentation of *Kaiser Friedrich der Zweite* (Berlin: Georg Bondi, [1927] 1963), 210/11.

28 Carl Schmitt, *Hamlet oder Hekuba: Der Einbruch der Zeit in das Spiel* (Düsseldorf: Diederichs, 1956), 62 ff. But see in detail Samuel Weber, "Taking Exception to Decision: Walter Benjamin and Carl Schmitt," *Diacritics* 22 (1992), 5–18; included in his book *Benjamin's – abilities* (Cambridge, MA: Harvard University Press, 2008), 176–94. Also Agamben, *Stato di eccezione*, 72 ff; *État d'éxception*, 94 ff.

29 One of the many proto-Hegelian motifs in Shakespeare, in which the spirituality of a bygone era becomes the aesthetic model of modern reflection. Unfortunately, the editors of Hegel's lectures on *Aesthetics* do not attend to many of the implied references. But there is little doubt that Hegel, who knew Shakespeare by heart, may have had *Richard II* in mind.

30 For the patristic debate of the term, see Helmut Kohlenberger, "Wandel des Katechon," *Tumult* 25 (2001), 87–91; for Carl Schmitt's own use and context here, *Der Nomos der Erde im Völkerrecht des Jus Publicum Europaeum* (Berlin: Duncker & Humblot, 1950, 1997), 28 ff. Raphael Gross, *Carl Schmitt und die Juden* (Frankfurt/M: Suhrkamp, 2000), 292 f. points to the historical center of the term *katechon* as *Aufschub* – not without reference to Derrida's *différance* by the way – in Schmitt's article "Der Staat als ein konkreter, an eine geschichtliche Epoche gebundener Begriff" (1941), *Verfassungsrechtliche Aufsätze aus den Jahren 1924–1954* (Berlin: Duncker & Humblot, 1956), 375–85.

31 Hans Blumenberg, *Arbeit am Mythos* (Frankfurt/M: Suhrkamp 1979), 602–4; *Work on Myth*, trans. Robert M. Wallace (Cambridge, MA: MIT Press, 1985), 554–56. See Ruth Groh, *Arbeit an der Heillosigkeit der Welt: Zur politisch-theologischen Anthropologie Carl Schmitts* (Frankfurt/M: Suhrkamp, 1998), 156–84: 175 f. For Peterson's critique of Schmitt on this point, see Gross, *Schmitt und die Juden*, 288 ff.

32 For the implications of this divide, see Anselm Haverkamp, "The Enemy Has No Future," *Cardozo Law Review* 26 (2004/5), 1400–12, a metaphorological commentary on Carl Schmitt, *Der Begriff des Politischen* (Berlin: Duncker & Humblot, 1927, 1931, 1933, 1963); trans. Georges Schwab, *The Concept of the Political*, expanded edition (Chicago: University of Chicago Press, 2007). Of particular importance for Schmitt is Reinhart Koselleck, "Zur historisch-politischen Semantik asymmetrischer Gegenbegriffe," *Poetik und Hermeneutik* VI (1975), 65–104: 103; repr. in *Vergangene Zukunft: Zur Semantik geschichtlicher Zeiten* (Frankfurt/M: Suhrkamp 1987), 211–259: 258 f. *Futures Past: On the Semantics of Historical Time* (Cambridge MA: MIT Press, 1985).

33 Louis Marin, *La parole mangée et autres essais théologico-politiques* (Paris: Klincksiek, 1986). Barbara Vinken, "The Concept of Passion and the Dangers of the Theatre: Une esthétique avant la lettre (Augustine and Port Royal)," *Romanic Review* 83 (1992), 43–59.

34 Contrary to Alain Badiou's presentation of Paul's politics, *Saint Paul: la fondation de l'universalisme* (Paris: PUF, 1997), 66; trans. Ray Brassier, *Saint Paul: The Foundation of Universalism* (Stanford, CA: Stanford University Press, 2003), 59.

35 Ivan Nagel, *Autonomie und Gnade: Über Mozarts Opern*, 3rd edn. (Munich: Hanser 1988), 133. Compare Reinhard Koselleck, reader of Carl Schmitt with Tacitus as an antidote, *Kritik und Krise: Eine Studie zur Pathogenese der bürgerlichen Welt* (Freiburg: Alber, 1959/Frankfurt/M: Suhrkamp, 1973), 58 ff; *Critique and Crisis: Enlightenment and the Pathogenesis of Modern Society* (Cambridge, MA: MIT Press, 1988).

36 E.K. Chambers, *William Shakespeare: A Study of Facts and Problems* (Oxford: Clarendon Press, 1930), II: 326. The utterance, obliquely documented, remains obscure.

37 Another anecdote of unclear proportions. Kenneth Muir, for example, muses in his *John Milton* (London: Longman, 1955, 1960), 22, about "Milton's discreditable sneer at Charles I for reading Shakespeare's plays in prison." Interestingly, Milton's "On Shakespeare. 1630" (first published as "Epitaph" to the Second Folio of 1632) ended with "And so Sepulcher'd in such tomb dost lie [i.e., in the monumental Folio]/ That Kings for such a Tomb would wish to die." The use of "sepulchered" and rhyme on "lie" indicate a theatrical function of the precursor for the sake of royal representation (including the ambition of young Milton), which took a conscientiously different turn in Milton's later career.

38 The relevant use of the term *arcana imperii* occurs in Tacitus, *Annales* 2.36.1, where it implicitly refers back to the exemplary *primum facinus* of the new principate 1.6.1, the usurpation of Augustus's successor Tiberius, beginning his succession with the murder of his competitor, Agrippa Postumus. See Ronald Syme, *Tacitus* (Oxford: Clarendon Press, 1958), I: 306, 399, II: 485.

39 Charles H. McIlwain, ed., *The Political Works of James I* (Cambridge, MA: Harvard University Press, 1918), 332, quoted by Kantorowicz, "Mysteries

of the State," 266. Note that James's very translation of *arcana imperii* as "Mysteries of the State" shifts the emphasis from the profane sphere of political *arcana* to the theological meaning of the competing Latin term *mysterium*.

40 Christoph Menke, "Gnade und Recht: Carl Schmitts Begriff der Souveränität" (1997), in *Spiegelungen der Gleichheit* (Berlin: Akademie Verlag, 2000/Frankfurt/M: Suhrkamp, 2004), 300–323: 317 ff. (173 ff.); "Mercy and Law: Carl Schmitt's Concept of Sovereignty," *Reflections of Equality* (Stanford, CA: Stanford University Press, 2006), 177–97: 191 ff.

5 The Death of a Shifter: Jupiterian History in *Julius Caesar*

1 As reviewed by Jennifer R. Rust, "Political Theology and Shakespeare Studies," *Literature Compass* 5 (2008), 1–17, with respect to the outcome of the preceding chapter.
2 *Shakespeare's Plutarch*, ed. T.J.B. Spencer (London: Penguin, 1964), here "The Life of Julius Caesar," 26/27.
3 See the latest supplement to Heinrich Meier's *Die Lehre Carl Schmitts: Vier Kapitel zur Unterscheidung Politischer Theologie und Politischer Philosophie* (Stuttgart: Metzler, 1994, 3rd edn. 2009), 269–300: "Der Streit um die Politische Theologie – Ein Rückblick."
4 Michel Foucault, *"Society Must Be Defended": Lectures at the Collège de France 1975–1976* (New York: Picador, 2003), 34 ff.
5 The only one among Dumézil's numerous works that has been translated is the late summary *Archaic Roman Religion*, 2 vols. (Baltimore, MD: The Johns Hopkins University Press, 1996), including an abstract of the most exemplary *Jupiter, Mars, Quirinus* (Paris: Gallimard, 1941) and its successors. The influence of Dumézil on Foucault is documented throughout the Foucault biography by Didier Eribon (Paris: Flammarion, 1989).
6 The appropriate etymological account is to be found in Emile Benveniste, *Le Vocabulaire des institutions indo-européennes* (Paris: Minuit, 1969), II: 267–73. Against the grain of Benveniste's preference for reading as the underlying force in *religio* – "le rapport entre *religio* et *legere*" (271) – I give priority to the double-binding force of *re-ligio* in a reading rebound in and by the binding: "l'explication de *religio* par *religare*" (272).
7 I am indebted in this point to the clarifying exposition of the problem by Friedrich Balke, "Die Maske des Kriegers: Foucault, Dumézil und das Problem der Souveränität," *Deutsche Vierteljahrsschrift für Literaturwissenschaft und Geistesgeschichte* 80 (2006), 128–70.
8 In the sense of Julia Reinhard Lupton, *Citizen-Saints: Shakespeare and Political Theology* (Chicago: Chicago University Press, 2005), 208 ff.
9 Lisa Jardine and Anthony Grafton, "Studied for Action: How Gabriel Harvey Read his Livy," *Past and Present* 129 (1990), 30–78.
10 Stephen Greenblatt, *Shakespearean Negotiations* (Berkeley, CA: University of California Press, 1988), vii. As Greenblatt specifies, "shared contingency" or, more to the point, the continual sharing of contingencies has found in the

institution of the Renaissance theatre a very congenial place of negotiation: it redefines the place of Quirinus between Jupiter and Mars. Shakespeare adds to the general "humanist" sense of the time called "Renaissance" a historical exemplarity, that is, he creates "history" in a new fashion as the most common place of political negotiation.

11 Stanley Cavell, "Coriolanus and Interpretations of Politics" (1980), in *Disowning Knowledge in Six Plays of Shakespeare* (Cambridge: Cambridge University Press, 1987), 143–77: 145.

12 See in a most exemplary fashion, Coppelia Kahn, *Roman Shakespeare: Warriors, Wounds, and Women* (London: Routledge, 1997).

13 See the politically apt distinction between *skopos* and *telos* in Samuel Weber, *Targets of Opportunity* (New York: Fordham University Press, 2006), 6 ff.

14 Even a more considerate account like Arthur Humphreys' Introduction to *The Oxford Shakespeare*'s edition of *Julius Caesar* (Oxford: Clarendon Press, 1984) cannot but repeat: "Nearly all the significant components of the play derive from . . . North's Plutarch" (8), only in order to specify in the following pages again and again that passages like "Brutus' enigmatic soliloquy . . . has no Plutarchan precedent" at all (12). We have come to realize that not everything in Shakespeare without nominal "precedent" is sheer invention.

15 Ronald Syme, *The Crisis of 2 B.C.* In Proceedings *Bayerische Akademie der Wissenschaften 1974, Philosophisch-historische Klasse*, 7 (Munich: Beck, 1974), last pages.

16 David Daniell, Introduction to *Julius Caesar, Arden Shakespeare*, Third Series (London: Nelson, 1998/Thompson, 2003), 25.

17 Oliver Arnold, *The Third Citizen: Shakespeare's Theater and the Early Modern House of Commons* (Baltimore, MD: The Johns Hopkins University Press, 2007), 14.

18 Andreas Kalyvas, "The Tyranny of Dictatorship: When the Greek Tyrant Met the Roman Dictator," *Political Theory* 35 (2007), 412–42: 420 f.

19 Paul Cantor, *Shakespeare's Rome: Republic and Empire* (Ithaca, NY: Cornell University Press, 1976). I do, however, agree with Cantor's contention that there is serious history at stake in *Julius Caesar*. Consequently, there is no Greek "conserving esotericism" to be registered and resisted, as Geoff Waite fears in his tableau of "Heidegger, Schmitt, Strauss: The Hidden Monologue, or, Conserving Esotericism to Justify the High Hand of Violence," *Cultural Critique* 69 (2008), 114–44.

20 Much more than Hugh Grady will allow in his assessment of *Shakespeare, Machiavelli, and Montaigne: Power and Subjectivity from Richard II to Hamlet* (Oxford: Oxford University Press, 2002), 44 ff. Jardine and Grafton (not cited by Grady) are right to stress the vicissitudes of Machiavellian readings as opposed to the simple progress from providence to the contingencies of luck.

21 Again, I am referring to the "Logic of Sovereignty," in Giorgio Agamben's in *Homo sacer: Il potere sovrano e la nuda vita* (Torino: Einaudi, 1995); trans.

Daniel Heller-Roazen, *Homo Sacer: Sovereign Power and Bare Life* (Stanford, CA: Stanford University Press, 1998), part I. For the anagrammatical return of the repressed – that most Roman mode of inscription – in Agamben and Benjamin, see my essay "Anagrammatics of Violence: The Benjaminian Ground of Homo Sacer," in *Politics, Metaphysics, and Death: Essays on Giorgio Agamben's Homo Sacer*, ed. Andrew Norris (Durham, NC: Duke University Press, 2005), 135–44.

22 Matthew Fox, *Roman Historical Myths: The Regal Period in Augustan Literature* (Oxford: Clarendon Press, 1996), 96 ff.

23 Georges Dumézil, *Fêtes romaines d'été et d'automne* (Paris: Gallimard, 1975), 141 ff. and 179 ff.

24 Ronald Syme, *The Roman Revolution* (Oxford: Clarendon Press, 1939), 59. Syme is famous among historians for his mastery of the prosopographic method; but what makes him truly exemplary for the purpose at hand is not the celebrated positivism of Syme's results, but the refinement of the readings grounding these results.

25 See William W. Batstone, and Cynthia Damon, *Caesar's Civil War* (Oxford: Oxford University Press, 2006), 136 ff.

26 Anselm Haverkamp, "Arcanum Translationis: Das Fundament der lateinischen Tradition," *Tumult* 30 (2006), 19–30.

27 Ernst Kantorowicz, "Mysteries of the State: An Absolutistic Concept and its Late Medieval Origins" (1953), *Selected Studies* (Locust Valley, NY: Augustin Publishers 1965), 281–398.

28 Naomi Conn Liebler, "Thou Bleeding Piece of Earth: The Ritual Ground of Julius Caesar," *Shakespeare Studies* 14 (1981), 175–96: 182.

29 Georg Wilhelm Friedrich Hegel, *Grundlinien der Philosophie des Rechts*, ed. Johannes Hoffmeister (Hamburg: Meiner, 1955), § 282; trans. T.M. Knox, *Hegel's Philosophy of Right* (Oxford: Oxford University Press, 1952), 186.

30 David Shotter, *The Fall of the Roman Republic* (London: Routledge, 1994), 85. One might go so far as to say Shakespeare's presentation, far from being imagination, had become history in the meantime.

31 See Richard Halpern, *Shakespeare Among the Moderns* (Ithaca, NY: Cornell University Press, 1997), 88 ff.

32 The structure of "giving in to the name" according to Samuel Weber, "In the Name of the Law," *Cardozo Law Review* 11 (1990), 1515–38.

33 Jonathan Goldberg, *James I and the Politics of Literature* (Baltimore, MD: The Johns Hopkins University Press, 1983), 168 ff. (my modification). Goldberg's fabulous critique of ideology suffers from, not to say thrives upon, and enjoys itself within – that is Foucault's point – the truthfully reproduced "sovereignty trap."

34 John Henderson, "XPDNC: Writing Caesar" (1996), in his *Fighting for Rome: Poets & Caesars, History & Civil War* (Cambridge: Cambridge University Press, 1998), 37–69, especially 48 ff.

35 Michel Serres, *Le Livre des foundations* (Paris: Grasset & Fasquelle 1983), 111;

trans. as *Rome: The Book of Foundations* (Stanford, CA: Stanford University Press, 1991), 124.

36 John Henderson, "On Getting Rid of Kings: Horace, Satires I.7" (1994), in *Fighting for Rome*, 73–107: 107. Brutus "holds us," let me add, as in some photographic moment of old, which is recalled, not without Roman traces, in Roland Barthes, *Camera Lucida* (New York: Hill & Wang, 1981), § 23, 55 ff.

37 See Margreta de Grazia, *Hamlet without Hamlet* (Cambridge: Cambridge University Press, 2007), 67 ff. after Stephen Orgel's perceptiveness of *The Authentic Shakespeare and Other Problems of the Early Modern Stage* (New York: Routledge, 2002), 241 ff.

38 Hans Jonas, *Gnosis und spätantiker Geist* (1934), citing "pseudomorphosis" according to Oswald Spengler, *Der Untergang des Abendlandes* (1920). See Hans Blumenberg's review article on Hans Jonas, "Epochenschwelle und Rezeption," *Philosophische Rundschau* 6 (1958), 94–119.

39 I adapt the term "speech situation" from Blumenberg's analysis of the literary avant-garde of the 20th century, "Sprachsituation und immanente Poetik" (1966), *Ästhetische und metaphorologische Schriften*, ed. Anselm Haverkamp (Frankfurt/M: Suhrkamp 2000), 120–35.

40 Elaine Fantham, "Caesar against Liberty? An Introduction," in *Caesar Against Liberty: Perspectives on his Autocracy*, ed. Francis Cairns and Elaine Fantham, PLLS [Papers of the Liverpool/Leeds/Langford Latin Seminars] 11 (Cambridge: Francis Cairns 2003), 1–18: 4.

41 Kurt A. Raaflaub, "Caesar the Liberator? Factional Politics, Civil War, and Ideology," in *Caesar Against Liberty*, 34–67: 65 ff. I am grateful to have heard, in the meantime, Joy Connolly's paper "Fear, Freedom, and the Right to Lie" on the younger Pliny's *Panegyricus*, a work that exhibits cleverly the new rules of speech a century later.

42 For the exemplary event of the *Bellum Catilinae* Ronald Syme's monograph *Sallust* (Berkeley, CA: University of California Press, 1964), ch. VI. A.J. Woodman, in the Introduction to his translation of *Catiline's War* &c. (London: Penguin, 2007), xvii, gives a pointed presentation of the historiographical method, which from Sallust via Tacitus informs Shakespeare's reception of Roman exemplarity: "the 'discovery' of what requires to be said in a given situation, the implied theory being that this is 'somehow' already there though *latent*" (xxiv, emphasis added); Woodman cites the rhetorical authority of D.A. Russell who, however, in his celebrated essay "Rhetoric and Criticism" from *Greece & Rome* 14 (1967), reiterates the modernist fallacy of discarding the "latent" as mere rhetoric (135). Writing and staging what is latent in history is what happens in *Julius Caesar* as well as in *Hamlet*.

43 Miriam Griffin, "Clementia after Caesar: From Politics to Philosophy," in *Caesar Against Liberty*, 157–82: 167 ff.

44 Ronald Syme's prominent title, *The Roman Revolution* (1939), refers back to

Theodor Mommsen's first use of the term, *Römische Geschichte* (vol. 1, 1855), whose preference for the word "revolution" was decisive and had been confirmed in Jacob Burckhardt's enormously influential late lecture series *Weltgeschichtliche Betrachtungen* (1868, 1st ed. 1905).

6 The Future of Violence: Machiavelli and Macbeth

1 The material of this chapter is in parts identical to another piece, "The gesture of execution," which deals not with the subject of "violence" but with that of "positing." Violence, as the medium of positing, touches upon problems that are of a representational logic and that result from the proto-syntactical questions of positing; the application in this sense is "illustration" in the technical sense of *enargeia* or *evidentia*: it strives to recapitulate the logic of representation of the object of "violence" and their futurity follows the demands that are at work in Machiavelli's and Shakespeare's texts. This aspect I find missing or in any case underrated in the static logic of representation reconstructed in Pierre Legendre's theory of "uncrossable distance," *Dieu au miroir: Études sur l'institution des images* (Paris: Fayard, 1994), Chapter I: 59; English trans. "Introduction to the Theory of the Image," in *Law and the Unconscious: A Legendre Reader*, ed. Peter Goodrich (London: Macmillan, 1997), 211–254: 228.
2 C.T. Onions, *A Shakespeare Glossary*, enlarged and rev. ed. Robert D. Eagleson (Oxford: Clarendon Press, 1986), 161: "intriguer, unscrupulous schemer."
3 Phyllis Rackin, *Stages of History: Shakespeare's English Histories* (Ithaca, NY: Cornell University Press, 1990), 74–76.
4 See, for example, Garry Wills, *Witches and Jesuits: Shakespeare's Macbeth* (New York: Oxford University Press, 1995). Alvin Kernan, *Shakespeare, the King's Playwright: Theater in the Stuart Court, 1603–1613* (New Haven, CT: Yale University Press, 1995), 77–80. Alan Sinfield, "*Macbeth:* History, Ideology and Intellectuals," *Critical Quarterly* 28 (1986), 63–77, adds the useful distinction, which is overthrown in the play and in fact shown to be an indifference, between state-supporting violence and state-destroying violence.
5 Jacques Derrida, *L'Écriture et la différence* (Paris: Seuil, 1967); "The Theater of Cruelty and the Closure of Representation" (1967), *Writing and Difference*, trans. Alan Bass (Chicago: University of Chicago Press, 1978), 232–94: 233, 236.
6 Claude Lefort, *Le travail de l'œuvre machiavel* (Paris: Gallimard, 1972, 1986), 259. Leo Strauss, *Thoughts on Machiavelli* (Glencoe, IL: Free Press/Chicago: University of Chicago Press, 1958), 176.
7 Niccolò Machiavelli, *The Prince*, trans. George Bull (London/New York: Penguin, 2005), 28. See the very common, but ridiculously naïve, presentation of the case by Harvey C. Mansfield, *Machiavelli's Virtue* (Chicago: University of Chicago Press, 1966), 186 f.
8 See Robert Hariman, "Composing Modernity in Machiavelli's 'Prince'," *Journal of the History of Ideas* 50 (1989), 3–29: 8.
9 Italian terms according to the original Niccolò Machiavelli, *Il principe*, nuova

edizione a cura di Giorgio Inglese (Torino: Einaudi, 1995), 45–47. For the "Fullness of Power" translated by R.W. Dyson see his edition of (so-called) Giles of Rome's *On Ecclesiastical Power* (New York: Columbia University Press, 2005), Introduction, xxvi. As the title of Aegidius Romanus' treatise *De ecclesiastica potestate* (elaborated around 1300) silently indicates, and Machiavelli's use ironically implies and reinforces, the specific point of the divine *plenitudo* lent to the pope is a principle to be applied occasionally only, and it is the specific *occasio* that informs the application of this term in this case and makes it exemplary, the *exemplum* to be stated and, that is, from now on, to be staged. See in the meantime also Giorgio Agamben, *Le règne et la gloire*, Homo sacer II.2 (Paris: Seuil, 2007), 158 ff.

10 John Freccero, "Medusa and the Madonna of Forli," *Machiavelli and the Dicourse of Literature*, ed. Albert Russell Ascoli, and Victoria Kahn (Ithaca, NY: Cornell University Press, 1993), 161–78: 166 ff. As well as Anselm Haverkamp, "Leo in nubibus: Dantes Allegorie der Dichter, Widerlegung der politischen Theologie" (1996), *Diesseits der Oder: Frankfurter Vorlesungen* (Berlin: Kadmos 2008), 37–41, for a reconstruction of Dante's model of a poetics that would literally "destroy" political theology (*interemit* is Dante's word). The poetical trajectory leads from Dante's Montefeltro via Machiavelli's Borgia to Shakespeare's Macbeth.

11 Roland Barthes, "Le discours de l'histoire" (1967), in *Essais critiques* II (Paris: Seuil, 1972). "The Discourse of History," *New Critical Essays*, trans. Richard Howard (New York: Hill and Wang, 1980).

12 Victoria Kahn, *Machiavellian Rhetoric: From the Counter-Reformation to Milton* (Princeton, NJ: Princeton University Press, 1994), 34. The translation of the term is awkward, as explained but not solved in the American edition of Jürgen Habermas's *Strukturwandel der Öffentlichkeit* (1962); *The Structural Transformation of the Public Sphere*, trans. Thomas Burger (Cambridge, MA: MIT Press, 1989), translator's note, xv.

13 Quentin Skinner, *Reason and Rhetoric in the Philosophy of Hobbes* (Cambridge: Cambridge University Press, 1996), 170, who does, however, counter the missing irony of Mansfield's *Machiavelli's Virtue* effectively enough.

14 Lefort, whom Skinner and Kahn ignore, alludes to this in his paraphrase (*Le travail*, 345); Kahn refers to the rhetorical-theoretical context from Ramus to Bacon; however, she mentions only "Machiavellian fraud" and with this speaks only to the rhetorical "threat," not to the analytical achievement of the "redescription" (*Machiavellian Rhetoric*, 114).

15 Carl Schmitt, *Politische Theologie: Vier Kapitel zur Lehre von der Souveränität* (Berlin: Duncker & Humblot, 1920, 1934, 1990), 49; trans. George Schwab, *Political Theology: Four Chapters on the Concept of Sovereignty* (Cambridge, MA: MIT Press, 1985), 36. For the rhetorical function of the miracle in Schmitt's context, see Anselm Haverkamp, "The Enemy Has No Future," *Cardozo Law Review* 26.6 (2004/5), 101–9: 102.

16 See already the young Hegel's sharp judgment, "Die Verfassung Deutschlands"

(1802), in *Hegels Schriften zur Politik und Rechtsphilosophie*, ed. Georg Lasson (Hamburg: Meiner 1913), 114 f.; "The German Constitution" *Hegel: Political Writings*, ed. Laurence Dickey, and H.B. Nisbet (Cambridge: Cambridge University Press, 1999), 82 f. Hegel refuses Machiavelli's theory of Borgia's bad luck but sees his borrowed legitimacy as constitutive of the Borgia pope's illegitimate son's failure.

17 Carl Schmitt, *Politische Romantik* (Berlin: Duncker & Humblot, 1919, 1925, 1998), 18, 92.
18 Walter Benjamin, *Ursprung des deutschen Trauerspiels* (1928), in *Gesammelte Schriften* I (Frankfurt/M: Suhrkamp, 1974), 392–93 (Baroque citations in italics); *The Origin of German Tragic Drama*, trans. John Osborne (London: Verso, 2003), 218/19 (translation modified where appropriate).
19 Giorgio Agamben's felicitous citation from Benjamin's "Critique of Violence," in *Homo sacer: Il potere sovrano e la nuda vita* (Torino: Einaudi, 1995), 115; *Homo Sacer: Sovereign Power and Bare Life* (Stanford, CA: Stanford University Press, 1998), 102.
20 All quotes according to Kenneth Muir's *Macbeth* edition, *Arden Shakespeare*, Second Series (London: Methuen, 1951).
21 Walter Benjamin, "Zur Kritik der Gewalt" (1921), in *Gesammelte Schriften* II (Frankfurt/M: Suhrkamp, 1977), 188; "Critique of Violence," trans. Edmund Jephcott, *Selected Writings* I (Cambridge, MA: Harvard University Press, 1996), 236–52: 239.
22 See Malcolm Evans, *Signifying Nothing: Truth's True Contents in Shakespeare's Texts* (Athens, GA: University of Georgia Press, 1986, 1989), 115 f. Harry Berger, *Making Trifles of Terrors: Redistributing Complicities in Shakespeare* (Stanford, CA: Stanford University Press, 1997), 75–7.
23 Emrys Jones, *Scenic Form in Shakespeare* (Oxford: Clarendon Press, 1971), 224, is right to emphasize the pointed contrast to *Richard III*.
24 James I, *The Trew Law of Free Monarchie* and also his *Basilikon Doron*, after Muir's paraphrases, introduction, *Arden*, lvii and lxiii.
25 See the famous article by Cleanth Brooks, "The Naked Babe and the Cloak of Manliness," in *The Well Wrought Urn: Studies in the Structure of Poetry* (New York: Harcourt, Brace & World, 1947), 22–49: 40, 41, 46, 49.
26 Harold C. Goddard, *The Meaning of Shakespeare* (Chicago: University of Chicago Press, 1951, 1960), II: 111.
27 See Stanley Cavell, *Disowning Knowledge in Six Plays of Shakespeare* (Cambridge: Cambridge University Press, 1987), 183.
28 It is a crass misapprehension of the emblematic moment of violence and not a good explanation of the situation when Quentin Skinner and Russell Price, in their edition of the *Principe* in the series of Cambridge Texts in the History of Political Thought (Cambridge: Cambridge University Press, 1988), describe the "due pezzi" in which Remirro d'Orco ends up as "probably decapitated."
29 Arthur Melville Clark, *Murder Under Trust: The Topical Macbeth and Other Jacobean Matters* (Edinburgh: Scottish Academic Press, 1981), 109.

30 Georg Wilhelm Friedrich Hegel, *Phenomenology of Spirit*, trans. A.V. Miller (Oxford: Oxford University Press, 1977), 446. See Chapter 3 on Lethe in this volume.
31 For the genealogical implication and transformation of the Roman "Fates" [*fata*], see Pierre Legendre, "Hermes and Institutional Structures: An Essay on Dogmatic Communication" (1993), in *Law and the Unconscious*, 137–63: 143, where the Fates' work is defined as "the speech which manufactures persons" [*personae*].
32 The gender- and family-political motifs of Lady Macbeth would deserve the elaboration – up until the fascistic, biopolitical consequences – that is still as good as absent. By no means is it as A.C. Bradley famously stated and carried to extremes in his criticism. "Whether Macbeth had children or (as seems usually to be supposed) had none, is quite immaterial," he wrote in *Shakespearean Tragedy* (London: Macmillan, 1904), 414, 421. He is admittedly right in doubting the lady's pathos, the false emphasis of "I have given suck" [1.7.54]. For this sentence makes the imagined child murder plausible only in the *irrealis* and cannot be imagined as a real project. It is absolutely decisive that Lady Macbeth (as Goethe suggested in a remarkable pun to Eckermann) deploys some sort of (rhetorical) "over-conception" [*Über-Zeugung*] – without of course bringing along her husband for this conception – that the king's murder implies another politics of reproduction through violence. Though this does not yet imply the biopolitical consequence itself, it exposes the medial condition of possibility: the literalization of the rights of blood and of the metaphor of blood-ties from the noble family politic to the violence of a consortium of murderers. A prophecy that led to Marinetti's grotesque, futuristic designs, as Barbara Spackman has usefully exposed, *Fascist Virilities: Rhetoric, Ideology, and Social Fantasy in Italy* (Minneapolis MN: University of Minnesota Press, 1996), 21, 24.
33 Thus, for example, Paul A. Cantor, *Macbeth und die Evangelisierung Schottlands* (Munich: Privatdruck Carl Friedrich von Siemens Stiftung, 1993), 54–7.
34 Christoph Menke, *Tragödie im Sittlichen: Gerechtigkeit und Freiheit nach Hegel* (Frankfurt/M: Suhrkamp, 1996), 23–5; continued in his Hamlet essay "Tragödie und Skepsis" (2001), in *Die Gegenwart der Tragödie* (Frankfurt/M: Suhrkamp, 2005), 61 ff.
35 See Anselm Haverkamp, "How to Take It (and Do the Right Thing): Violence and the Mournful Mind in Benjamin's Critique of Violence," *Cardozo Law Review* 13 (1991), 1159–71.
36 Martin Harries, *Scare Quotes from Shakespeare: Marx, Keynes, and the Language of Reenchantment* (Stanford, CA: Stanford University Press 2000), 132 ff.
37 Ulrich Beck, *Die Erfindung des Politischen: Zu einer Theorie reflexiver Modernisierung* (Frankfurt/M: Suhrkamp, 1993), 254. For the term "Risikopolitik," see also his *Risikogesellschaft* (Frankfurt/M: Suhrkamp, 1986).
38 Hartmut Böhme, "Gewalt im 20. Jahrhundert: Demozide in der Sicht von Erinnerungsliteratur, Statistik und qualitativer Sozialanalyse," *Figurationen:*

Gender Literatur Kultur, No. 0 (1999), 139–57: 141. Böhme's seductive presentation has overpowering aspects, under whose superiority the possibility of every consequence evaporates – including the particular detail. Within this excessiveness, statistics appears as the equivalent of futurity, its quasi "transcendental" horizon (that is, as is well known, "without any measure" according to Kant). Bodiless, it appears as the ghost, that drives history.

7 A Whispering of Nothing: *The Winter's Tale*

1 Heinrich Heine, *Deutschland – Ein Wintermärchen* (1844), in *Sämtliche Schriften*, ed. Klaus Briegleb (Munich: Hanser, 1968–76) IV, commentary: 1015, 1016 (unfortunately without explanation of the – very common at the time – Shakespeare allusion).
2 Wolfgang Preisendanz, *Humor als dichterische Einbildungskraft* (Munich: Fink Verlag. 1963), 126 ff. Anselm Haverkamp, "Humor: Latenz der Form," *Deutsche Vierteljahrsschrift für Literaturwissenschaft und Geistesgeschichte* 76 (2002), 171–80: 179.
3 See Christoph Menke, *Die Gegenwart der Tragödie: Versuch über Urteil und Spiel* (Frankfurt/M: Suhrkamp, 2005), Excursus on tragic irony.
4 See the concise overview in Stephen Orgel's Introduction to the Oxford edition, *The Winter's Tale* (Oxford: Clarendon Press, 1996), 2 ff.
5 Northrop Frye, *A Natural Perspective: The Development of Shakespearean Comedy and Romance* (New York: Columbia University Press, 1965), 113 (my additions). Slightly before Frye, C.L. Barber's *Shakespeare's Festive Comedy* (Princeton, NJ: Princeton University Press, 1959) had proposed a framework that had no problem including, without further qualification, the late work of Shakespeare; the last word of this book, however, without having dealt with any of it at length, is, like Frye's, "the renewal of life, after tragedy, at the festival in *The Winter's Tale*" (261).
6 Emrys Jones, *Scenic Form in Shakespeare* (Oxford: Clarendon Press, 1971), gives priority to the scene as unit, with the result that "the two-part structure" was for Shakespeare pertinent "at all stages of his career" (68, 85, 163 for *The Winter's Tale*). As far as the development of the five-phase sequence in tragedy is concerned in this case, see Ruth Nevo, *Tragic Form in Shakespeare* (Princeton, NJ: Princeton University Press, 1972), 17 ff.
7 In Herbert Anton, *Der Raub der Proserpina: Literarische Traditionen eines erotischen Sinnbildes und mythischen Symbols* (Heidelberg: Carl Winter, 1967), Shakespeare plays no role; Anton resumes, however (15), the direction the "moralization" is to take in the historical future according to Walter Benjamin's seminal investigation *Ursprung des deutschen Trauerspiels* (1928), in *Gesammelte Schriften* I (Frankfurt/M: Suhrkamp, 74), 257: "to determine the true, the demonic nature of the ancient gods for Christianity" (my translation).
8 Edgar Wind, *Pagan Mysteries in the Renaissance* (New York: Norton 1958, 2nd ed., 1968), 126 f. with long note 47.

9 For this Augustinian formula (from his *Epistolae* 53.39), see Pierre Legendre, "The Masters of Law" (1983), in *Law and the Unconscious: A Legendre Reader*, ed. Peter Goodrich (London: Macmillan, 1997), 98–133: 107 ff.
10 Gerhard Regn was kind enough to have made me aware of passages in Poliziano, which not only illustrate Botticelli's use of Petrarch, but provide the missing philological link that may connect Botticelli's Ovid with Shakespeare's use of him.
11 Robert Greene, *Pandosto: The Triumph of Time* (1588, 1592, 1595), in the Appendix of *The Winter's Tale*, ed. J.H.P. Pafford, Arden Shakespeare, Second Series (London: Methuen, 1963/Routledge, 1988, 1996), 185: "that contrary to the law of nature he (Pandosto) had lusted after his own daughter, moved with these desperate thoughts, (...) fell into a melancholy fit, and, to close up the comedy with a tragical stratagem, he slew himself." Magisterial statements like Stanley Wells's "Shakespeare and Romance," in *Later Shakespeare*, Stratford-upon-Avon Studies 8 (New York: St. Martin's Press, 1967), 49–79, while stressing Greene's popularity for the tale's sake, underestimate his cunning (approaching Romantic, namely, alienating) irony (64 ff.) and falls for the very appeal of popular Romantic Shakespeare, "humanizing his source, giving it greater relevance to normal life" and what-not (66).
12 See the common design expertly documented by Willard Farnham, *The Medieval Heritage of Elizabethan Tragedy* (Oxford: Blackwell, 1936, 1956, 1963). For "recent studies," see Louis Montrose, *The Purpose of Playing* (Chicago: Chicago University Press, 1996), Ch. 1.
13 Robert Burton, *The Anatomy of Melancholy* (1621, 1624, 1628, 1632, 1638), ed. Thomas C. Faulkner, Nicolas K. Kiessling, and Rhonda L. Blair (Oxford: Clarendon Press, 1989–2000), cites Saint Augustine ("Austin," III: 406) all the time (according to the Frobenius edition, Basel, 1596), but does not mention him on jealousy (or envy). But he records and defines, precisely enough for the purpose at hand, "small occasion, cum amicissimis, & without a cause, datum vel non datum, it will be scandalum acceptum" (I: 390.10–11).
14 Howard Felperin, "Tongue-tied our queen? The Deconstruction of Presence in *The Winter's Tale*," *Shakespeare and the Question of Theory*, ed. Patricia Parker, and Geoffrey Hartman (New York: Routledge, 1985), 3–18: 6.
15 Stanley Cavell, "Recounting Gains, Showing Losses: Reading *The Winter's Tale*" (1983), in *Disowning Knowledge in Six Plays of Shakespeare* (Cambridge: Cambridge University Press, 1987), 193–221: 194. For Augustine's theory of memory and the role of sight replacing the loss of memory, see Gerald O'Daly, *Augustine's Philosophy of Mind* (Berkeley, CA: University of California Press, 1987), 146 ff. For the allegorical, *avant la lettre* Freudian function of original sin, see Peter Brown, *Augustine of Hippo* (Berkeley, CA: University of California Press, 1967), 261 ff.
16 *Saint Augustine's Confessions*, trans. William Watts, 1631 (Loeb Classical Library), ed. W.H.D. Rouse (London: Heinemann, 1912/Cambridge, MA: Harvard University Press, 1977), I: 21–23. The editor mentions that Watts'

translation of the first books seems to be the reworking of some older translation by Sir Tobie Matthew (London 1624 and Paris 1638), "to whom he alludes in his notes with often upbraiding as 'the Papist' " – and whom he consequently tries to demystify into a more harmless, i.e. secular, version.
17 For the standard historicist view on the other hand – without or against Cavell – see Leonhard Tennenhouse, *Power on Display: The Politics of Shakespeare's Genres* (London/New York: Methuen, 1986), 175.
18 Cf. David Wilbern, "Shakespeare's Nothing," in *Representing Shakespeare: New Psychoanalytical Essays*, ed. Murray Schwartz, and Coppelia Kahn (Baltimore, MD: The Johns Hopkins University Press, 1980), 24–63: 248 f.
19 William Empson, *Some Versions of Pastoral* (London: Chatto & Windus, 1935/ Penguin, 1966), 29.
20 Friedrich Nietzsche, *Die Geburt der Tragödie* (1871), in *Werke*, ed. Karl Schlechta (Munich: Hanser, 1966), I: 48 f. Nietzsche specifies: "Der Satyrchor (. . .) ist die rettende Tat" ("The satyr chorus . . . is the saving deed"). The corresponding line from Hölderlin's *Andenken* ends: "Was bleibet aber, stiften die Dichter" ("What remains, however, the poets establish").
21 See Anselm Haverkamp, *Figura cryptica: Theorie der literarischen Latenz* (Frankfurt/M: Suhrkamp, 2002), 7 ff., 13.
22 Jonathan Bate, *Shakespeare and Ovid* (Oxford: Clarendon Press, 1993), 223, see also 227, 232, 236 f.
23 Leonard Barkan, *The Gods Made Flesh: Metamorphosis and the Pursuit of Paganism* (New Haven, CT: Yale University Press, 1987), 283–87.
24 James Ellison, "*The Winter's Tale* and the Religious Politics of Europe," in *Shakespeare's Romances* (New Casebooks), ed. Alison Thorne (New York: Palgrave 2003), 171–204: 185.
25 As prominently overlooked by Alain Badiou, *Saint Paul: la fondation de l'universalisme* (Paris: PUF, 1997), 44; trans. Ray Brassier, *Saint Paul: The Foundation of Universalism* (Stanford, CA: Stanford University Press, 2003), 42 f.
26 See Katrin Trüstedt, "Secondary Satire and the Sea Change of Romance: Reading William Shakespeare's *The Tempest*," *Law and Literature* 17 (2005), 345–64.
27 The allegorical Climax of the topos of *veritas filia temporis* in Francis Bacon is of a peculiar significance here, as Hans Blumenberg, *Lebenszeit und Weltzeit* (Frankfurt/M: Suhrkamp, 1986), has remarked. Bacon outdoes even Ovid: *materiam superabat opus* in Ovid has become *materiam superabit opus* in Bacon (161). Pierre Hadot, *Le voile d'Isis: Essai sur l'histoire de l'idée de Nature* (Paris: Gallimard, 2004), follows Blumenberg and sharpens Bacon's point: "il n'y a rien de caché qui ne sera découvert" (187).
28 See Peter Goodrich on the Freudian metaphorology of "Dogmatics and Domesticity" from the legal point of view, "Psychoanalyis and Law," in *Law and the Unconscious: A Legendre Reader*, ed. Peter Goodrich (London: Macmillan, 1997), Introduction, 1–36: 30 ff.
29 Christoph Menke, *Die Gegenwart der Tragödie*, 98 (my translation). See also

Hans-Thies Lehmann's term *Postdramatisches Theater* (Frankfurt/M: Verlag der Autoren, 1999).
30 Thus, as I tentatively read him, also Stanley Cavell in his late conclusion, "Shakespeare and Rohmer: Two Tales of Winter" (1999), in *Cities of Words: Pedagogical Letters on a Register of the Moral Life* (Cambridge, MA: Harvard University Press, 2004), 421–43, literally imagining: "Leontes has visited Hermione's burial place every day for sixteen years, and at the same time Shakespeare has deferred to Hermione's wish for a merry tale by providing a happy ending at the grave site" (441/42).
31 Walter Benjamin, "Schicksal und Charakter" (1921), in *Gesammelte Schriften* II (Frankfurt/M: Suhrkamp, 1977), 171–79: 176 (my rendering); similarly "Critique of Violence" (1922); "Fate and Character," trans. Edmund Jephcott, *Selected Writings*, ed. Michael W. Jennings (Cambridge, MA: Harvard University Press, 1996–2006), I: 201–6: 204 (translation only partly useful).
32 Karl Marx, *Grundrisse der Kritik der politischen Ökonomie* (1857/58), Introduction, last pages (my translation).
33 Heinrich Heine, *Shakespeares Mädchen und Frauen* (1838), in *Sämtliche Schriften* IV: 251 ff. Heine lists Jessica and Portia in this coffee-table collection of portraits under "Tragedies." Paulina, unfortunately, did not make it into the list commissioned from him for the purpose of this commercial project. See Chapter 8 in this volume.
34 Theodor W. Adorno, "Die Wunde Heine" (1956), *Noten zur Literatur* I (Frankfurt/M: Suhrkamp 1958), 144–52: 146; *Notes to Literature*, trans. Shierry Weber Nicholson (New York: Columbia University Press, 1991), I, 80–5: 81 (translation modified).
35 Juliane Rebentisch, "Theatrokratie und Theater: Philosophie als Literatur in Benjamin und Brecht," *Literatur als Philosophie – Philosophie als Literatur*, ed. Eva Horn, Bettine Menke, and Christoph Menke (Munich: Fink, 2006), 297–318: 301.
36 Benjamin, "Zentralpark" (compiled by Adorno in 1956), § 44, in *Gesammelte Schriften* I: 689, where the term is cited, not without pathos, according to Melanchthon's Rhetoric: "*Melencolia illa heroica.*"

8 But Mercy is Above: Shylock's Pun of a Pound

1 I use the term "index-fossil" (*Leitfossil*) in the intensified sense it receives in Hans Blumenberg's theory of "non-conceptuality": "Theorie der Unbegrifflichkeit" (1979), in *Ästhetische und metaphorologische Schriften*, ed. Anselm Haverkamp (Frankfurt/M: Suhrkamp, 2001), 193.
2 See Anselm Haverkamp, "Anagrammatics of Violence: The Benjaminian Ground of Homo Sacer" (2000), in *Politics, Metaphysics, and Death: Essays on Giorgio Agamben's Homo Sacer*, ed. Andrew Norris (Durham, NC: Duke University Press, 2005), 135–44; *Latenzzeit: Wissen im Nachkrieg* (Berlin: Kadmos, 2004), 167 f.
3 Rudolf Eberstadt, "Der Shylockvertrag und sein Urbild," in *Jahrbuch der*

deutschen Shakespeare-Gesellschaft 44 (1908), 1–35: 4 ff. gave a concise overview of the juridical discussion of the play's Roman underpinnings during the nineteenth century (Simrock, Ihering, Kohler, Strasser). All these by now forgotten reconstructions of the legal setting confirm the procedural correctness of Shakespeare's presentation of the case; but they unnecessarily take this condition of possibility of representation as proof of an undoubted veracity and of the "real" possibility of the story itself. Hegel's reference is decisive because he is the first to include Shylock in the reception-history of this opaque piece from the Twelve Tables, whose notoriety is not least based on the reference to it in Quintilian's rhetoric, the only reference to the Twelve Tables in this work (*Institutio oratoria* 3.6.84). For Quintilian it serves as the very case in point in which, in Donald A. Russell's new *Loeb Classical Library* translation, "a legal action" must be regarded as "not justifiable" (Cambridge MA: Harvard University Press, 2001). What Russell still reads, in the spirit of the nineteenth century, as an agreement on Quintilian's part (II: 90), had been thoroughly questioned way before Hegel: the commentaries of Quintilian by Georg Ludwig Spalding (5 vols. Leipzig: Crusius/Vogel, 1798–1829) and his predecessor Peter Burmann (2 vols. Leyden: Issac Severin, 1720), looked back to the magisterial treatment of the matter in Cornelis van Bynkershoek's *Observationes Juris Romani* of 1710, where the dubious commonplace seemed settled for good (Burmann, I: 261; Spalding, I: 534). The skeptical view that was, after all, already most manifest in Quintilian's own citation of the law, went against the grain of the new topicality that the Twelve Tables had gained through the first reconstruction of their corpus by Francois Hotman in 1564 and Jacob Gotofredus in 1616. For Shylock's motif, this may have been an additional context, but the authority of Quintilian in general, and for the Inns of Court in particular, is more than sufficient. See for the latter Samuel E. Thorne, "The Early History of the Inns of Court" (1959), *Essays in English Legal History* (London: Hambledon, 1985), 137–154; or Kenneth Charlton, "Liberal Education and the Inns of Court in the Sixteenth Century," *British Journal of Educational Studies* 9 (1960), 25–38. The sheer "virtuality" of the archaic construct, in which no piece is genuine, but which is instead constituted entirely by hearsay – mostly fragments from indirect citation – is splendidly highlighted in the phantasmagoria of juridical consequences by Marie Theres Fögen, *Römische Rechtsgeschichten* (Göttingen: Vandenhoeck & Ruprecht, 2002), 69 ff.

4 Georg Wilhelm Friedrich Hegel, *Philosophy of Right*, trans. S.W. Dyde (New York: Cosimo, 2008), Introduction, xxvii–xxviii (my additions in parentheses); for the German original, see *Grundlinien der Philosophie des Rechts*, ed. Johannes Hoffmeister (Hamburg: Meiner, 1955, 1967), Einleitung § 3: 26. For the historical context, see Gerald Hartung, *Die Naturrechtsdebatte: Geschichte der Obligatio vom 17. bis 20. Jahrhundert* (Freiburg/Breisgau: Alber, 1998), Excursus on Shylock, 266 ff. who develops the post-Hegelian debate of the late nineteenth century to the strong hypothesis that Shylock's case marks a

turning point in the legal *principium obligationis* and preludes Nietzsche's *Genealogy of Morals* (273).

5   On the depth and debts of Hegel's Shakespeare-reading, see Anselm Haverkamp, "Shakespeare. Wieland. Hegel: Wortzeichen auf dem Strand der Endlichkeit," in *Wieland–Übersetzung*, ed. Bettine Menke (Munich: Fink, 2010), 1–30.

6   Compare the richly suggestive chapter "Verbal Usury in *The Merchant of Venice*," in Marc Shell, *Money, Language and Thought* (Berkeley, CA: University of California Press, 1982), 47 ff.

7   See the Restauration version *The Jew of Venice: A Comedy* (London: Lintott, 1701), in *Five Restauration Adaptations of Shakespeare*, ed. Christopher Spencer (Urbana, IL: University of Illinois Press, 1965), 345–402.

8   See the remarkably balanced Introduction to the play by Katharine Eisaman Maus for the *Norton Shakespeare* (New York: Norton, 1997), 1081–9, which she edited with Stephen Greenblatt.

9   Anton Schütz, "Structural Terror: A Shakespearean Investigation," in *Law, Text, Terror: Essays for Pierre Legendre*, ed. Peter Goodrich, Lior Barshack, Anton Schütz (Oxford: Routledge-Cavendish, 2006), 71–92. For Heine and Rahel Varnhagen, see the first part of Hannah Arendt, *The Origins of Totalitarianism* (New York: Harcourt Brace Jovanovitch, 1951); *Elemente und Ursprünge totaler Herrschaft* (Munich: Piper, 1958, 1986), esp. 119 ff.

10 See Klaus Briegleb in the commentary of his edition of the collected works of Heine's *Schriften* IV (Munich: Hanser, 1971), 890 ad 259. Heine's occasional work of 1838/39 was entitled "Shakespeare's Mädchen und Frauen" and the passage in question appears in the section on "Jessica," IV, 251–61: 256 ff. Both the provocative irony of Heine's presentation and the reaction formation cited in the form of "a private letter" (presumably, even easy to guess, Rahel Varnhagen's) are worth a much closer reading than is possible here.

11 John Dover Wilson, "The Merchant of Venice in 1937" (1938), in *Shakespeare's Happy Comedies* (London: Faber & Faber, 1962), 94–119: 114. On Dover Wilson, see Terence Hawkes' latency-rich masterpiece "Telmah" (1985), *That Shakespeherian Rag* (London: Methuen, 1986), 110 ff.

12 Stanley Cavell, "Hamlet's Burden of Proof" (1984), in *Disowning Knowledge in Six Plays of Shakespeare* (Cambridge: Cambridge University Press, 1987), 179–91: 190.

13 J.L. Austin, *How to Do Things with Words* (Cambridge, MA: Harvard University Press, 1962), 22. On mercy's status "above" as literary theme, see Otto Kirchheimer, *Political Justice: The Use of Legal Procedure for Political Ends* (Princeton, NJ: Princeton University Press, 1967), ch. 10.

14 Julia Reinhard Lupton, *Citizen-Saints: Shakespeare and Political Theology* (Chicago: The University of Chicago Press 2005), 72 and, extensively in the following, 101.

15 On René Girard's hypothesis, "To Entrap the Wisest: A Reading of *The Merchant*

of Venice" (1980), see Richard Halpern's reply, *Shakespeare Among the Moderns* (Ithaca, NY: Cornell University Press, 1997), 176 ff.
16 Thus the political-scientific genealogy of the "separation of charity and justice" by Edward Andrew, *Shylock's Rights: A Grammar of Lockian Claims* (Toronto: University of Toronto Press, 1988), 54 ff.
17 For an overview, see the relevant paper by Oona Eisenstadt, "*The Merchant of Venice* Through the Lens of Continental Philosophy," *Journal for Cultural and Religious Theory* 8 (2007), 1–6: 3 f.
18 Eberstadt, *Jahrbuch der deutschen Shakespeare-Gesellschaft* 44 (1908), who elaborates the historical veracity of Portia's role in every detail (3–12), does not recognize the forced theatricality of the scene, although he admits, on the other hand, the "scholastic play" with the "concept of flesh" and the formula "*plus minusve*," which "does not at all fit" the Roman Law frame (20 f.).
19 Unmatched on this point is Harold C. Goddard, *The Meaning of Shakespeare* (Chicago: Chicago University Press, 1951), I: 103 ff. One cannot wholly do justice to the finesse of the staged trial, especially not to the "double plot" (in Empson's, not Goddard's terms), through which the scale is brought to a precarious balance. "In the twinkling of an eye, the angel reverts to the Doctor of Laws," shows Goddard (106) and proves Bassanio (in the choice of the three caskets that I have to neglect here) "worthy of the leaden casket" (108). In the fact that "Portia the lover of mercy is deposed by Portia the actress" (107) a latency of the legal order prevails – as Goddard's generous reading intuits – a latent content, which the stage brings to the light of day.
20 Ken Jackson, "Shylock: The Knight of Faith," *Journal for Cultural and Religious Theory* 8 (2007), 67–82: 75.
21 Anselm Haverkamp, "Dialektisches Bild: Die Konstellation der Geschichte" (1992), in *Figura cryptica: Theorie der literarischen Latenz* (Frankfurt/M: Suhrkamp, 2002), Ch. 2.
22 Johannes Lohmann, *Philosophie und Sprachwissenschaft* (Berlin: Duncker & Humblot, 1965, 1975), 88, who at this place translates Heidegger's *Alétheia* with "Illatenz" and supplements the result with Hegel.
23 For the specific dramatic paradoxes of this type of – in Austin's understanding – "parasitic" speech-acting in Shakespeare, see Björn Quiring, *Shakespeares Fluch* (Munich: Fink, 2009). For the legal consequences taken by Hobbes, see Karen S. Feldman, *Binding Words: Conscience and Rhetoric in Hobbes, Hegel, and Heidegger* (Evanston, IL: Northwestern University Press, 2006), 34 ff.
24 *The Oxford English Dictionary*, 2nd edn. (Oxford: Clarendon Press, 1989), XII: 832. Cf. Henriette Michaelis, *Dizionario pratico*, 15th edn. (Lipsia: Brockhaus, 1907), I: 612 f.
25 Charles Talbut Onions, *A Shakespeare Glossary*, 3rd edn. (Oxford: Clarendon Press, 1986), 213. Shakespeare's technically elaborate metaphorics of fencing, oriented towards the handbooks of the time, not only bear notorious sexual connotations, but serve rhetorical-poetological specifications, as is decisive – already recognized in Hegel's *Aesthetics* – in the ominous *punto riverso* of

Hamlet's final scene, which offers virtually an ironic allegory of the final tragic outcome. See the unraveling of the scene in the language of fencing-technique by James L. Jackson, "They Catch One Another's Rapiers," *Shakespeare Quarterly* 41 (1990), 281–98: 285.

26 P.G.W. Glare, *Oxford Latin Dictionary* (Oxford: Clarendon Press, 1982), 1520. Cf. *Le Petit Robert*, 20e Éd. (Paris: Le Robert, 1975), 1336 as well as, of course, Roland Barthes, *La chambre claire* (Paris: Gallimard-Seuil, 1980), 49, where the semantics of the *punctum* are unfolded anew in their poetological aspects.

9 Habeas Corpus: The Law's Desire to Have the Body

1 Walter Benjamin's "Critique of Violence" (1922), Martin Heidegger's *Nietzsche* (1959), Michel Foucault's *Discipline and Punish* (1975), Jean-François Lyotard's *Kafka-Interpretation* (1985), as well as Niklas Luhmann's *Sociology of Law* (1972) and Robert Cover's "Violence and the Word" (1985) – all use the metaphor of the law's shadow, whose reason lies way above the clouds, a motif from political theology which I have touched upon elsewhere: "Leo in nubibus: Dantes Allegorie der Dichter in Zeiten politischer Theologie" (1995), and "Stranger than Paradise: Dantes irdisches Paradies als Antidote politischer Theologie" (1997), both reprinted in *Diesseits der Oder* (Berlin: Kulturverlag Kadmos, 2008), Chs. 3 and 4.

2 Walter Benjamin, "Zur Kritik der Gewalt" (1922), in *Gesammelte Schriften* (Frankfurt/M: Suhrkamp, 1972–77), II: 188; first trans. Edmund Jephcott as "Critique of Violence," in the Benjamin collection *Reflections* (New York: Schocken 1979), 277–300: 286; in the following cited according to the new edition of *Selected Writings*, ed. Michael W. Jennings (Cambridge, MA: Harvard University Press, 1996–2003), I: 236–52: 242.

3 Robert Cover, "Violence and the Word," *Yale Law Review* 95 (1985), 1601–29: 1628/29; now in the collection of his essays *Narrative, Violence, and the Law*, ed. Martha Minow, Michael Ryan, and Austin Sarat (Ann Arbor, MI: University of Michigan Press, 1993), 203–38: 236/37. See Austin Sarat, and Thomas R. Kearns (Eds.), *The Rhetoric of Law* (Ann Arbor, MI: University of Michigan Press, 1994), Editorial Introduction, 1–27: 2 ff.

4 For the dialectics of the literal and the metaphorical used here, see Nelson Goodman, *Languages of Art* (London: Oxford University Press, 1968), 68–70.

5 In our use of speech-act theory we are indebted to Ted Cohen's account and amendments in "Figurative Speech and Figurative Acts," *Journal of Philosophy* 72 (1975), 669–84. See Anselm Haverkamp, "Rhetoric, Law, and the Poetics of Memory," *Cardozo Law Review* 13 (1991/92), 1639–53: 1645.

6 Owen Barfield, "Poetic Diction and Legal Fiction" (1947), a unique essay in the metaphorology of law, repr. *The Importance of Language*, ed. Max Black (Ithaca, NY: Cornell University Press, 1962, 1969), 51–71: 64.

7 The *locus classicus* is J.L. Austin's *How to Do Things with Words* (Cambridge, MA: Harvard University Press, 1962), Lecture VIII, 99; but see also the

notorious critique by Jacques Derrida, "Signature Event Context" (from *Glyph* 1, 1977), *Limited Inc*, ed. Gerald Graff (Evanston, IL: Northwestern University Press, 1988), 14.

8 Edward Jenks, "The Story of the Habeas Corpus," *Law Quarterly Review* 18 (1902), 64–77: 67. See in the following the specimen in Baker's *Introduction to English Legal History*, 626/27.

9 Here and in the following we refer, if not otherwise mentioned, to J.H. Baker's *Introduction to English Legal History*, 3rd edn. (London: Butterworths, 1971, 1979, 1990), 165 ("the rule of law"), 168/69, 537–40 (*Habeas corpus*). We restrict ourselves to the English development.

10 M.T. Clanchy, *From Memory to Written Record: England 1066–1307* (Cambridge, MA: Harvard University Press, 1979), 220. See already Theodor Mommsen, *Römisches Staatsrecht* of 1871–88 (Darmstadt: WBG, 1955), 324.

11 Baker, *English Legal History*, 112/13, citing the prominent *Case of Prohibitions del Roy* (1608).

12 Ernst H. Kantorowicz, *The King's Two Bodies: A Study in Medieval Theology* (Princeton, NJ: Princeton University Press, 1958), 140, 146 (chapters on Frederick II and Bracton). For the crucial role of Bracton, his discussion of the King's "placet" and Kantorowicz's interpretation of it, see Ewart Lewis, "King Above Law? Quod principi placuit in Bracton," *Speculum* 39 (1964), 240–69: esp. 256: "ut in omnibus iudiciis aequitatem praeceperit et misericordiam" (Bracton, *De Actionibus*). Bracton does not fail to underline the political function of the law: *opus iustitiae pax*, quoting the old version of the coronation oath (drawn from Jesaia 32.17).

13 As more recently in Martha Nussbaum's impressive attempt to reinstate mercy as a principle of justice in her article "Equity and Mercy," *Philosophy and Public Affairs* 22 (1993), 83–125. In spite of her emphasis on Seneca, Nussbaum finally succumbs to a Christian reading of mercy as primarily motivated, and justified, by sympathy; she gives away Seneca's point but may have a rhetorical point of her own with respect to what counts as an argument in today's legal debate.

14 The text of *Hamlet* is cited according to Harold Jenkins' edition, *Arden Shakespeare*, Second Series (London: Methuen, 1982/Routledge, 1989).

15 As far as procedure is concerned, *Habeas corpus* belongs with yet another writ, the *Certiorari*, another means of removing the proceedings from an inferior to a higher court, finally to the king. See here and in the following, Naomi Hurnard, *The King's Pardon for Homicide before A.D. 1307* (Oxford: Blackwell, 1969), 47. Baker, *English Legal History*, 170.

16 See, besides Hunard, Thomas Andrew Green, *Verdict According to Conscience: Perspectives on the English Criminal Jury 1200–1800* (Chicago: University of Chicago Press, 1985), 72 ff., 97 ff. Also Natalie Zemon Davis, *Fiction and the Archive: Pardon Tales and their Tellers in 16th Century France* (Stanford, CA: Stanford University Press, 1987).

17 Shakespearean theater and theatricality, to come back to one subtext of

our study, reflect the exploitation of this economy, say, in the management of "salutary anxiety" most forcefully described by Stephen Greenblatt, *Shakespearean Negotiations* (Berkeley, CA: University of California Press, 1988), 133, 137. What the theater does achieve in pointing out the "[institutional commitment] to the arousal of anxiety," thus exposing its inbuilt theatricality, is the thematization, or deconstruction, of the law's logic of representation rather than the mere enforcement of, or ironic detachment from, ongoing exchanges.

18 Michel Foucault, *Surveiller et punir: Naissance de la prison* (Paris: Gallimard, 1975), 22; trans. *Discipline and Punish: The Birth of the Prison* (New York: Pantheon 1978, Vintage, 1993), 29.

19 Baker, *English Legal History*, 168, citing from *R. v. Lord Warden of the Cinque Ports* (1619). See the example of James's handling of the Bye Plot, as interpreted by Greenblatt, *Shakespearean Negotiations*, 136. Some rather circumstantial evidence we find in Catherine Drinker Bowen, *The Lion and the Throne: The Life and Times of Sir Edward Coke* (Boston, MA: Little, Brown & Co., 1956), 220–2.

20 *Habeas Corpus Act*, cited after William Stubbs, *Select Charters and Other Illustrations of English Constitutional History* (1858), Standard 4th edn. (Oxford: Clarendon Press, 1905), 518.

21 F.M. Maitland, *Justice and Police* (London: Macmillan, 1885), 130. It is the tradition of Maitland's optimistic modernism, from which Ernst Kantorowicz takes his departure.

22 See, for example, and only in the most general manner, Alan Hunt, and Gary Wickhamm, *Foucault and Law: Towards a Sociology of Law and Governance* (London: Pluto, 1994), 61–4, with note 135.1.

23 Stanley Fish, "The Law Wishes to Have a Formal Existence," in *The Fate of Law*, ed. Austin Sarat, and Thomas Kearns (Ann Arbor, MI: Michigan University Press, 1991), 159–200; reprinted in his collection *There's No Such Thing as Free Speech* (New York: Oxford University Press, 1994), 141–79.

24 Jacques Derrida, "The Force of Law," *Cardozo Law Review* 11 (1990), 919–1045: 971. See also Stanley Cavell, "The Conversation of Justice: Rawls and the Drama of Consent" (1980), in *Conditions Handsome and Unhandsome* (Chicago: University of Chicago Press, 1990), 101–26: 113.

25 H.L.A. Hart, "Legal Powers" (1972), *Essays on Bentham* (Oxford: Clarendon Press, 1982), 194–219: 217.

26 See "Rhetoric, Law, and the Poetics of Memory," as well as Peter Goodrich, "Anti-Teubner: Autopoiesis, Paradox, and the Theory of Law," *Social Epistemology* 13 (1999), 197–214.

27 Georg Wilhelm Friedrich Hegel, *Grundlinien der Philosophie des Rechts*, ed. Johannes Hoffmeister (Hamburg: Meiner, 1955), § 282; trans. T.M. Knox, *Hegel's Philosophy of Right* (Oxford: Oxford University Press, 1952), 186. See Jean-Luc Nancy, "La jurisdiction du monarque hégélien," *Rejouer le politique* (Paris: Galilée, 1981); trans. Mary Ann, Peter Caws, "The Jurisdiction of the Hegelian Monarch," *Social Research* 49 (1982), 481–516: 486.

28 For example, Kenley R. Dove, "Logik und Recht bei Hegel," *Neue Hefte für Philosophie* 17 (1979), 89–108: 96.
29 See the Austin essay by H.L.A. Hart, "Sovereignty and Legally Limited Government" (1967), in *Essays on Bentham*, 220–42: 223.
30 Chiara Frugoni, *La citta lontana* (Torino: Einaudi, 1983), 147. Anselm Haverkamp, *Figura cryptica: Theorie der literarischen Latenz* (Frankfurt/M: Suhrkamp Verlag, 2002), 153 ff.
31 Francis Barker, *The Culture of Violence* (Chicago: University of Chicago Press, 1993), 170.
32 Benjamin, "Critique of Violence," *Reflections*, 286; *Selected Writings*, I: 242. For the connection of this motif with Benjamin's later work *The Origin of the German Trauerspiel* (1928) see my contribution to the second Cardozo Conference, "How to Take it (and Do the Right Thing): Violence and the Mournful Mind in Benjamin's Critique of Violence," *Cardozo Law Review* 13 (1991), 1159–71; "Ein unabwerfbarer Schatten: Gewalt und Trauer in Benjamins Kritik der Gewalt," *Gewalt und Gerechtigkeit: Derrida–Benjamin*, ed. Anselm Haverkamp (Frankfurt/M: Suhrkamp, 1994), 162–84.
33 Robert Cover, "Nomos and Narrative – Foreword, The Supreme Court, Term 1982," *Harvard Law Review* 97 (1983/84), 4–68; *Narrative, Violence, and the Law*, 95–172. In defense of Cover's counterpart Ronald Dworkin – notably *Law's Empire* (Cambridge, MA: Harvard University Press, 1986) – see Klaus Günther, *Der Sinn für Angemessenheit: Anwendungsdiskurse in Moral und Recht* (Frankfurt/M: Suhrkamp, 1988), 345 ff. For my own reservations (in favor of Cover, against Dworkin), see *Gewalt und Gerechtigkeit*, 26 ff. with note 48 f.
34 Hegel, *Grundlinien der Philosophie des Rechts*, § 228; trans. *Hegel's Philosophy of Right*, 145 (our paraphrase). See Hans Kelsen, *Reine Rechtslehre* (1934), revised and enlarged edition (Vienna: Österreichische Staatsdruckerei 1960, 1992), Ch. 33, "Rechtssubjekt, Person." For the intricate post-Hegelian consequences, see the impressive phenomenology of procedure developed by Niklas Luhmann, *Legitimation durch Verfahren* (Neuwied: Luchterhand, 1969), 91 ff.
35 Peter Goodrich, *Languages of Law* (London: Weidenfeld, 1990), 265.
36 We borrow this phrase, time and again, from Stanley Cavell, *Disowning Knowledge in Six Plays of Shakespeare* (Cambridge: Cambridge University Press, 1987), 191, where the sentence summarizes the evidence to be gained through "Hamlet's Burden of Proof" (1982). The sentence ends, of course, "like philosophy."

The last chapter was written with Cornelia Vismann, to whom I owe more in this book than meets the eye.

Names, Words, and Things

Abraham, Nicolas 11, 15, 29, 30, 136n, 138n
Adelman, Janet 61, 138n
Adorno, Theodor W. 105, 142n, 160n
Aegidius Romanus/Giles of Rome 154n
Aeschylus 54
Agamben, Giorgio 4–5, 49, 50, 53–6, 58, 69, 109, 115, 144n–7n, 150n, 151n, 154n–5n, 160n
Alexander, Peter 136n
allegory: ironic 42–3, 113, 163n; juridical 49; of latency 116; mythic 91; neoplatonic 92; philosophical 44; political 55, 76; of skepticism 97; of the stage 98; temporal 89, 103, 125, 159n; typological 70
ambiguity 22, 42, 45, 70, 83, 96, 101, 106, 144n
anamorphosis 20, 27, 29, 45, 132n, 135n, 139n
Andrew, Edward 162n
Anton, Herbert 157n
Arc, Joan of 13
Arendt, Hannah 161n
Aristotle 10, 42, 92, 98, 110, 130n, 143n
Arnold, Oliver 62, 150n
Artaud, Antonin 3, 76, 88, 130n
Augustine 48, 60–2, 64, 71, 92–100, 103, 105, 145n, 148n, 158n
Augustus 62–70, 109, 148n, 151n
Austin, John L. 112, 126, 158n, 162n–6n
Axton, Marie 34, 140n

Bacon, Francis 3, 23, 41, 137n, 142n, 154n, 159n
Badiou, Alain 148n, 159n
Baker, John Hamilton 124, 164n–5n
Balke, Friedrich 149n
Barber, C.L. 157n
Barfield, Owen 118, 164n
Barkan, Leonard 159n
Barker, Francis 126, 166n
Baroque 8, 44, 76, 79, 86, 133n
Barthes, Roland 78, 152n, 154n, 163n
Bate, Jonathan 15, 41, 101, 142n, 146n, 159n
Batstone, William W. 151n
Battenhouse, Roy W. 133n
Beck, Ulrich 156n
Beckett, Samuel 40, 45, 130n, 142n
Belleforest, François de 33
Benjamin, Walter 2, 4–5, 8, 11, 12, 14, 18, 43, 76, 79–81, 85–8, 93–4, 97, 100, 104, 106, 112, 115–17, 127, 131n, 133n, 140n, 142–3n, 147n, 151n, 155n–7n, 160n, 163n, 166n
Benveniste, Emile 149n
Berger, Harry 155n
binding, double bind, *re-ligio* 9, 41, 43, 59, 66, 109, 113, 149n
biopolitics 85, 156
Bloom, Alan 63
Bloom, Harold 15, 39, 52, 129n

Blumenberg, Hans 2, 4, 48–9, 54, 56, 131n, 144n–5n, 147n, 152n, 159n–60n
Böhme, Hartmut 156n–7n
Boleyn, Anne 31, 103, 137n
Bolingbroke, Henry of 50–1
Borgia, Cesare 5, 76, 77–9, 81–4, 154n, 155n
Botticelli, Sandro 90–2, 94, 98, 100, 158n
Bowen, Catherin Drinker 165n
Bracton, Henry 4, 47, 50–4, 56, 144n, 146n, 164n
Bradley, A.C. 33, 139, 156
Brecht, Bertolt 3, 12, 92, 130n, 160n
Breuer, Horst 135n
Briegleb, Klaus 157n, 161n
Brook, Peter 3, 14, 130n
Brooks, Cleanth 155n
Brown, Peter 158n, 165n
Brutus, Marcus Junius 63, 65–8
Burckhardt, Jacob 71, 153n
Burton, Robert 3, 93, 139n, 158n

Caesar, Julius 4, 57–60, 62–71, 82, 149n, 151n–2n
caesura 11, 71, 82, 115
Camden, William 35
Canterbury, Anselm of 43
Cantor, Paul 63, 150n, 156n
Cassirer, Ernst 146n
catharsis, anti-catharsis 68, 76, 78–9, 93, 98, 113
Catiline, Lucius Sergius 62–5, 70, 152n
Cato the Younger 65
Cavarero, Adriana 140n
Cavell, Stanley 4, 13, 15, 30, 43, 60–1, 69, 95, 97–9, 111, 116, 131n, 136n–7n, 139n, 143n, 150n, 155n, 158n–60n, 162n, 166n–7n
Chambers, E.K. 148n
character 8–10, 21, 42, 84, 104, 113, 133n–5n, 144n
Charles I, King 55, 121, 148n
Christianity 70, 84–5, 109, 112, 157n
Cicero, Marcus Tullius 65, 68, 109
Clanchy, M.T. 164n
Clark, Arthur Melville 155n
Cohen, Ted 164n
Coke, Edward 120, 122, 126–7, 165n
Collingwood, R.G. 1
comedy 88–9, 92–3, 103, 105, 112–15, 158n; see also tragic humor under tragedy
Connolly, Joy 152n
constantia 67–8, 71

contingency 11, 49, 55–6, 62–9, 82, 149n; see also fortuna
conversio 91–93, 97, 101–2, 112, 125; catastrophe 12, 78, 92–4; metamorphosis 91–2, 97, 100–2, 104
Copernicus, Nicolaus 18, 131n
Cover, Robert 5, 74, 117–18, 163n, 166n
Cox, Lee Sheridan 132n

Damon, Cynthia 151n
Daniell, David 150n
Dante Alighieri 23, 24, 40, 52, 77, 79, 92, 94, 101, 133n–4n, 142n, 145n, 154n, 163n
D'Avenant, William 134n
Davis, Natalie Zemon 165n
deferred representation 22, 24, 30, 69, 71, 75, 110–11, 116, 160n; belatedness (*Nachträglichkeit*) 18, 30, 69, 111, 116, 125, 141n; retrospection 18, 24, 30, 69, 141n
Defoe, Daniel 77
Derrida, Jacques 11, 15, 76, 124, 129n–31n, 138n, 142n–3n, 147n, 153n, 164n, 166n
deus ex machina; see machine
dialectical image 104; dialectics at a standstill 104, 115
Diana, Princess of Wales 28, 37
Divine Right of Kings 36, 49, 55, 59, 70, 74, 80, 84–5
Douglas, Garvin 83
Dove, Kenley R. 166n
Dumézil, Georges 4, 59, 61–4, 66, 68, 149n, 151n
Dworkin, Ronald 166n

Eberstadt, Rudolf 160n, 162n
Eden, Kathy 42, 130n, 143n
Eisaman Maus, Katharine 161n
Eisenstadt, Oona 162n
Eliot, T.S. 14, 135n
Elizabeth I, Queen of England 12, 20, 31, 34–6, 52, 55, 62, 74, 103, 137n, 140n–1n
Elizabeth II, Queen of the United Kingdom 37
Elizabeth of Bohemia 102
Ellison, James 159n
Empson, William 12, 14, 95, 100, 106, 133n–6n, 159n, 162n
enargeia – energeia 3, 10–12, 90, 106, 130n, 153n
Enlightenment 30, 87, 97, 102, 106, 109–10, 113

Eribon, Didier 149n
Evans, Malcolm 15, 155n
evidence, *evidentia* 153n; *see also enargeia*; historical evidence 8, 42, 141n, 147n; legal evidence 42, 100, 123, 127; self-evidence 8, 100; of the stage 10, 43, 66, 68; textual 130n, 167n
exemplarity: legal, historical precedent 1–5, 9, 150n; legal, historical unprecedentedness 85, 113, 115; Machiavellian exemplarity 76–7, 79, 82; paradoxical non-exemplarity 113; Roman exemplarity 60–5, 69–71, 152n, 154n

Fantham, Elaine 152n
Farnham, Willard 158n
Feldman, Karen S. 163n
Felman, Shoshana 131n
Felperin, Howard 158n
Fernie, Ewan 137n
Festus, Sextus Pompeius 109, 115
Fineman, Joel 11, 13, 15, 53, 61, 136n, 139n, 151n
Fish, Stanley 165n
fortuna 77, 81, 83, 142n, 146n; *see also* contingency
Foucault, Michel 1, 4, 58, 59, 61, 71, 74, 117, 122, 124–5, 127, 149n, 151n, 163n, 165n
Fox, Matthew 151n
Frazer, James G. 90
Freccero, John 133n–4n, 154n
Frederick II of Hohenstaufen 120–1, 164n
Freud, Sigmund 1–2, 4, 11–14, 18–19, 21, 24, 30–2, 44–5, 61, 69, 78, 90, 93, 97–9, 105, 131n–2n, 136n, 138n, 142n, 158n–9n
Frugoni, Chiara 166n
Frye, Northrop 89, 92, 157n

George, Stefan 49
ghost, spirit 7–8, 11–13, 19–36, 39–45, 74, 82, 85, 103, 105, 133n–9n, 144n, 157n
Gilman, Ernest B. 135n
Girard, René 11, 15, 112, 162n
Glare, P.G.W. 163n
Goddard, Harold C. 14, 155n, 162n
Goethe, Johann Wolfang von 9, 32, 44, 81, 130n–2n, 135n, 156n
Goldberg, Jonathan 151n
Goodman, Nelson 164n
Goodrich, Peter 153n, 158n–9n, 161n, 166n–7n

Grady, Hugh 150n
Grafton, Anthony 60–1, 63, 149n–50n
Grazia, Margreta de 15, 131n, 138n, 143n, 152n
Green, André 11, 15
Green, Thomas Andrew 165n
Greenblatt, Stephen 2, 10–11, 15, 30, 60, 129n, 131n–2n, 134n, 149n, 161n, 165n
Greene, Robert 89, 92–95, 103, 158n
Griffin, Miriam 152n
Groh, Ruth 147n
Gross, Raphael 147n
Günther, Klaus 166n

Habermas, Jürgen 58, 78, 130n, 154n
Hadot, Pierre 159n
Halpern, Richard 15, 146n, 151n, 162n
Hamacher, Werner 143n
Hamilton, Donna 147n
Hariman, Robert 153n
Harries, Martin 134n, 138n, 143n, 156n
Hart, H.L.A. 166n
Hartung, Gerald 161n
Harvey, Gabriel 60–2, 66, 149n, 153n
Hawkes, Terence 162n
Hayward, John 51, 146n
Hegel, G.F.W. 1, 3–4, 10, 12, 14, 29, 44–5, 56, 67, 83–8, 97, 109–10, 113, 126, 128, 133n, 136n, 143n–4n, 147n, 151n, 154–6n, 161n, 163n, 166n–7n
Heidegger, Martin 74, 85, 115, 117, 150n, 163n
Heine, Heinrich 5, 87–8, 103–5, 110–12, 157n, 160n–1n
Henderson, John 61, 69, 151n–2n
Henry VIII, King 31, 103
Henry, Prince of Wales 102
Herder, Johann Gottfried 144n
Hesiod 142n
Hewitt, Andrew 142n
Heywood, Thomas 74, 77
Hirsch, Emanuel 143n
history: and character 10, 29; contingency of 36, 49; *see also* contingency and *fortuna*; counter-history 58–9; credit-history, as futurity 70, 85; exemplary histories 1–2; as genealogy 1–5, 10, 110, 156n; as *Geistesgeschichte* 1, 3, 7, 44–5; as haunting 11–12, 20, 24, 30, 40, 43, 82, 157n; of ideas 48, 90; as invention 39, 150; irony of 36, 42, 56, 68, 71, 77; legal 3, 109, 118, 125–6;

as mortgage 1, 44; as natural history 7, 10; as pre-history 5, 12–13, 22–3, 26, 73–5, 85, 110; as reception-history 3–4, 18; and/of revenge 24–33, 106, 134; rewriting of 5, 18, 45, 70; Roman, Jupiterian 19, 59–61, 67, 70; salvation-history 93; sovereign as representative of 140; as theater 1–2, 8–10, 14, 41–2, 101–2, 150n, 152n; tragic 18, 57–8, 67, 70–1, 88, 102, 116; World History 98

Hobbes, Thomas 49, 53, 154n, 163n
Hölderlin, Friedrich 17, 49, 90, 131n, 145n, 159n
Holinshed, Raphael 51, 74, 146n
Homer 87, 138n
homo sacer 50, 53–5, 66, 109, 144n–6n, 150n–1n, 160n
Hoppe, Marianne 12, 130n
Horace 69, 90, 152n
Humphrey, Arthur 150n
Hunt, Alan 165n
Hurnard, Naomi 165n
Hutson, Lorna 144n, 147n

ideology 1, 36, 59, 70, 103, 144n, 151n; as blindness 115–16; as the law 124, 127; as political theology 4, 36, 47, 59, 142n
inheritance 21, 25, 27, 29, 94, 103, 104–5, 138n
institution 1–2, 49, 63, 65, 93, 110, 115, 119, 128, 132n, 150n, 165n
irony: allegorical 42–3, 163n; dramatic 68–9, 78, 114, 135n, 137n; historical 13, 36, 42, 56, 62, 68, 70–1, 77, 141n; infernal 45, 85, 134n; legal 2, 110, 124, 154n; literal 33, 43, 67, 110; *see also* literalization; poetological 4, 158n, 161n; rhetorical 77; tragic 19, 87, 92, 100–1, 105, 157n, 165n
Iser, Wolfgang 146n–7n

Jackson, James L. 136n, 163n
Jackson, Ken 144n, 162n
James I, King of England 35–6, 55–6, 65, 74, 76, 80–4, 102, 141n, 148n–9n, 151n, 155n, 165n
James IV, King of Scotland 74
James, William 135n
Jardine, Lisa 60, 61, 63, 149n–50n
Jarvis, Simon 134n
Jenkins, Harold 132n, 139n, 165n
Jenks, Edward 122, 164n

Jonas, Hans 70, 152n
Jones, Emrys 14, 155n, 157n
Jones, Ernest 11, 14
Jonson, Ben 130n
Joyce, James 40, 57, 142n
justice, *Iustitia* 19, 29, 118; as mercy 111, 126, 162n, 164n; *Iustitia mediatrix* 121; as law's fulfillment 118, 121, 124, 126; legal 49, 56, 78, 81, 118, 132; mock-justice 21, 27, 110–11; revenge-justice, wild justice 23, 41, 45

Kafka, Franz 102, 163n
Kahn, Coppelia 61, 150n, 159n
Kahn, Victoria 78, 141n-2n, 146n, 154n
Kalyvas, Andreas 150n
Kant, Immanuel 157n
Kantorowicz, Ernst H. 2, 4, 12, 14, 48–56, 71, 121–2, 140n, 142n–8n, 151n, 164n–5n
Kearns, Thomas R. 164n–5n
Keats, John 2
Kelsen, Hans 146n, 166n
Kernan, Alvin 140n–1n, 153n
Keynes, Maynard 86, 134n, 138n, 143n, 156n
Kluge, Alexander 130n
Knight, G. Wilson 14, 135n
knowledge, non-knowledge 13, 20, 58–9, 97, 103, 128, 136n, 138n
Kohlenberger, Helmut 147n
Koselleck, Reinhard 148n
Kott, Jan 9, 14
Kyd, Thomas 23, 41

Lacan, Jacques 11, 15, 33, 61, 131n–2n, 136n, 138n, 142n
Ladner, Gerhart B. 147n
Langhoff, Matthias 12, 130n
latency: allegory of 113, 116, 132n; *see also* literalization; *ars adeo latet arte sua* 2, 100–1; (con)textual 18; of death 135n; economy of 3, 45, 98, 111; effectivity of 11, 111, 116, 136n; *see also* deferred representation; historical 1–5, 10, 14, 83, 110–11, 152n; *Illatenz* 163n; Latinity's 5, 71, 104, 113, 116; law's 4, 105, 109, 113, 162n; linguistic, pun 56, 113–15; mythical 45, 54, 85, 98–9, 104–5, 112; performative 30, 33, 90; psychological 2, 91, 96; semantic 3, 133n; theater's 3, 14, 98–9, 103
law: execution of 51, 78–81, 118–28, 153n; (supra legal) foundation of 10, 31, 43, 51,

53, 71, 82; *see also* positing; punishment 120–8
Lefort, Claude 76–7, 153n–4n
Legendre, Pierre 110, 153n, 156n, 158n–9n, 161n
legitimacy 1, 27, 31, 34, 48–50, 58, 155n
Lehmann, Hans-Thies 160n
Leiner, Markus Konradin 130n
Lessing, Gotthold Ephraim 112, 130n
Lever, J.W. 132n
Levin, Harry 129n, 131n, 135n–6n
Lewis, C.S. 14, 52–3, 135n
Lewis, Ewart 146n, 164n
Liebler, Naomi Conn 151n
life 8, 80, 103, 128
Lipsius, Justus 56, 67
literalization 12, 28, 33, 43, 49, 67, 98, 101, 106, 110, 118, 127, 156, 158n
Livy 5, 60–6, 69, 149n
Lohmann, Johannes 115, 162n
Longinus 68
Lorenz, Philip 146n
Lorqua, Ramiro de 79
Lucan 61–2
Lucretius 90
Lugowski, Clemens 142n
Luhmann, Niklas 5, 74, 117, 163n, 167n
Luis-Marínez, Zénon 146n
Lupton, Julia Reinhard 15, 112, 114, 138n, 149n, 162n
Luther, Martin 22
Lyotard, Jean-François 117, 163n

Machiavelli, Niccolò 5, 24, 34, 49, 56, 60–3, 65, 68–9, 73, 76–86, 106, 133n, 146n, 150n, 153n–5n
machine 3, 7–11, 22, 39, 130n; *deus/diabolus/rex ex machina* 25, 50
Maitland, Frederic William 122–3, 165n
Manlius Capitolinus, Marcus 69
Mannheim, Karl 144n
Manning, John J. 134n
Mansfield, Harvey C. 153n–4n
Marc Antony 64, 68
Marin, Louis 148n
Marinetti, Filippo Tommasi 156n
Marius, Gaius 64
Marquard, Odo 145n
Marx, Karl 5, 10–11, 15, 87, 104–5, 134n, 138n, 142n–3n, 156n, 160n
McIlwain, Charles H. 148n

mediation, mediatization 13, 75–6, 121, 136n
Meier, Heinrich 144n, 149n
melancholia 3–4, 9, 12, 21, 27–8, 32, 39–42, 71, 75, 79, 83, 87, 93, 95, 106, 132n–5n, 139n, 143n, 158n
Melanchthon, Philipp 160n
memoria 18, 39, 83; immemorial 104–5, 115; Mnemosyne, mnemotechnics 39–40, 43, 45, 95; remembrance 8, 31, 40–3, 137n
Menke, Christoph 149n, 156n–7n, 159n
mercy 56, 97, 105, 111–12, 117, 120–2, 126–8, 149n, 162n, 164n; *clementia* 65–70, 78, 111, 121–3, 126, 152n
metamorphosis 91–2, 97, 100–2, 104; *see also conversio*
metaphor 1, 33–4, 43, 48–50, 53–4, 74, 100–1, 106, 110, 118, 125, 128, 156n, 163n–4n; catachresis 49, 101; fencing-metaphor 116, 173n; metaphorology 48, 54, 148n–9n, 164n; metonymy 118; pun of the pound 110–6; substitution 56, 119, 122, 128, 132n
Michaelis, Henriette 163n
Milton, John 56, 75, 148n, 154n
Minetti, Bernhard 130n
modernity, 12–13, 18–19, 23–4; melancholic 40, 44–5, 106; as meta-drama 18, 105, 147n; modern audience 10, 24, 29, 94, 112; modern subject, individuum 9, 19, 23, 32, 44, 124; postmodern 40; prehistories of 3, 12–13, 39, 45, 85–6, 111, 146n; violent politics of 47–9, 59, 73–7, 113, 115
Mommsen, Theodor 71, 153n, 164n
Montaigne, Michel de 5, 86, 150n
Montrose, Louis 147n, 158n
mortgage 1, 4, 20, 30, 32, 44, 69, 83, 92, 104–6, 134n, 137n–8n
Mountagu, Henry 122
Mühe, Ulrich 130n
Muir, Kenneth 148n, 155n
Müller, Heiner 3, 7, 10, 12, 15, 41, 88, 129, 130n–1n, 141n–2n
myth 13, 37, 39, 45, 48, 84, 131n; Christian Latin metamorphoses of 90–106, 157n; after classical tragedy 18–19, 92; mythic latency 95, 99, 104–5, 112; *see also* mythical *under* latency; and law 5, 14; theology's mythic function 50, 54–5, 85, 107, 141n–2n

Nagel, Ivan 55, 148n
Nancy, Jean-Luc 166n

Neale, John E. 140n
Nero, Claudius Augustus 19–20, 70, 139n
Nevo, Ruth 157n
New(er) Historicism 9–10, 18, 45, 51, 58, 74, 81, 94, 141
Nietzsche, Friedrich 4, 8, 13–14, 19, 24, 32, 44–5, 85, 88, 97, 100, 103, 105, 131n, 138n–9n, 159, 161, 163
Norbrook, David 144n, 147n
North, Thomas 58–9, 150n
nothingness 28, 30, 33, 36, 75, 87–106; 142n, 155n, 159n; annihilation 32, 75, 121, 137n, 139n; as being 32; as castration 32, 98, 139n; *creatio ex nihilo* 99; negative capability 12; nihilism 85
Nussbaum, Martha 164n
Nuttal, Anthony D. 143n

occasion, *occasio* 14, 20–3, 26, 34, 68, 71, 78, 82, 154; *causa et occasio* 34, 79, 154
O'Daly, Gerald 158n
Oedipus Complex 9–10, 19, 24, 44, 99, 131, 138
Onions, C.T. 83, 116, 153n, 163n
Orco, Messer Remirro de 77, 82
Orgel, Stephen 102, 152n, 157n
Ovid, 2, 14, 90–3, 97, 100–1, 105, 146n, 158–9n

Parker, Patricia 133n, 158n
Pater, Walter 52, 71, 147n
Paul, Saint 53, 55, 148n, 159n
Peterson, Erik 4, 48, 53, 54, 145n, 147n
Petrarch, Francesco 32, 91–2, 158n
Plato 86, 92, 105
Pliny, the Younger 152n
Plutarch 58–63, 66, 149n–50n
political theology 2, 4, 47–63, 68–70, 74, 79, 109, 141n, 144n–9n, 154n, 163n
positing, *Setzung* 49, 78–9, 81–2, 126–8, 153n; *see also* theatricality
Preisendanz, Wolfgang 157n
Price, Russell 155n
prophecy; *see* typology
Prosser, Eleanor 133n
Proust, Marcel 97
psychoanalysis 9–10, 61, 93
Pucci, Pietro 142n
pun 28, 39, 67, 71, 73, 93, 109–16, 156n
Pye, Christopher 135n

Quintillian 116, 161n
Quiring, Björn 139n, 163n

Raaflaub, Kurt A. 152n
Rackin, Phyllis 153n
Rawls, John 124, 166n
Readings, Bill 134n
Rebentisch, Juliane 160n
recognition, misrecognition 24, 44, 47, 58, 89, 96, 106, 126, 133
Regn, Gerhard 158n
Reinhard, Kenneth 15, 138n
Renaissance 3, 12–13, 19, 71, 84, 90, 100, 103–4, 130n, 150n
Republicanism 58, 62–70, 97, 103, 105
revenge, vengeance 4, 21–33, 41–5, 66–7, 83, 95, 106, 132n–4n, 136n, 142n
reversal 18, 25, 29, 83, 115
revolution 8, 11–13, 18, 40, 51–3, 56, 63, 71, 97, 153n
rhetoric 24, 68, 70, 116, 128, 138n–9n, 147n, 152n; and latency, *actualitas* 2–3; and the law 20–1, 164n; mnemotechnical 39–45; *see also* memoria; rhetorical reading 133n; as redescription 78–9, 154n; as *techne* 118; and theology, poetry 52–3
Richards, I.A. 147n
Richardson, Samuel 130n
Robespierre, Maximilien 12
Romanticism 2, 5, 9–12, 19, 21, 25, 79, 87–8, 103, 111, 158n
Ronell, Avital 13, 130n
Rousseau, Jean-Jacques 1, 105
Russel, D.A. 152n
Rust, Jennifer R. 146n, 149n
Rüter, Christoph 130n

Sallustus 61–3, 70, 152n
Sarat, Austin 164n–5n
Scarisbrick, J.J. 137n
Schiesari, Juliana 142n
Schiller, Friedrich 75, 98, 110
Schlegel, August Wilhelm 14
Schmitt, Carl 2, 4–5, 14, 47–50, 52–6, 58, 63, 70, 76, 79, 140n–1n, 144n–50n, 154n–5n
Schmitt, Jean-Claude 137n
Schramm, Percy Ernst 48, 145n
Schütz, Anton 110–11, 161n
Schwarzkopf, Herbert Norman 12, 130n
secularization 41, 47–51, 134n, 145n
Shakespeare's plays cited: *A Winter's Tale* 2,

4–5, 64, 87–106; *Antony and Cleopatra* 67, 69; *Coriolanus* 57, 59–60, 63, 66–7; *Cymbeline* 57; *Hamlet* 3–45, 51, 55, 57, 61, 67, 69, 75–6, 80, 82–9, 93, 99–102, 111, 121; *Julius Caesar* 4–5, 57–71, 115; *King Lear* 36, 89, 99; *Macbeth* 4–5, 8, 36, 44–5, 56, 73–86, 93, 106; *Measure for Measure* 47; *Othello* 23, 66, 89, 97, 133n; *Richard II* 4, 12, 27, 47–58, 69–70; *Richard III* 8, 12, 73, 80, 83; *The Merchant of Venice* 4, 105, 109–16, 113, 116; *The Tempest* 4–5, 88, 103; *Titus Andronicus* 41, 57–8; *Twelfth Night* 35
Seneca 19, 40, 61, 70, 121, 139n, 164n
Serres, Michel 69, 151n
Servilia Caepionis 66
Shell, Marc 11, 15, 52, 91, 139n
Shotter, David 151n
Shuger, Deborah K. 47, 144n
Sinfield, Alan 153n
singularity 8, 86, 113; *see also* exemplarity
skepticism 13, 61, 71, 97
Skinner, Quentin 78, 154n–5n
Sophocles 131n, 138n
sovereignty: *arcana imperii* 56, 65, 148n–9n; deposition, self-deposition 51–2, 69; dictator 63–8; High Treason 31, 74; Jupiter function 4, 59, 64–71, 150n; King's Two Bodies 34, 48–56, 140n–6n; *plenitudo potestatis* 52, 78–9, 147n, 154n; prerogative 56, 66–70, 120–4; *translatio imperii* 59, 83
Spackman, Barbara 156n
speech act; *see also* positing; illocution 118, 128; performative 3, 30, 32–3, 56, 67, 90–1, 96, 104, 116, 118, 126–7; perlocution 32–3, 118, 126, 128
Spencer, Hazelton 134n
Spengler, Oswald 70, 152n
state of exception 20, 27, 34, 53, 56, 65, 78, 80
Stengers, Isabelle 129n
Stierlin, Helm 137n
Stoppard, Tom 14, 133n
Strauss, Leo 63, 76, 150n, 153n
Stuart, Maria 31, 34–5, 141n
Stubbs, William 123, 165n
succession 1, 22, 25–37, 55–8, 64, 74–8, 82–5, 93–4, 99, 102, 135n, 137n, 140n, 148n–9n
Sulla, Lucius Cornelius 64–5, 67
Syme, Ronald 61–3, 65, 148n, 150n–2n

Tacitus 5, 19, 56–63, 65–7, 70, 139n, 148n, 152n

Taubes, Jacob 48, 145n
Taylor, Neil 132n
Tennenhouse, Leonhard 159n
theatricality: anti-theatricality 36; of history 8, 23, 41; as mediality of reflection 11, 32, 76, 94, 114; as performative latency 90, 112; and political theology 52, 54, 62, 68; retrospective 1, 24, 30; *see also* deferred representation; of the secret 23, 55; of the *Trauerspiel* 76, 136n; of the trial 35, 165n; theatrical positioning 2–3, 10, 23, 95, 103; theatrical positing of violence 78–9, 83–4
Thompson, Ann 132n
Tiberius 56, 148n
Tillyard, E.M.W. 14, 146n
tragedy: classical, Aristotelian 8, 181–9, 42, 76, 83; Elizabethan 35; end of tragedy 44–5; revenge 21, 30, 133n; Roman 41, 71; tragic humor 83, 87, 94, 97–106
Trauerspiel 4, 42, 53, 76, 79, 86, 88, 92, 104, 136n, 140n, 146n
Traversi, Derek 146n
Trousdale, Marion 139n
Trüstedt, Katrin 159n
Tuve, Rosemond 130n
typology 70; *see also* deferred representation; fulfillment 11, 21, 25, 33, 55, 75, 121, 130n; prophecy 9, 11, 56, 73, 75, 84–5, 136n, 156n

Valéry, Paul 17, 129n, 131n
Varnhagen, Rahel 111, 161n
Vinken, Barbara 134n, 148n
violence: future of 5, 73–96; of history 10, 13; and language 75–6; and the law 105, 117–18, 124–8; as medium, as reproduction 76, 82, 84, 156n; of positing 78–9, 126, 153n
Virgil 83

Waite, Geoff 150n
Warburg, Aby 45
Weber, Samuel 131n, 140n, 142n–3n, 147n, 150n–1n, 160n
Wells, Stanley 158n
Whitehead, Alfred North 129n
Whitman, James Q. 144n
Wickhamm, Gary 165n
Wilbern, David 159n
Wills, Garry 153n

Wilson, John Dover 41, 86, 111, 132n, 135n, 139n, 141n, 144n, 146n, 162n
Wind, Edgar 90–2, 157n
Woodman, A.J. 152n

Yates, Frances 14, 43, 45, 143n

Names by Florian Fuchs, Words and Things by Barbara Natalie Nagel